A CASTLE IN TUSCANY

The remarkable life
of Janet Ross

A CASTLE IN TUSCANY

The remarkable life of Janet Ross

SARAH BENJAMIN

PIER 9

For my parents, Pattie and Robert

Contents

Preface

When I was a student in Florence in my twenties, sometimes, after a long day in the archives, I would take the bus into the centre of the old city and make my way to the Via Tornabuoni. To my mind, the grand old street was the essence of Florentine style. It represented the faded remains of life lived there a hundred years before. I was in Florence on a research trip; my days spent delving through manuscripts. My area of scholarship was Renaissance Florence — female religious experience in the early sixteenth century, to be precise — but I was always fascinated by the city's more recent past. The past represented in this street a century ago.

Here on the Via Tornabuoni were traces of the life of the Anglo-Florentine community, the writers, aesthetes and others who did much to shape our present day romantic image of the city — Henry James, E.M. Forster, John Ruskin, Mary McCarthy and others. Here was the fashionable Café Doney at one end, the beautiful neighbourhood church of Santa Trinità opposite and the English Pharmacy with its immense apothecary jars and generous wooden counters across the way; on the other side of the street, magnificent and overwhelming, stood the Palazzo Strozzi.

Whenever I passed by the Via Tornabuoni, I could not miss a visit to the old Café Giacosa. Located midway up the street, a little further along from the Seeber bookshop with its comforting collection of English and Italian authors, it stood at the intersection with the Via della Spada and the Via degli Strozzi. The café was opposite what is now the IntesaBci Bank — formerly the Banca Commerciale — into whose vast foyer I would venture once a month to receive my meagre university stipend and hope vainly that the monies might see me through another four weeks.

I entered the café and ordered a coffee. If my money had come through at the bank, I would privately celebrate the happy event by taking a sweet yeasty brioche from the counter. For the ten minutes or so it took to slowly sip one perfect coffee, I would then imagine I was part of the chic world of Giacosa.

The place was an institution. It was famous for creating the Negroni cocktail in the 1920s — equal parts gin, vermouth and Campari — and had stood on the same site for over a hundred years, an enduring haven for Florence's elite society. Giacosa was not expensive but it was unfailing in its supply of perfect service. The men behind the espresso machine practised their art with an understated flourish. They were immaculate, from the combing of their hair to the filing of their fingernails. Not one bad coffee passed through their hands. They were masters.

As for the edibles, I always thought it interesting that in a country not often praised for its patisserie, the morsels served here were the height of refinement. Everything about them was right — their size, smell and the texture. And every day the performance was repeated with the same enthusiasm and perfection. Part of the fascination was the elegance of the clientele; they were extremely fashionable but never overdone, a balancing act achieved by few, even in Italy. These were the heirs to the street's halcyon days. Mostly I enjoyed this ritual alone but sometimes I would go with a boyfriend or family visitor and every time, I came away feeling deeply satisfied, as if I had partaken in some special communion.

Since those days, whenever I am in Florence, I make a point of walking up the Via Tornabuoni to Café Giacosa. It is always the first thing I do. It reminds me of times past and gives me a sense of comforting continuity. I remember the first time I was in Florence with my husband, and I was anxious that he would appreciate Giacosa as I did. On that occasion, we stayed at a lovely and well-run *pensione* down the street towards the river. We had a plainly furnished room with polished bricks underfoot and tall airy ceilings. Every morning we took the tiny elevator downstairs and stepped out onto the stone footpath and headed straight for Giacosa. To my great pleasure, he enjoyed it every bit as much as me.

I first went to Florence with my parents when I was twelve years old and since then, I have returned at various times to live and study. As a schoolgirl, I liked to read stories about the Medici and the great painters of the Renaissance and daydreamed about what it might have been like to live there in the fifteenth century. I was intrigued by the pragmatic practice of commerce and politics, and the striving for beauty and perfection in art. When I was twenty, I returned to the city, first to learn Italian and then to prepare for entrance exams to the prestigious art restoration lab at the Opificio della Pietra Dura. The Opificio was established in 1588 to produce the intricate inlay work of semi precious stone, known as Florentine mosaic.

Before taking the exams, it was mandatory to study for a year under the eye of an experienced restorer. When I was accepted by a grand old master of the craft to study in his studio, the rhythm of my days was set. Every afternoon I attended the studio tucked behind the church of Santa Felicità, a stone's throw from the Pitti Palace and the Ponte Vecchio. To enter the little doorway on the right-hand side of the church was to enter another world. It was presided over by the tall and solemn maestro who demanded total concentration from his eight students. For hours at a time, we sat on hard benches silently copying images placed in front of us, mixing colours and preparing plaster using the ancient methods. I was the only foreigner in the small group.

Mornings were spent either at the Uffizi Gallery looking intently at pictures or at art history lectures given at the University of Florence. Without formal enrolment, I would join the other students in the overcrowded lecture hall and, aided by slide illustrations, try to make some sense of it all.

In the evenings, I ambled home to eat and after dinner would pull out Cennino Cennini's *The Book of Art*, which we had been instructed to absorb in its entirety. Though the book is generally thought to have been written at the end of the fourteenth century, it remains a primary text for instruction in the principles of painting. The preparation of glues from animal's feet, the grinding of materials into colours and the mixing of plaster ready for fresco — it is all covered in Cennini's old-style Italian.

As fascinating as all this was, I did not complete the year and I did not take the examination. I finally came to realize that the whole process was more science than art. More discipline than creative application, and probably something I did not want to do for the rest of my working life.

At this point, I returned to university and to Italian history, seeking another way to engage with the old city. My mind turned to women of the Renaissance. Firstly, I spent time on Alexandra Strozzi, the widow of a fifteenth-century Florentine merchant, and the mother of Filippo, builder of the famous Strozzi Palace. She was a strong and resourceful woman who managed the family's fortunes while her two older sons were exiled in Naples.

The Strozzi boys, Filippo and his brother Lorenzo, had been on the wrong side of political manoeuvring in Florence and found themselves banished from the city. Overnight they were removed from the day-to-day running of their commercial and banking interests. Their father was dead and so for the years of their banishment they relied on their mother, Alexandra, to manage their commercial and political interests. She was from an old patrician family herself and so understood the social and political networks that were the life force of the city. She worked these with all the deftness she might apply to a work of elaborate needlepoint. Letters and notes here, a quite word in the right ear there, or some assistance rendered to a potential ally.

What is more, she was determined that the temporary loss of political prestige suffered by her sons' exile would not jeopardize the arrangement of advantageous marriages for her daughters. She was determined that the family would not go under. In large part because of her efforts, the family thrived. When her sons were eventually allowed to return they did so as proud and rich men. So proud in fact, that Filippo soon began plans for his massive and grand palace, a testament to family success and endurance.

Later I came across the unstoppable Domenica Narducci, later known as Domenica dal Paradiso (Dominica from Paradise), a woman without family connections who managed to found a convent and become an influential religious figure in a city where religion really mattered.

Domenica grew up the daughter of a market gardener living on the outskirts of Florence in a little place called Paradiso. It is on the other side of the river Arno and today forms part of the spreading suburban city. She was a woman of twenty-five when the Dominican monk and religious zealot Savonarola was burned at the stake in Piazza della Signoria. Like many of her generation, Domenica had been influenced by his reforming zeal and used his message to inspire others to join her in a movement embracing mysticism and extreme religiosity.

Eventually she established a closed convent of Dominican nuns, which attracted the daughters of some well-known Florentine families. Like Alexandra Strozzi, she had a keen understanding of *realpolitik*.

She ensured her independence from the Dominican hierarchy of San Marco by placing herself directly under the authority of the Bishop of Florence. She could swim in the wake of Savonarola, but she was not about to be told what to do by his Dominican brothers.

This remarkable and unorthodox woman became the focus of a postgraduate thesis. I returned to the city for three cold winter months in 1986 to work in the convent archive in Via Aretina. Only ten nuns remained as a testament to Domenica's vision. They were making a last ditch effort to have the Vatican recognize her as a saint and my arrival from the other side of the world was an excellent omen.

Each day I would wait in the little parlour at the front of the building where nuns might occasionally talk to family members through a small grill in the wall. Then a small ageing nun who doubled as archivist and convent nurse, would lead me through the only door, a heavy wooden thing that bolted from the inside only. I would silently follow her along a bare corridor, up a narrow stairway and into the reading room. There I would spend the next four hours looking at manuscripts taken from a stack inside an oversized closet of dark carved wood.

In that freezing convent archive I sat quietly, one hand resting on the heater and one transcribing entries made in barely legible fifteenth-century handwriting. There were volumes describing her visions and revelations, others of memoirs of her achievements and many convent ledgers and accounts relating to the life lived in the convent by Domenica and the Florentine women who came to live with her. At the end of such a session, I was ready for some small comfort. I would take the bus back into the city centre and head towards Via Tornabuoni and the Café Giacosa.

Now years later, I was in Florence again, this time with my husband and our young son. Just as soon as we had showered and settled, it was our intention to head directly for Café Giacosa. There would be coffee for us, and a little brioche for our young boy.

I had come back in search of the more recent past, the one that existed on the Via Tornabuoni that had captured my imagination years before when I was a young student. My purpose was to track down documents that I hoped would reveal more to me of the life of an Englishwoman who had lived in the city over a hundred years before. Her name was Janet Ross. In her twenties, she had moved to Florence and made her home there. Over the remainder of a long life she came, to me, to embody the late-nineteenth-century Anglo-Florentine experience.

My interest in her had begun as a private thing. Since I was a young girl, I have enjoyed reading cookbooks. I take great pleasure in all sorts of cookbooks — the beautifully illustrated books that breathe life into the modern kitchen as well as out of print, hard-to-come-by books. These old cookbooks inspire me in a different way, transporting me back in time into the households that used them.

In the best cookbooks, I find great comfort in the details of place and time, of rituals and forms that were the daily routine of a different epoch. I delight in the lists of ingredients, the arrangement of tables and the order of meals, grand and modest: Eliza Acton's elaborate instructions for dishes standing on pedestals and whole animals stuffed and brought to table or, by contrast, Elizabeth David's beautiful descriptions of simply prepared dishes eaten in the French countryside. I love to imagine the care taken in the preparation of such food as much as the pleasure to be had in the eating.

Sometimes I am happy simply to create visual pictures of the dishes described, but other times I am provoked to practical imitation. I have a particular fancy for moulds of different shapes and sizes. This is something of an Edwardian fascination but one that I have adopted, and which I attempt to realize from time to time. I am curious too, to know something of the lives of the authors of some of my treasured tomes. Did they actually cook or were they more historians and writers? Some were clearly all of these.

In the last century, arguably the greatest food writer in English was Elizabeth David, although on the other side of the Atlantic, M.F.K. Fisher was her equal as a writer if not as a chronicler and advocate. Both have a timeless quality in their descriptions of food and eating. From an earlier period, I find Eliza Acton to be a revelation. Isabella Beeton too has a capacity to draw me in. I love to pore over the menus at the back of her book — menus for each of the seasons, for dinners and lunches, large and small. Then there are Mrs Beeton's menus for special occasions, wedding breakfasts, christenings, Christmas and other traditional feasts.

It was my love of cookbooks that had led me to the story of Janet Ross. She was the author of a little cookbook called *Leaves from Our Tuscan Kitchen*, first published in 1899. This slender work has, in one edition or another, been with the women in my family for generations and I have taken much pleasure in cooking recipes from it. For many lovers of cookbooks, Janet's name and book are quite recognizable, but few know much about the life she lived. I had noted references to her in history books and other cookbooks and was interested to find out more.

So here we were hardly installed in our apartment on Via Maggio, the street that runs directly on from the Via Tornabuoni on the other side of the beautiful Santa Trinità Bridge. More importantly for me, it was just around the corner from the library that held most of the material on Janet Ross I had come to look at.

There was great anticipation in getting to work. I was making a break from the Renaissance city with which I was so familiar and fast tracking forward to the late-nineteenth century. I was entering the world of Via Tornabuoni and the last glory days of the Anglo-Florentines.

But first, the pilgrimage across the bridge and up the Via Tornabuoni to Café Giacosa. And so, sure in the knowledge of the pleasure awaiting us, we set off. Only as we were about halfway up the street did I have a strange sense of unwelcome change. My husband and I both felt it, but neither was prepared to be the first to acknowledge it. As we passed the English Pharmacy, we were confronted by the first irrefutable proof. It was closed. A notice at the front made it plain it was about to be redeveloped for use as a shoe shop. Seeber bookshop was also closed for renovation, to be reincarnated as an outpost of an international — albeit Italian in origin — dress shop chain.

At second glance it was obvious that a number of shop fronts were boarded up and temporarily dressed in loud billboards announcing coming attractions. Prada, Max Mara and Versace, opening soon! Even the shop of the city's beloved Count Pucci — or at least the business that carries his name and is now run by the next generation — had proudly staked its claim alongside some of its flashier cousins. Gone was the discreet Pucci boutique in nearby Via della Vigna Nuova that in my youth had appeared like a meeting place for some secret fashion society.

Behind the hoardings, the old spaces were being restyled into temples of cream and white sleekness — retail heavens of glass showcases and lighting on a par with their sister stores in so many other cities around the world. And while they lacked the charm of their predecessors, they were certainly more accessible for the average shopper.

But I did not care for accessibility. For me the appeal of Via Tornabuoni was its remnant sensibility of times past and faded. This was now being uprooted with unseemly haste. Intellectually, I understood the inevitability of the change and I knew the Florentine's reputation for being notoriously unsentimental about the past.

Yet, there was more. As we drew towards the Café Giacosa, it appeared that crude hoardings had been erected across its front. At first, I thought this must be temporary restoration work. The cafe must surely have relocated close by for the duration of such an extensive refurbishment. But it had gone. The last living incarnation of Via Tornabuoni's Anglo-Florentine past was being converted into another dress shop.

Nursing an unwelcome sense of alienation we wondered whether we had made a terrible mistake to come back again. Were we the only ones so affronted by the indecent rush to make over the old street?

There is a tendency, unrealistic though it is, to assume that certain landmarks that identify a city in one's experience will be there every time one goes back to enjoy the experience all over again.

In reality, the life of the old Anglo-Florentines had long gone. It had really been in decline since World War One. The *pensioni* frequented by writers, the cafés — including Giacosa — and clubs where poets and politicians met to talk over coffee were all but gone. Couples sharing gelatos and cold drinks, young girls selling freshly picked flowers and ladies driving past in their carriages — all had inevitably succumbed to the new ways. What remained was memory and imagination.

All that was left for me was to turn to the documents and photographs residing in the archives. And this became the backdrop to my research into the life of one of the grand figures of the times, Janet Ross.

Florence

She sat in the sunshine beside her yellow river
like the little treasure-city she has always seemed ... with nothing
but the little unaugmented stock of her mediaeval memories,
her tender-coloured mountains, her churches and palaces,
pictures and statues.

HENRY JAMES
ITALIAN HOURS (1909)

HENRY JAMES suggests Florence as a place apparently immune to change, a monument more than a real city. But when Janet Ross came for a two-week holiday in the spring of 1867, it was in the midst of a major makeover. The old city had been proclaimed the capital of the newly united Kingdom of Italy and was now in a hurry to look the part.

The first king of the new realm was Victor Emmanuel II, formally King of Sardinia-Piedmont in the north. The path to Italian unification was complex, slow and initially not conceived as a complete vision, but can be traced back to the Congress of Vienna signed in 1815. The Congress attempted to undo the work of the then recently defeated Napoleon, exiled on the island of Elba, by carving up the Italian peninsula into many parts and handing them back to former 'legitimate' masters. So the House of Savoy regained Piedmont and Sardinia and added Genoa. The Pope was returned to the Papal States. Much of the rest was divided up between Austria and others close to her. Lombardy and Venetia were controlled by Austria; and other Hapsburgs — relatives of the main Austrian branch of the royal family — regained the Grand Duchy of Tuscany. Other minor Hapsburgs were given the duchies of Moderna and Parma. The King of Sicily — whose wife was Austrian — took the kingdom of Naples, and the Duchy of Lucca was created for the house of Bourbon-Parma.

The Austrians remained dominant until uprisings spread in Lombardy-Venetia in 1848, a year of widespread upheaval across Europe. Although these revolts were eventually suppressed, the movement towards unification had begun and its centre was King Victor Emmanuel of Sardinia-Piedmont and his liberal-minded minister Camillo Cavour. They sought support from the French and the British by, among other things, introducing social reforms in Sardinia and joining the allies in the Crimean War.

In the south, the charismatic Guiseppe Garibaldi, after suffering earlier defeats and exile, finally succeeded in marshalling a sizable national army aimed at seizing power. Once he crossed from Sicily to the mainland he met the army of Victor Emmanuel and the two proclaimed a united kingdom. Garibaldi's cause had been assisted by private English money and sympathy from the British Government, which was the first Government to recognize the new Kingdom of Italy. This was in 1861, though it would be another five years before the Austrians were overthrown in Venice and another nine years before the Papal States were included in a unified peninsula.

In recognition of the union of previously independent Italian duchies, King Victor Emmanuel moved his court to a more central location. Rome was the obvious choice, but it was the one part of the peninsula still beyond his grasp. French troops were stationed there, protecting the papacy — a remnant of the diplomatic vicissitudes leading to unification. In an arrangement made by Napoleon's nephew, Louis Napoleon and Cavour, the French would protect the Papal States in return for allowing Victor Emmanuel to move into Naples, Umbria and other provinces. In the meantime, Florence, the birthplace of modern civilization and possessing a history going back to ancient Rome, was a worthy consolation.

As a native of Turin, Victor Emmanuel was disinclined to move south and sceptical that the old Florentine families with their natural reserve and caution would pay him much regard. Nonetheless, he made the move, relocating to newly decorated apartments in the Pitti Palace. He formally entered the city in February 1865 and to his great relief was warmly welcomed by the crowd.

Two years after this Janet arrived from Alexandria, Egypt, where she had been living with her husband Henry Ross, for the previous five years. Her trip to Florence was planned as a short holiday. She booked a berth on a run-down steamer that took a route out from Alexandria across the Mediterranean to the southern Italian port of Brindisi. From there she went by carriage northwards up the peninsula, through beautiful countryside with hills of old knotted olive trees and swathes of perfumed lavender, beneath a brilliant blue sky. Her plan was to arrive in Florence and stay for a fortnight as the guest of an old family friend and relative by marriage, Sir Henry Elliot, the British Ambassador to Italy.

She had read about Florence, its treasures and its history. She was familiar with its great writers, Dante and Boccaccio, the unsurpassed beauty created by its painters, and the understated order achieved by its architects. She had heard stories of the proud patrician families with their age-old feuds and allegiances — names like Medici, Pazzi and Strozzi — and she new something of the story of Savonarola and how he was burnt at the stake in the Piazza della Signoria. This was her opportunity to witness for herself the history that till now she had only read about in books. Above all it was a change of scenery and she was in need of some distraction.

She knew something of Italian politics, because it had been a topic of discussion among her parents and their friends in the liberal-minded household of her childhood. The plight of the Italian people had long been of interest to the British. Since the days of the Grand Tour and through the years of Napoleonic occupation and subsequent Austrian domination, the British had developed a romantic view of the peninsula's history and her possible future freedom from foreign interference. Through her parents, she had met Italian refugees living in England, fleeing because their aspirations for independence would have them imprisoned in their homeland. She knew of Garibaldi's brave exploits against occupying forces and the part played by the clever politician Cavour. What she had heard of the courage and determination of those that led Italy to be free and united increased her enthusiasm for the place.

For as long as she could remember, Janet had been an enthusiastic traveller. One of her great pleasures was to explore new places, aided by a sharp eye and a quick facility with languages. It was this talent with languages that enabled her to quickly immerse herself in the local culture. At twenty-five she spoke and wrote in French, German and Arabic; and since her early teens she had been translating for others and for herself. She was quick to add Italian to her list of languages.

For her, the discomforts of travel were far outweighed by the excitement of experiencing new things. As a girl she had spent time in Germany and France and, since her marriage, she had become something of an authority on life and politics in Egypt. A woman of her times, she had a well-developed Victorian fascination with the exotic. Moreover, she was physically adventurous, healthy and strong.

In her mid-twenties, Janet was at the peak of her physical beauty, a beauty that dominated any room she entered. Her looks, however, were not conventional and references throughout her life tended to describe her appearance in masculine terms. Henry James, when he met her years later, described her as the least feminine woman he had ever set eyes on, although he emphasized that he did not mean ugly. The first impression of her was of her penetrating eyes, emphasized by dark, thick eyebrows. She had well-proportioned cheekbones and clear healthy skin. Her hair was dark too, thick and shiny, parted in the middle and tied at the back in a chignon. Her voice was a firm contralto.

Janet, aged twenty-three, when she was living in Alexandria and working as a correspondent for *The Times*. Portrait by Vanetine Princep.

She exuded a robust, almost sexless beauty. She was lively, fun and spirited, and most likely to say yes to a challenge, especially if it was physically daring and in a saddle. She enjoyed the company of both men and women and was comfortable talking to either sex on almost any subject. But if she had to be categorized, she would probably be described as a man's woman. She had characteristics that were considered masculine ideals — she was serious and forthright. She liked to dance and go to parties, but if she was up half the night, she would just as likely still rise at dawn to go riding, fast and furious on a magnificent horse.

She loved to participate physically with men. When she was living in Egypt in the early years of her marriage, one of her favourite pastimes was to canter out across the desert, the only woman among the Bedouin chieftains. She admired the skill and courage of their horsemanship, and was never intimidated by it. These noble Bedouin, whose wives and daughters were confined to the harem, enjoyed her company, and she was easy and comfortable with them. She knew how to flirt, but really she treated them as her equals and received the same in return.

Her dress sense tended to the simple, highlighted by the addition of some beautiful artifact, a gold Arab bangle or a magnificent piece of woven material collected on her travels. Sometimes, though, she had no hesitation in wearing something bold to attract attention. On special occasions in Alexandria, she liked to dress head to foot in local costume, in part as a way of paying a compliment to her hosts, but also as a way of setting herself apart from other expatriate women.

Indeed she had no aversion to attention at all. She welcomed it as someone who had enjoyed it from an early age. She had an expectation of, indeed seemed to actually require it, to function well. Outwardly at least, she had all the confidence of a young woman assured of her attractiveness and intelligence.

At the time of this trip to Florence, she had been married for five years and had one child, a son. But no sense of obligation stopped her doing very much as she liked. Her husband remained in Egypt working as a banker and the little boy was in England. In general terms, she enjoyed her freedom and did as she pleased.

Her first trip to Italy had been a year before. Then, Janet had accepted an invitation from old family friends, the Layards, to travel with them to Venice to witness the formal entry of Victor Emmanuel up the Grand Canal to the Piazza San Marco. The Austrians had finally been pushed out of the watery city and the new king was received with great pomp and ceremony. Janet described how:

> Victor Emmanuel, ugly though he was, looked every inch a king as he stood on the prow of the 'Bucentoro', hailed with the wildest enthusiasm from the fleet of gondolas on the Grand Canal and by the crowd on the shore. All the palaces had magnificent sheets of damask or embroideries hanging from their windows, even the poorest quarters of the town had something suspended, a counterpane, a shawl or a small flag. The tricolour waved everywhere, and patriotic songs resounded on all sides. The review on St Mark's square roused the Venetians almost to a frenzy.

Henry Layard was famous for his discovery of the great bas-reliefs of the Assyrian kings from Nineveh, which he donated to the British Museum. Henry Ross, whom he introduced to Janet, had accompanied Layard on his expeditions. Layard had grown up in Florence and had always enjoyed keeping Janet abreast of Italian affairs. He was typical of the English liberal who longed for the time when Italy would thrive under a unified banner. His enthusiasm for the Italians had rung in Janet's ears ever since she could remember.

That trip to Venice had been a great success. The magnificent spectacle and the optimistic enthusiasm of the liberated populace were infectious. Now in Florence, Janet was hoping this holiday would be just as enjoyable. Besides, a few weeks away from Egypt would, she hoped, provide some diversion from the problems she and Henry were having.

The English had long held the old medieval city of Florence in special affection and, over the centuries, many visitors had recorded their impressions for posterity. The Florentines may have been considered aloof and the heavy stone palazzos impenetrable, but the handsome streets and cultivated hills always held a certain allure.

Since the days of the 'Grand Tour' when young men of leisure completed their classical education by making an extended pilgrimage to France and Italy, literary visitors both famous and lesser-known have been moved to describe their impressions of Florence. Inevitably, the results are a mixed bag, but the best examples are delightful. The eighteenth-century writer Hester Piozzi wrote one such. She was formerly Hester Thrale, wife of the wealthy London brewer and close friend of Samuel Johnson. (Most recently she was depicted as the problematic mother in *According to Queeney*, Beryl Bainbridge's recreation of Hester's relationship with her daughter.) After the death of Henry Thrale, Hester married Gabriel Mario Piozzi, who had recently been music teacher to her children. This second marriage was not well received in London, so the Piozzis set off on an extended visit to Italy and settled for a time in Florence.

Hester's appreciation of Italy is infectious to those who have read her accounts; Elizabeth David was one who enjoyed her writing. Her travel writings are among the earliest to be published by a woman and they reveal a great deal about the many English comforts to be found in Florence, as well as the peculiarly Italian delights she discovered. The durability of the writing lies in Hester's ability to capture the charm of everyday domestic detail.

She writes of being very happy staying in an English-style hotel that served English-style food. She was especially impressed with the currant tarts on offer. But this was minor compared to the quality and abundance of the fruit:

> The fruits in this place begin to astonish me; such cherries did I never yet see, or even hear
> tell of, as when I caught the Laquais de Place weighing two of them in a scale to see if they

came to an ounce. These are in the London street phrase, cherries like plums, in size at least but in flavour they far exceed them, being exactly of the kind that we call bleeding-hearts, hard to the bite, and parting easily from the stone which is proportionately small. Figs too are here in such perfection, that it is not easy for an English gardener to guess at their excellence; for it is not by superior size, but taste and colour that they are distinguished; small, and green on the outside, a bright full crimson within, and we eat them with raw ham, and truly delicious is the dainty. By raw ham, I mean ham cured, not boiled or roasted. It is no wonder though that fruits should mature in such a sun as this is; which, to give a just notion of its penetrating fire, I will take leave to tell my countrywomen is so violent, that I use no other method of heating my pinching-irons to curl my hair, than that of poking them out at a south window, with the handles shut in, and the glasses darkened to keep us from being actually fired in his beams ... The flowers too! how rich they are in scent here! how brilliant in colour! how magnificent in size! Wall-flowers perfuming every street, and even every passage; while pinks and single carnations grow beside them, with no more soil than they require themselves; and from the tops of houses where you least expect it, an aromatic flavour highly gratifying is diffused.

A half century later, Charles Dickens, a contemporary and friend of Janet's parents, published in 1846 his popular *Pictures from Italy*. In it, he describes in more masculine terms how:

Magnificently stern and sombre are the streets of beautiful Florence; and the strong old piles of building make such heaps of shadow and a different city of rich forms and fancies, always lying at our feet. Prodigious palaces, constructed for defence, with small distrustful windows heavily barred, and walls of great thickness formed of huge masses of rough stone, frown, in their old sulky state, on every street.

These contrasting descriptions of the city are two among the countless number that have trickled down over the years. In England, there was a ready market for such writing about Italy — and Florence and Tuscany were perennial favourites. In time, Janet would become one of the best exponents of the genre.

May, when Janet arrived, is perhaps the ideal month for Florence. It is the time when warmth returned to Dickens's huge masses of rough stone and flowers covered the hillsides. Bunches of flowers were stacked around the bases of the great palaces ready for sale to passers by, locals meandered the streets, open carriages went out for pleasure in the parks and children delighted in their gelati.

This was the Florence Janet entered when she ventured out from the Ambassador's residence. But she would just as quickly have noticed the noise and mess of construction all about. The city which now spilled out beyond its old medieval walls and towering gates, nestled in a long valley, intersected down its middle by the river Arno. But now there were grand plans to modernize the place. Local grandees had given the go ahead for plans to revamp the town in readiness for the arrival of the new court. Florentine officials wanted to update their city in the style of the great European capitals, Paris being the apogée of their aspiration. What they envisaged involved massive works.

The authority controlling all this was the Florence Land and Public Works Company, an affiliate of the Anglo-Italian Bank. The Bank's directors were a mix of Anglophile Italians and Englishmen with Italian associations. Men who had sympathized and supported a free and united Italy were now figures of influence.

Areas around the great church of San Lorenzo were cleared of houses and, in other parts, where communities had been housed for centuries, parks and gardens were pencilled in. In the frenzy of works, the boldest plans were reserved for the historical centre — whole chunks of which were earmarked for demolition. Perhaps the greatest loss in all this was the Ghetto, a densely populated area of about 200 square metres (2,150 square feet) in the centre of the city. The Ghetto had been decreed on this site in 1571, but its buildings were medieval and its foundations Roman. It was to be replaced with grand squares and neo-classical facades — the most notable being the oversized and rather lifeless Piazza della Repubblica.

Walking through the Piazza della Repubblica today, there is no hint at the labyrinth of alleyways and towers that once stood there. The large and somewhat ungainly square lined by swathes of fashionable café tables and the Savoy Hotel on its eastern side, was built on the very site where most of the Ghetto was razed to the ground in the name of progress.

Today all that remains of the old buildings with their distinctive Hebrew inscriptions and decorative motifs can be seen in the Museum of San Marco, the Dominican convent once home to Savonarola and where Fra Angelico painted his beautiful frescos exhorting the monks on their spiritual path.

Janet became intrigued by the vanished life of the old Ghetto and some years later penned one of the finest descriptions of the place, which she saw as it was being readied for destruction:

> A characteristic portion of old Florence will soon be a thing of the past; the Ghetto, where
> but a few months ago no decent person could enter without a guardian angel in the shape
> of a policeman, stands empty and deserted, doomed to disappear like the ancient city walls
> … Over one of the doors outside, some wag had written under a half-effaced coat of arms:
> 'Lasciate ogni speranza, voi che 'ntrate' (leave all hope, those that enter here). Sad words,
> well suited to the unhappy Jews in old times …

It was during this period of 'modernization' that the now characteristic slow-twisting avenues known as the Viale dei Colli were laid down. They wind their way up the southern hills to another grand works project, the Piazzale Michelangelo. This was designed as a huge terrace providing an elevated and

The Ghetto in Florence before it was pulled down.
Etching by Carlo Orsi to accompany Janet's article
on the subject.

suitably grand view back towards the city. The piazza gave a nineteenth-century perspective to the city, quite different to the intimate human scale of earlier times. Today, it is a favourite with sightseers and Florentines alike, but in the process of its construction, many of the ancient walls that once fortified the old city were torn down.

Oddly enough, amid all this activity, the most famous landmark of all, the Duomo, retained an incomplete façade. Since its construction in the fourteenth century, the western wall of the great church had been bare of decoration, showing only its exposed brickwork and masonry. A number of neo-gothic designs incorporating the distinctive green and white marble geometric patterns common in Tuscany had been proposed for the front, but none had ever been chosen. It was not until some years later that work began on the present façade, which was finally completed in 1887.

It is a testament to the enduring spirit of the city that despite all the renovations, it retained an evocative sense of history. Like Henry James, anyone who knew something of its past could feel it in every street and piazza, every church and palace.

When Victor Emmanuel moved south from Turin, he moved with a massive retinue. Almost overnight, the compact medieval city had to accommodate large numbers of people associated with the royal household and government. Estimates suggest that as many as 20,000 to 30,000 additional people came to work and live in Florence during the few short years it was the capital.

Socially, it was catapulted from a provincial town where the old families hosted the occasional ball to a scene of endless formal receptions and private parties. Foreign delegations and the Court itself hosted numerous of these occasions. Dances and dinners were on offer most nights of the week. The cafés and bars became crowded, and the main public park, the Cascine, built on the former Medici farms on the north-western edge of the city — 'the great Bois de Boulogne of Florence' as Henry James called it — was filled with a crush of social strollers, and carriages almost end to end.

Another favourite place to congregate and be seen was the Via Tornabuoni. People came to sit at cafés and browse at displays in shop windows, much as they do today. In the same street, the local noblemen established the Club dell'Unione, along the lines of a smart London club. The club was housed in a Palazzo belonging to one of the old patrician families, the Gherardi; the same family that owned an old castle in the hills below the town of Fiesole — the same castle that Janet would discover years later.

Across the street, one of the most popular places to gather was the Café Doney. It was founded in 1827 and had long been a beacon to fashionable Florentines and tourists. Inside were three large salons with cream-coloured columns built the full height to the ceiling. The space between them was arranged with marble-topped tables where customers sipped coffee, ate pastries or delicately consumed gelato. In the poem 'Aurora Leigh' written in 1856, Elizabeth Barrett Browning wrote:

To eat their ice at Doni's tenderly, –
Each lovely lady close to a cavalier
Who holds her dear fan while she feeds her smile
On meditative spoonfuls of vanille,
He breathing hot protesting vows of love,
Enough to thaw her cream, and scorch his beard.

There were also tables of elderly ladies taking tea, finely dressed men engrossed in conversation and young friends catching up on gossip. Between them would wander flower girls with their baskets of fresh picked blossoms and hawkers selling souvenir photographs.

Like many Englishwomen before and since, Janet felt an immediate affection for Florence. The English influence that had penetrated this Tuscan heartland over many years produced a comforting sensation of familiarity among so much that was foreign. There were the established English residents who lived most of the year in or near the city, and then there were more visitors, among them Germans and Americans arriving for the winter months.

To meet the needs and tastes of these foreigners, there were all sorts of shops supplying 'indispensable' English items such as mackintoshes, tea, marmalade, shortbread and English novels, journals and newspapers. There were popular tearooms serving muffins and English cakes like the currant tarts of Hester Piozzi's time. There were English doctors and English bankers, pharmacies like Roberts and Co. and the English Pharmacy in Via Tornabuoni. There was the English Church in Via Lamarmora and Anglican services also at the church of San Marks in Via Maggio directly across the Ponte Santa Trinità from Via Tornabuoni.

The best hotels were along the river. Here were the expensive places like The Grand Hotel Continental and De La Paix, the Hotel D'Italie and The New York. Less grand was the Porta Rossa still in operation today, or the Hotel Pensione Suisse where George Eliot became a regular. More affordable, but still good, were the *pensioni*, often named after the proprietress; Miss Earle in the Palazzo Corsi in Via Tornabuoni, Fräulein Selbon on the Via della Colonna or, on the other side of the river, Madame Kirch in the Lungarno Serristori. For those staying longer, furnished apartments were available and affordable. At the centre of English life in the city was the British Embassy, and it was here that the energetic Janet Ross stayed as the guest of the ambassador Sir Henry Elliot.

Florentine society consisted of the newly arrived court and the old patrician families that traced their lineage back to the thirteenth and fourteenth centuries — names such as Corsini, Ridolfi and Rucellai. Even during the fortnight of this first short stay, Janet caught a sense of the social whirlwind. She attended the balls and receptions and private parties, all the more enjoyable for being less formal than English balls. In between such invitations, she was happy to go to museums and take in sights that until now were only known to her through books. She discovered a city exciting and civilized, friendly and exotic, beautiful and affordable. It was, she concluded, 'a delightful city'.

Her Florentine sojourn ended after two short weeks when, as planned, Henry arrived and they prepared to leave for England. The respite was over and once more she to face the realities temporarily left behind in Egypt. Janet and Henry were on the verge of financial ruin.

England

AFTER seven years living abroad, the Rosses travelled back to England in June 1867 at the end of Janet's Italian holiday. Having concluded that there was no future for them in Egypt, it was in Britain that the Rosses sought refuge. Janet had family and friends there, and while Henry's immediate family lived in Malta, he had connections in London.

Coming back in such uncertain circumstances was far from what Janet had envisaged when she left home seven years before. She and Henry had planned to return in their own time, and with success to proclaim in the form of a healthy bank balance. It was not a naive plan either. Henry at forty-seven was a successful banker with many years of experience in the East, earlier with Layard's expeditions and more recently working for British financial interests.

Theirs was not some fly-by-night scheme. There was money to be made in the East and until now, the Rosses had been taking a reasonable share of it and faring very well — certainly well enough for Henry to expect to be able to retire comfortably in England. Suddenly, however, all that had been dashed and their future was uncertain. The Egyptian economy had crashed and many people including the Rosses saw their savings disappear overnight.

Janet and Henry were still accounting for the extent of their losses. For weeks and months Henry tried to assess what, if any, monies might be retrievable. In Alexandria, he had done as much as he could, and they were both relieved to finally leave the city and their debacle behind. England too was where their son, Alick, was being cared for, and the place of Janet's own childhood. Up until her marriage to Henry, it had been her home. It was the land of her forebears and much she held dear.

Janet was the eldest child of Sir Alexander and Lady Lucie Duff Gordon. He was glamorous, and she was beautiful and clever. Together they were a popular couple in liberal and artistic circles in early Victorian London. The influence of these parents resonated throughout Janet's life. She idolized her father and at the same time, identified herself as the custodian of her strong maternal heritage. She came from a long line of distinguished feminine achievement, something that would prove both a blessing and a burden throughout her life.

Alexander was heir to an impoverished baronetcy, inherited when he had barely left Eton. Unable to afford the cost of university, he found himself a modest paying job in the civil service. Fortunately, he was able to compensate for the lack of financial security with charm, manners and good looks. He was an immensely likeable young man who, like his wife, was a good linguist and keen reader. Although he came from a socially conventional family he was open to ideas and discussion on all manner of subjects.

Lucie came from an overtly intellectual and less conventional tradition, one barely known to the Duff Gordons; a tradition committed to ideas and public-spirited work. These values applied to the daughters as much as the sons. Lucie and her mother, Sarah Austin, and even Sarah's mother before her, Susannah Taylor, had been beneficiaries of the tradition and each enjoyed a reputation as women of intellect and accomplishment. It was a bloodline of remarkable achievement that expected nothing less of its daughters than they apply their ability in whatever situation they found themselves.

In the earlier part of the 1800s, Sarah Austin was known as a first rate translator of European literature. Lucie was later to gain acclaim for her adventures on the upper reaches of the Nile in her excellent and very popular *Letters from Egypt*, published posthumously. Like her mother she too was sought after as a translator.

Janet's forebears on Sarah's side were Unitarians; liberal-minded Protestants. Unitarians were anti-dogmatists who saw Christ as an exemplar rather than a focus of worship, and tended to see social ills as humanly created rather than acts of God. Not surprisingly, Unitarians were drawn to campaigns for social and political justice. The family always had empathy for the vulnerable or weak, both human and beast.

Lucie was an only child, and although the family finances were often in a perilous state, her mother made every effort to ensure she received a broad, if somewhat idiosyncratic, education — she even spent one brief, highly unconventional spell as the only girl at a boys' school. While she had few friends her own age, she did play with the children of some of her mother's illustrious friends, including the young John Stuart Mill who lived next door. Lucie was very close to her parents, especially her mother, with whom she spent a lot of time. Her mother especially encouraged her broad reading and immersion in the world of ideas and current affairs.

She was doubly fortunate to be both intelligent and attractive. She was a healthy girl with a clear complexion and thick dark hair worn in a braid twisted up at the back of her head. As a young woman, she liked to dress according to personal style rather than fashion — sometimes understated, at other times leaning towards the theatrical with bright colours and exotic patterns. Either way, she stood out in a crowd as beautiful and confident.

When Alexander first met her at a London party in 1839 he was fascinated, and in short time set about convincing her that they had every chance of being happy together. Lucie was eighteen and Alexander twenty-eight. Although he still held only a relatively junior clerkship at the Treasury, Alexander anticipated further promotion. On this basis, the family he and Lucie looked forward to would enjoy a comfortable, if not extravagant, life. Sarah Austin was realistic about Duff Gordon's limited financial prospects, but seemed happy for the marriage to go ahead. Indeed, she seemed more at ease with the idea than Alexander's formidable mother, Lady Duff Gordon, who finally accepted her eldest boy's choice to marry an independent-minded young woman of limited means without celebration.

The fact that her prospective husband actually had a job at all would likely have convinced Lucie that her marriage would be a happier union than that suffered by her parents. John Austin and Sarah Taylor were married in August 1819 after a five-year engagement — protracted by the length of preparation time John Austin required before being called to the Bar. Before taking up the law, John had spent an unhappy five years in the army. He turned to legal studies in the hope it would better suit his interests and temperament.

Although her intellectual equal, to Sarah's great frustration her husband never ended up achieving his latent potential. John Austin's passion was legal philosophy, but a chronic mixture of inhibition and anxiety held him back from anticipated public achievement and success. Indeed, within the first couple of years of their marriage it became clear that her husband was ill-equipped for any courtroom appearance. To enter the room made him so anxious he could barely speak a word. The fact that he is remembered today within legal circles for his contribution to the law is due, in large part, to Sarah's determination to edit and publish his best work.

Socially, he was often withdrawn or terse and privately he was too preoccupied to show any affection to his wife. Worse still, his psychological state often spilled over into hypochondria.

26

A CASTLE IN TUSCANY

At a practical level, John Austin's failure to thrive meant almost constant money worries for Sarah. This meant that Sarah had to earn as much as possible from translation work, although it was hardly ever enough. There was a demand for her skills and the work could be done at home and fitted around other obligations.

Sometimes the family was obliged to move out of London to find affordable living. With John out of work for long periods, it was economical for the Austins to close or let their London house and take lodgings elsewhere, occasionally in the countryside, sometimes abroad. A few times, they simply travelled across the channel to Boulogne and took rooms in a pleasant little seaside inn there. Relieved of the expense of running a house in London and with the lower cost of living on the continent, the Austins could make their income go further. Over the years they also spent time in Germany. In 1827–8 they rented a house in Bonn where John Austin prepared a lecture series on jurisprudence he had been invited to deliver at London University. In the end he did not manage to complete the lectures.

Finally, seventeen years after their marriage, John Austin had some success. He was appointed to head a government commission in Malta — an important naval base for the British — inquiring into colonial grievances on the island. For the two years he was there, he carried out his work with enthusiasm and authority and was promised a good salary. When they returned to England, however, they came back to many of their old financial difficulties. Indeed, it took some time for the Colonial Office to pay the two years' salary that was outstanding. In Malta, Sarah had managed to get by on a living allowance attached to her husband's prestigious position. After Malta there would be more time spent on the continent trying to save money, finally returning to England in 1848 to escape the civil unrest in Paris. Ultimately the Austins retired to a rented cottage in the country at Weybridge, in Surrey.

As if in compensation for him, Sarah became the antithesis of her husband. She managed all the details of the household and the upbringing of her daughter, she became the emotional crutch John relied on, carrying his anxieties and disappointments day in and day out. Often anxious herself, she nonetheless determined to become a success in her own right. Although friends knew something of the domestic reality she endured, she did not complain. There was little to be gained by doing so. Out of loyalty to the marriage, she stoically avoided mention of her husband's failings.

Instead, she channelled her energy into conversation and company. From childhood her intellectual gift had been obvious. One admirer, intending a great compliment, described her mind as 'masculine'. Her house became a meeting place for some of the most able minds in London. Originally, they came to talk with John Austin, but as he increasingly withdrew into inaction and disappointment, it was clear they kept coming to enjoy the company of his wife. Thomas Carlyle, Sydney Smith and well-known Unitarians John Stuart Mill and Jeremy Bentham were among her admirers.

Some years after Malta, during an extended period of financial exile in Paris, Sarah established a modest salon in their apartment. Because she spoke French, German and Italian, and because her intellect and conversation were so admired, her house became a focal point for some of the brightest in Europe, all interested in talking about ideas in a convivial environment. These were the years after Lucie's marriage, when Sarah had only herself and her husband to care for. She also kept busy with translations, with works by French, Italian and German authors, and became an established authority on the latter, especially Goethe.

How Sarah managed the various elements of her life is a story of ability and will, but the frustrations and unhappiness of her marriage could not be suppressed forever. Her private despair eventually revealed itself in a most unexpected way. In her late thirties after about twelve years of marriage, Sarah, almost in defiance of her own character, began an extraordinary correspondence with a German author. He was Herman von Pückler-Muskau, best known as a travel writer. He was an extravagant minor German nobleman with a reputation as a libertine. Everything about him was in contrast to Sarah; his background, values and character. But she was deeply unhappy and he recognized her vulnerability and spoke directly to it. She was an attractive woman; emotionally and physically ignored by her husband.

This unlikely pair crossed paths in 1830 when Sarah began the job of translating Pückler's latest bestseller, *Briefe eines Verstorbenen* (*Letters from a Dead Man*). At some point in their professional relationship he began to encourage her to write to him in the most open and frank way, urging her to reveal everything of her intimate self and she agreed to the suggestion.

It was a seduction via correspondence. The relationship, though never physical, was intense and highly sexual. Having embarked on an intimate correspondence she had no regrets, and over the coming years she wrote in her articulate and firm hand about her life, 'heart, passion, imagination, gaiety, all crushed under this weight of care and anxiety', and of her fantasies and longings:

> *Would to Heaven, dear one, I could sit … at your feet; my head on your knees, my arms clasped around them and yours around my neck, or better, would I were laid by your side, tranquilly, your head upon my shoulder, or my face in your bosom and that you could tell me all you wish or hope; all that troubles or annoys you.*

Their intimate letters corresponded to some of the most difficult years of Sarah's marriage and were exchanged via diplomatic bags. Pückler had a friend in the German embassy in London and this method was safer than the regular post. Over time, the ardour diminished and when, after nearly four years of letter writing, the two did meet briefly in Berlin, they had little to say to each other. The meeting marked the end of the correspondence.

It is only by chance that the letters came to light. After Sarah's death, the family, including Janet, chose to overlook the unhappiness of the Austin marriage. Sarah had destroyed her copies of the letters, but lived in fear that Pückler might be less discreet. And indeed her letters to him and his draft responses remained part of his papers. Some time after his death, his executor placed them in the Berlin State

Janet's grandmother, Sarah Austin, much admired
for her intelligence and dignity despite her
domestic difficulties.

Library, and until World War II they were available for research; though those who read them preferred to deal with them only in the most general way.

During the War, parts of the library's collection were moved for safekeeping. Pückler's papers were included and ended up in Silesia, an area subsequently ceded to Poland. Polish authorities then hid the German material from the Soviets and until the 1970s the papers were described as war losses. Finally, in 1980 they turned up in the Jagiellonian University in Kraków. Maturing like a rich archaeological dig, the correspondence sheds new light on Sarah Austin's experience. More recently, the letters themselves have become the subject of study by two American scholars — precisely what Sarah Austin wished to avoid.

Sarah had good reason to think that her daughter would enjoy a more successful marriage than she had, and the wedding took place on May 16, 1840 in Kensington Old Church in London's West End. Removed from the complications of her parents' marriage, Lucie, now Lady Duff Gordon, was free to make a happier life. The young couple were handsome, clever, shared an interest in politics and enjoyed books and languages; their popularity was assured, both with Sarah Austin's friends and the many more they made of their own.

They moved into a rather large house at 8 Queen Anne's Gate, Westminster. Before long they had acquired a close circle of friends including many talented artists and writers. Some of the better known were William Thackeray, who would soon publish *Vanity Fair*; the popular playwright and later, editor of *Punch* magazine, Tom Taylor; Richard Doyle, an illustrator for *Punch* and a household name in Victorian England; Alexander Kinglake, the author of the hugely popular *Eothen*, a fictionalized travelogue from the East, and Caroline Norton, a writer and later model for the heroine of one of the most enduring of Victorian novels, *Diana of the Crossways*, written by George Meredith.

There were dinners and informal gatherings, Lucie often with a cigarette in hand mingling among her friends, enjoying the conversation and entering into forthright debate. Her adored husband, less voluble by nature, was an easy host who obviously enjoyed his wife's company.

On February 24, 1842, Lucie gave birth to her first child, Janet Anne. Although they had hoped for a boy, the new parents were delighted. From the start, Lucie and Alexander agreed on a relaxed approach to their daughter's upbringing. There was limited formal structure and little formal education in their instruction, an attitude that caused considerable anxiety to Sarah Austin. Even as a young child still in the nursery, Janet revelled in her parents' world of conversation and merriment with friends. Visitors came and went, and the household enjoyed the company of some of the most witty and talented minds in the city. The rooms were alive with ideas and politics, books and writing.

In Janet's world, she knew nothing of lessons or discipline. She was socially sophisticated but lacked any rudimentary education. Sarah Austin wrote to a friend that the child, just three, 'continues deaf to all suggestions about learning her letters and the like'. Despite these misgivings, Sarah was not prepared to take on the role of formal tutor. Nor was she approached by her daughter to assist, though in her own way she encouraged Janet by taking her along when she visited old friends. On one such visit Sarah called on Charles and Georgiana Babbage. Charles Babbage was the mathematician credited with originating the idea of a programmable computer. Being naturally curious, the little girl was delighted to get informal lessons in the workings and advantages of Mr Babbage's calculating machine.

Lucie and Alexander also gave generous latitude to Janet joining gatherings outside the house. One fixture especially looked forward to by the well-mannered little girl who charmed all the adults she was presented to, were the long and elaborate Sunday morning breakfasts at the house of Samuel Rogers. Rogers, a very successful poet in his day, had been a banker. He collected art and supported emerging artists and writers, among them Charles Dickens. Alexander and Lucie were regulars at his extended breakfasts and sometimes Janet would receive a special invitation from the elderly man, asking her to be brought over — presumably by a household servant — in time to join the other guests for the desserts and fruit. She would be placed on a chair supported by cushions and fed grapes that had been specially reserved for her. It didn't matter that she was the only child in the room.

The result of so much adult company was that, by her own assessment, Janet was precocious but also lonely. At home, her father was away for long hours at the office, and Lucie's time was taken up with work on translations. One book she worked on was Berthold Neibuhr's *Stories of the Gods and Heroes of Greece*, published in 1843. This translation was accredited to her mother, whose name was better known. The following year, Lucie translated under her own name, Wilhelm Meinhold's *The Amber Witch* from the German. Soon afterwards she completed the somewhat dryer, *The French in Algiers* by M. de France and Clemens Lamping, then came the *Narratives of Remarkable Criminal Trials* by Anselm Ritter Von Feuerbach. Alexander negotiated her contractual arrangements and payment for the work was made to him.

Like Sarah, her knowledge of languages and sensitivity to style made her good at the work. This was a welcome asset, because there had always been a need to supplement household finances. Also like her mother, Lucie found she could not rid herself of money problems, although her own were nowhere near the magnitude of Sarah's. More to the point, money problems did not stop the early years of her marriage being among the happiest of her life.

Meanwhile, one significant exception to young Janet's loneliness was a young servant boy named Hassen el Bakkeet, known to the family by Janet's nickname for him, Hatty. He came to live at Queen Anne's Gate when Janet was still a toddler. He had worked as a servant in another London house, but he was going blind and was of little further use to his employer. Africans in London working as domestic servants were not uncommon, and a young unattached boy like Hatty would be at the mercy of his employer. He was turned out with nowhere to go and was found one night by Lucie, returning home after a party at the Dickens'. She literally tripped over him on the doorstep and took him in. He was about twelve years old and probably Sudanese. Lucie and Alexander decided English missionaries likely raised him because he spoke with an English accent and his speech was heavy with curiously pious terms and phrases. Hatty did some light work around the house and played with and read to Janet. He was warmly welcomed by the family and repaid the kindness with total devotion.

About this time, just before Janet's third birthday in 1845, Lucie had another child. Hatty announced triumphantly to all callers 'we have got a boy'. He was, recalled Janet, 'so elated that I wished to change my sex, a boy being evidently so much more important than a girl'. Her precocious ways seemed to count for very little in the face of a baby boy.

The baby was healthy enough at birth and his parents had every expectation for him. They named him Maurice. He was christened at the end of July and there was a breakfast at home to celebrate. The very next day, however, Maurice caught a fever. All the remedies applied were useless to save him and within a week he was dead. He was a little over five months old. Lucie and Alexander were devastated.

Despite the shadow hanging over the house, with her parents' efforts Janet's life went on much as before. The great event in her year was of course her birthday. On this day, she was allowed to dine downstairs and to invite her particular friends. This meant the guests in attendance were not children, but rather the adult friends of her parents, mostly men twenty or thirty years older than Janet. At her fifth birthday were Tom Taylor, Caroline Norton, William Thackeray and Richard Doyle, as well as Lord Lansdowne, a distinguished statesman who would serve under eight prime ministers and after whom Maurice had been named. Also at the table was C.P. Bayley, another journalist, known as 'the thunderer of *The Times*'. Bayley was a bachelor and had been introduced to the Duff Gordons by Thackeray. He had recently moved into their house as a paying lodger.

It was four years after the death of Maurice that another baby arrived, a boy. He too was named Maurice, a practice common in the nineteenth century, and, mercifully, he survived. The happiness helped Alexander and Lucie to compensate for the earlier loss. They had their male heir at last. Janet, now seven, was less convinced of the happiness of the occasion. Though she wanted her parents to be pleased, she found their new enthusiasm difficult to bear. The extra fuss over the boy and the high expectations held for him were the talk of the house. Nor did her irritation pass with time; throughout her life it would rankle with her that she was not the chosen heir, for she believed, with some justification as it turned out, that she would have made a better job of it.

It was about this time that the Duff Gordons came to know George Meredith. While Lucie, Janet and Maurice were staying with the Austins at Weybridge in Surrey they visited a nearby boarding house called The Limes. One of the residents was their friend Tom Taylor and it was through him that they first met the aspiring young writer Meredith, barely twenty-one years old, and his then wife, Mary Ellen who were also staying at the boarding house. George Meredith was the son of a humble Portsmouth tailor. From an early age he was ambitious to overcome his background and make a success in the world of letters. His intelligence and literary aspirations were accompanied by a generous temperament. Mary Ellen was the bright and talented daughter of well-known Victorian novelist Thomas Peacock. When she married George Meredith — seven years her junior — she was a young widow with a small daughter and aspirations to be a writer. At first they were happy but the relationship would suffer under constant financial constraints, miscarriages and, it has been suggested, the revelation that Meredith had misled his wife about his family background — tailors being then held in low regard. In the end their relationship would descend into acrimony and bitterness.

When the Duff Gordons first met them the Merediths were newly married and Mary Ellen's daughter Edith was a couple of years younger than eight-year-old Janet. The two girls soon became friends, and Janet came often to play in the garden at The Limes. At the end of these visits George Meredith would walk with Janet back to her grandparents' house. As the writer and his new little friend ambled, he would invent stories to keep her entertained. One he devised was a tale called 'The Queen of the Serpent'. Later, he renamed the tale 'Bhanavar the Beautiful', and it became one of the best-loved stories of his Arabian fiction *The Shaving of Shagpat*. When it came out in 1855, *Shagpat* was deemed a great success, and considered by many critics an achievement in the realm of the *Arabian Nights*. From the first days of their friendship when Meredith told her beautiful stories, she christened him 'My Poet'.

Toward the end of their stay at Weybridge, Hatty, who had accompanied them, developed a persistent cough. As the cooler weather closed in, the cough developed into bronchitis. He became weak and feverish and short of breath. By the time the family returned to London it was clear that the boy had consumption, as tuberculosis was known then. Towards Christmas, Hatty's condition worsened and he finally died in Alexander's arms on Christmas Day. For the whole family it was an awful loss. For Janet it was the loss of her intimate playmate. For Lucie and Alexander it was an echo of the death of their first son. Caring for Hatty as well as her own children for the last couple of months, Lucie hardly noticed that she too had developed a cough that was proving difficult to shake off.

The following year on a subsequent visit to her parents' house, Lucie came down with serious bronchitis and then pneumonia, which took her months to get over. She and Alexander thought that fresh country air might be the best long-term remedy and, recalling the lovely summer they had enjoyed at Weybridge two years before, the Duff Gordons decided to move out of the city permanently.

Queen Anne's Square would be let and they would be better off financially. After a short search, they found a place at Escher, just four miles away from the Austins and close enough to the train line for Alexander to be able to commute daily to London for work. Their new home was called Belvedere House and was perched on top of a hill; it was dry and warm and pretty. It had once been an inn with a cottage to one side, and sat in an old-fashioned garden of grassy slopes and attractive walks. The garden was full of beautiful shady trees, the sort that young children love to climb. The place became known as the 'Gordon Arms' and it was the backdrop for the last years of happy family life.

When not playing with friends or visitors, Janet was free to ride her new pony, which she named Eothen in honour of Kinglake. Since moving to the country, she had become a fearless rider. Before long, the family was settled into country life. There was hunting with the Surrey Union Foxhounds, which Janet joined when she was a bit older, and fishing and boating on the River Mole in the summer. If fish were scarce, she liked to watch her pet bull-terrier chase water rats or hens in and out of the bulrushes. Sometimes there would be idyllic picnics with her parents' friends by the river, their wine bottles tied over the sides of boats to cool in the water.

For a spirited nine-year-old, life at Escher was a dream. But even her rather unconventional parents could see that Janet was in danger of running wild. She was overdue for some formal education. A governess was the answer.

Lucie and Alexander's attitude to date, while it might appear charmingly bohemian, had been little short of neglect. And it had persisted despite Sarah Austin's early concerns and the value that Lucie herself placed on learning and the family lineage of well-educated intelligent women. Perhaps Lucie was reacting against her mother's fastidiousness on the subject, or perhaps she lacked the time and energy for the task. (Maurice, by contrast was destined from the first for Eton, to be paid for by his godfather, Lord Lansdowne.)

The young woman chosen to take on Janet's education was one Mathilde von Zeschau, the daughter of a retired Major of the Saxon army who had come to see England and do some teaching while she was there. Her principal task was to teach Janet to speak and read German. But progress was slow, so it was decided that Janet be sent to a school in Dresden accompanied by Mathilde whose family lived nearby.

Janet loathed the place so much that after only two weeks she fell ill and was forced to withdraw. She went to stay with Mathilde's family instead, where she was much happier. Each morning she attended classes in a little day school run in the same house. Although it was better than the boarding school, Janet still found it tough going. The schoolmistress disliked her for her boyish, independent ways, chiding her for teaching the other girls boy's games during the hour of recreation in the small garden. After years of being the centre of attention, it was difficult for Janet to adjust to being one of a group. It was a hard lesson. At the end of the German experiment Janet and Fraulein von Zeschau returned to England.

Despite the difficulties, the German experience did began to show dividends. Janet's German was finally declared excellent. At the age of thirteen, Janet was asked to do her first translation work by Kinglake. Recognizing that she had the concentration and determination required, he approached her with a German text on the Crimea — one of his favourite subjects. Her German must have been very good indeed. The book was *Unter dem Doppeladler* (*Under the Double Eagle*) written by the famous Russian military engineer General Todleben. It was dreary stuff for an active young mind but she was of course flattered to be asked. Though it proved a tedious drudge, she persevered and finished the job.

Not long after completing the work for Kinglake, Janet became ill with scarlet fever. For a month and a half she lay in bed with little consolation but the complete novels of Sir Walter Scott, borrowed from the library by her father.

In addition to the limited formal teaching she was now getting, Janet, entering her teenage years, benefited from the interest of her parents' friends. A number of them, generally men, enthusiastically took on some aspect or other of her education. These men admired Lucie because she was clever and generous and, recognizing these traits in her daughter, they too welcomed the opportunity to encourage her further. Janet liked the attention. From her perspective it was a more adult version of sitting in Samuel Rogers's special seat when she had been requested to join his breakfasts as a small child. Kinglake now appointed himself as her informal guardian. As an unmarried man (he claimed never to have wed because he had observed that women always prefer other men to their own husbands) he had spare time to devote to Janet and would continue to do so for the rest of his life. He took her to hear debates in the House of Commons and encouraged her reading.

Lord Lansdowne was another supporter. He invited her stay at Lansdowne House in Berkeley Square in central London and to ride in the park, and happily accompanied her to concerts and other outings, including the opening of Parliament. With Janet in mind, in autumn 1857, Lucie and Alexander decided to travel with the children to Paris. The previous year, Alexander at last received a worthy promotion to become a Commissioner of Inland Revenue. The accompanying rise in salary was very welcome and a couple of months in Paris would be quite affordable. The trip, it was hoped, would assist Janet's French, and she would also benefit from some informal tutoring from a couple of her grandmother's old intellectual friends. Among those who took her on were Jules Barthélemy-Saint-Hilaire, philosopher, journalist and statesman, who steered her away from reading novels in an effort to turn her mind to more serious matters. Another was the philosopher Victor Cousin who spent an hour at a time with Janet talking, not about Plato, but about the beautiful ladies of the 1700s. The family stayed in a flat on the Rue de Chaillot not far from the Champs-Elysées. Throughout her adolescence, Janet continued to be an avid horse rider, and even in Paris when she wasn't reading or being 'educated' in some way, she still liked to get on a horse — the wilder the beast the better.

The intense young Janet with cropped hair who caught
the eye of G.F. Watts.

As Janet's interests were expanding, her physical presence was becoming more striking. As part of the treatment for scarlet fever, Lucie had cut her daughter's hair short and it was kept that way until she was sixteen. The effect was to make her look more like a beautiful young boy than a girl.

Her unusual looks caught the eye of Victorian painter George Frederic Watts. He was another friend of her parents, and Janet took to visiting his studio and sitting for hours at a time watching him work. On one of these occasions, he asked her to keep very still for a moment, time enough for him to complete a little study of her head. Shortly after, he made another, this time as part of a group of classical figures commissioned for Lord Lansdowne's country house in Wiltshire, Bowood House. Janet was dressed in armour as Patroclus, one of the Grecian chiefs during the Trojan war and the intimate of Achilles. Watts caught the firm jaw, the strong brow and the penetrating gaze. The study suggested the androgynous quality of both the subject and sitter, more complex and provocative than merely tomboy. The painter caught the beauty of her face just as she entered adulthood.

A Life of Her Own

It was Rose, living and glowing; Rose, who was the brilliant
young Amazon, smoothing the neck of a mettlesome gray cob.
Evan's heart bounded up to her, but his limbs were motionless.

GEORGE MEREDITH
EVAN HARRINGTON (1860)

AS Janet was on the cusp of adulthood, Lucie gave birth to her third child. The baby girl they named Urania was born in late 1858. Arriving many years after her brother and sister — she was nine years younger than Maurice and sixteen years younger than Janet — she was the absolute darling of her mother's affections. Lucie's happiness though, was tinged with lurking anxiety over her own health.

Ever since Hatty's death, she had been vulnerable to recurrent chest infections, each illness followed by periods of recuperation that never really delivered back her full strength. She was careful about overexerting herself, but sometimes not careful enough — as when she went to look after her father during his last days. For the last ten years since their return from Paris, the Austins had lived quietly at Weybridge. Janet would make the 6.5-kilometre (4-mile) trek almost daily on horseback to visit her grandparents, and she began to recognize that her grandfather was getting very ill. At first she wanted to shield her mother from the fact so as not to alarm her, but as her grandfather deteriorated she told Lucie.

Though not well herself, Lucie immediately went to nurse her father, who was diagnosed with acute bronchitis. She was anxious to be with him and comfort him. John Austin, who had suffered so much in his life, was very dear to his only child. As soon as she saw him, Lucie must have realized how sick he was because she stayed by his bed day and night.

She was already ill before she went to nurse him and immediately after he died, physically and emotionally exhausted, she relapsed completely and began coughing blood. This was the telltale symptom of consumption. Coughing blood was a clear indication that the germs, probably dormant in her body for many years, were now active and forming tubercles on the surface of the lungs. For her own sake and for her new baby, Lucie's priority was to get well. It fell to Janet to stay and comfort her desolate grandmother, who despite all the problems of her marriage could barely think of life without her husband. Janet stayed in the cottage with Sarah Austin for a week or so before bringing her to the Gordon Arms just before Christmas.

With Lucie's illness, Janet and her father increasingly looked to each other for companionship. They had long been known among family and friends as 'the inseparables', but the bond became more intense than ever. As always since they had moved to Escher, Janet rode to the station every afternoon to meet Alexander off the London train. On weekends, they would ride together, often venturing out on long excursions. Their idea of a great time was to ride the horses up to fifty or sixty miles in a day, only arriving home for dinner.

Other times they would set off on overnight trips. Once, when they visited Great Marlow in Buckinghamshire — a place Alexander had known as a boy — and tried to book two rooms at an inn, the landlady would not believe they were father and daughter. She pointedly told them that she had lived with titled families and had never heard any young lady address her parent as 'dear old boy' as Janet did. Father and daughter thought this was very funny. They adored each other and the comfort and closeness they enjoyed was a relief from the creeping ill health settling on the Gordon Arms.

⁂

In 1858, one afternoon on her way to Alexander's train, Janet pulled up in front of a little boy who had fallen on the road. She asked him if he was all right and offered to accompany him home. When they arrived at a nearby cottage, they were greeted at the door by the father who kissed the child and looked hard at the young woman accompanying him. As Janet later recalled, the attractive man with kindly eyes turned to her and asked, 'Are you not Lady Duff Gordon's daughter?' and before the answer was out he clasped her in his arms and exclaimed, 'Oh my Janet! Don't you know me? I am your Poet'.

Since leaving Weybridge, Meredith's literary success had been mixed and by the time he rediscovered Janet his marriage to Mary Ellen had disintegrated completely. She had left him for the painter Henry Wallis and had taken her children to stay with her former mother-in-law, Lady Nicolls, to

39

whom she was still close. While Mary Ellen was travelling in Italy, Meredith went to the Nicolls's house and took his five-year-old son back to live with him. Edith (the girl) remained with her grandmother. The Arabian stories he had invented for Janet years before, though they enjoyed critical praise, had not sold well. The acclaimed writer of later life was still the unsure author working as a reader in a publishing house — Chapman and Hall — to make ends meet. For now his immediate preoccupation was the search for a place for himself and his young son to live. Janet and Meredith were quick to renew their early friendship. She enthusiastically assisted in the search and together they secured a cottage on Copsham Common not far from the Gordon Arms.

It was obvious from the beginning that they enjoyed each other's company. Increasingly, they spent time walking in the woods and talking about his books and poetry. He was no longer the avuncular storyteller, but rather a companion on an equal footing. The fourteen-year age difference between them was of slighter significance than it may have been to many girls of sixteen; indeed, it was what Janet was used to. Like other older admirers, Meredith enjoyed her firm opinions and independent ways. As Kinglake had, he recognized her talent for languages and nominated her to translate the work of German historian, Herr von Sybel, *Geschichte und Literatur des Kreuzzuge* (*The History and Literature of the Crusades*) for Chapman and Hall. It was edited by Lucie and published in 1861 under her name.

In a fragile emotional state after the failure of his marriage, the companionship of an uncomplicated, well-connected girl was a pleasant relief. An added advantage to their friendship was Janet's willingness to look after little Arthur when Meredith was working or in London. Meredith also enjoyed the warmth shown to him by the Duff Gordons and most of their friends, although some of them clearly left him ill at ease. Acutely sensitive to class, Meredith had not yet enough success to compensate for the shortcomings of his family background, as he perceived them.

Janet appreciated his anxieties. 'My Poet', she remembered, 'in the early days when I saw so much of him, was a delightful companion when he knew he was liked; before strangers his shyness took the form of asserting himself rather loudly, and trying to be epigrammatic and witty; he gave one the impression that he was not quite sure on what footing he stood'.

All the time spent with Meredith did not affect Janet's relationship with her 'dear old boy' father, but Lucie viewed things differently. She found herself increasingly aware of the depth of feeling between Janet and Meredith. Fond as she was of the 'Poet', the idea of him as a son-in-law was alarming. There was the age difference, Janet's lack of experience and Meredith's financial insecurity to consider.

Lucie was not the only one concerned for Janet. The sight of a spirited, apparently carefree, young woman going about without a chaperone alarmed some more conventional members of society. One who commented was Janet's godmother, Lady Antrobus, a cousin on the Duff Gordon side. She thought there were altogether too many men in Janet's life, even though most of them were old enough to be the girl's father — a fact that may have further fuelled her alarm. She was particularly taken aback on one occasion when Janet, staying with her as a guest in London, organized an outing with Meredith on an omnibus to visit the Tower of London. Lady Antrobus was horrified and felt compelled to try to send send her daughter's maid along to accompany the couple. Janet, though fond of her godmother, found her concern amusing and politely turned down the offer of the maid.

Among the Duff Gordons and some of their friends and acquaintances, it was still considered appropriate for young ladies to be presented at Court. Even Sarah Austin in her straitened financial situation, had felt compelled to have Lucie presented. Little had changed, and, in a rare nod to convention, Lucie began preparing her daughter for the event. The relationship with Meredith probably encouraged her to have Janet 'come out'; it would formally open the field for potential suitors.

At seventeen, Janet was presented to Queen Victoria. She wore a dress given to her by Lady Antrobus, who also saw to it that her goddaughter's hair was fashionably styled. For the first time in her life Janet was fitted with a whalebone corset. The attention and fuss that preceded the event were exciting, but when the day arrived, Janet had never felt more shy and frightened in her life, and also very uncomfortable. Her curtsey was awkward and worse still, she dropped her glove in front of the Queen and was too anxious to pick it up. She was now officially 'out', although the fact made little difference to the way Janet chose to conduct herself.

Lucie need not have worried so much that her daughter would make an unwise match with Meredith. Janet was first and foremost a practical person, a characteristic underestimated by her family. She understood perfectly well that marrying a man in Meredith's position would put her in a precarious financial situation. She only had to observe her grandmother's marriage and the financial worries of her own parents to see the perils of too little money.

In any event, time would tell that Janet had no interest in romantic love as a foundation for marriage. Nor was physical intimacy a priority for her, at least not with Meredith and probably not with men generally.

The possibility that Janet was a lesbian is something her descendents have certainly considered — one view holds that she had lesbian tendencies but they were repressed. Janet's great-great-nephew, the historian Antony Beevor — well known for his bestselling works *Stalingrad* and *Berlin — The Downfall 1945* — is of this view. He tells of a cache of postcards showing nude nubile girls found among Janet's papers. If these belonged to Janet, there is no way of telling when she began collecting them. Another great-great-nephew is a psychotherapist and the editor of the last edition of *Leaves from Our Tuscan Kitchen*, Michael Waterfield. He views her latent lesbianism simply as one part of a complex sexuality, which did not necessarily exclude men.

If Meredith ever wondered about Janet's sexuality, it did not inhibit his feelings for her. Despite the ruins of his marriage, he was very much drawn to women, and as a writer, the female character intrigued him. Janet's unobtainable status only firmed the bond between them. Their familiarity posed no danger to either of them because it would not be consummated and in their hearts they both understood as much.

In the meantime, their mutual affection was heartfelt. One day when Janet complained of the dullness of the German words to one of Meredith's favourite songs, Schubert's 'Addio', he composed some English verses for her.

The pines are darkly swaying:
The skies are ashen-gray:
I mock my soul delaying
The word I have to say.

As if above it thundered
That we, who are one heart,
Must now for aye be sundered
My passion bids me part.

I dare not barely languish,
Nor press your lips to mine;
But with one cry of anguish,
My darling I resign.

Our dreams we too must smother:
The bitter truth is here
This hand is for another
Which I have held so dear.

To Pray that at the altar
You may be blessed above:
Ah, help me if I falter,
And keep me true to love.

But once, but once, look kindly,
Once clasp me with your spell:
Let joy and pain meet blindly,
And throb our dumb farewell.

In 1860 Meredith's new novel, *Evan Harrington*, began serialization in the *Fortnightly Review*. Much to Janet's delight, his heroine Rose Jocelyn had marked similarities to herself. With strong autobiographical overtones, the novel traces the story of the son of a tailor from Lymport. Evan's sisters have all married well and they are keen that he follows their example. By contrast, his mother wants him to continue in the debt-ridden family business. Ultimately, Evan marries Rose Jocelyn, a forthright and independently minded young woman, typical of the type that Meredith championed in many of his novels, and they live happily ever after. There were similarities too in Rose Jocelyn's parents with Janet's own parents, who are presented in a sympathetic light. When it came out, the novel was a popular success. Meredith was particularly pleased with a review in *The Saturday* that described Rose Jocelyn as 'a heroine who deserved to be a heroine'.

In Janet, Meredith had a willing receptacle for the projection of his female ideal, and Janet was deeply flattered. Moreover, he saw her as a young woman, not a child, and that too must have been appealing. With him, she was more than simply the daughter of the redoubtable Lady Duff Gordon. There is no doubt that he adored her and she delighted in the attention, and despite Janet's claims in later life that she had no idea Meredith was in love with her, they did, for a time, share a deeply intimate, though not sexual, friendship.

One weekend Janet and Alexander took the horses by rail to Aldermaston. The plan was to ride back as best they could. This was just the sort of adventure they relished; they arranged to meet up with an old friend of Alexander's, Austin Henry Layard, known to Janet as the man who dug up the beasts in the British Museum — the man with whom she would later travel to Venice to witness the entry of the King Victor Emmanuel. Though not a professional archaeologist, he was acclaimed as the excavator of Nineveh, the ancient Mesopotamian city on the banks of the Tigris River (in what would become Iraq). Born in Paris to English parents, he grew up in Florence and later went on to have a long career as a politician, English diplomat, art connoisseur and man of letters. He had embarked on his first expedition East three years before Janet was born and remained there for the next eight years. It was during this time that he made his great discovery.

Layard arrived for the weekend with an old friend he had made in the East, Henry James Ross. Ross was in his early forties and was a partner in the English-based bank Briggs and Co in Alexandria. He grew up in Malta where his father was also a banker. Early in his career, he spent a few years in the British consular service, but left to pursue greater adventures. To a young woman, Henry's overseas experience gave his conversation an extra sense of excitement. Besides he was a good horseman and a charming addition to the little party.

Janet later recalled that he sat next to her at dinner and told stories about the sport of pig sticking. This was a favourite pastime of the English in far-off places, the object being to hunt and spear wild boar and remain on your horse at the same time. With perfect dramatic timing, he recounted how once when his horse put its foot in a hole and rolled over him, the wild boar he was in pursuit of turned upon him, and would have gored and perhaps even killed him, had not Layard galloped up and drawn the beast's attention off. He talked too of the excavations they had done together at Nineveh and the wild life among the Yezidis — a Kurdish sect. Janet found Henry to be the most wonderfully vivid raconteur she had ever met. A horse loving, archaeologist-banker who had lived in far off exotic places — perfect!

After the weekend Ross left for a pre-arranged trip to Scotland, but Janet invited him to the Gordon Arms when he returned — which he did soon afterwards. Lucie was unwell and at the time convalescing at the seaside, so a maiden aunt was asked to oversee the visit. Janet took Ross to the local hunt and was impressed by his riding as much as his conversation and gentle manners. He too must have been impressed, because before the end of the visit he had proposed marriage to her. This was their second meeting. The proposal was made in the understanding that she would move to Alexandria with him. She agreed immediately, 'to the dismay of many of my friends, who did not at all approve of my going to live in Egypt'.

Ross's proposal was a way out for Janet. Life at Escher, though idyllic for a young girl, was less appealing now. The Gordon Arms was no more the lively place of friends and family that it had been in its best days. Lucie's ill health had fractured the rhythm of the place and she was often away recuperating. Maurice was away at school so Janet and Alexander, who was still commuting to London, were left to make do. Urania stayed close to her mother and the household servants who oversaw much of her day. The family, though surprised at the news of Janet's sudden engagement, took it well. Sarah Austin seemed to represent the general feeling when she wrote to a friend in Paris:

> Our little Janet is going to be married, and is to live in Alexandria! In a month you will see Mr and Mrs Ross at Paris, en route for their Egyptian home. It is like a clap of thunder, and I feel quite stunned. Mr Ross is a banker, clever and agreeable, an intimate friend of Mr Layard, whom he aided in his excavations at Ninevah [sic]. There is a little too much difference in their ages, but Janet never liked young men. We are all charmed with Mr Ross, but less so with the notion of Alexandria. However, he means to settle in England in the course of a few years. She is too young, and had he resided here the marriage would have been delayed.

Henry Ross seemed to understand from the start that his prospective wife did not love him in a romantic way and quite probably the feeling was mutual. Yet, they obviously had much in common. He possessed both the initiative and kindness she wanted and, importantly, he was financially secure. She was intelligent, enthusiastic and wonderful to look at. Marriage offered Janet the excitement of living in the near East and, at a practical level, of making enough money so that they could return to live comfortably in England. In a frank letter to Meredith she wrote, 'Henry makes 5,000 pounds a year and

Henry epitomized experience and adventure.

Janet in the year of her marriage, 1860.

Henry in the year of his marriage.
Drawing by G.F. Watts.

we will live on 1,000 pounds and put by 4,000 pounds — and at the end of five or six years, Click'. It was an opportunity to make a life of her own out of the shadows of her family.

Lucie's fears that her carefree daughter would make an unsuitable marriage were happily not realized. To her mind, Ross was 'excellent and agreeable; and there is quite enough money and a new country to see, and an interesting life ahead'. Meredith may have been crushed, but knew Janet well enough not be surprised. She knew exactly what she was doing.

Janet spent some of her last weeks in England in the company of Meredith, who wished her well. 'God bless you, my dear girl. If you don't make a good wife, I've never read a page of woman. He is a lucky fellow to get you, and the best thing he can do is to pray he may always know his luck.' If Janet was sentimental about leaving Meredith, friends and family, she hid it well. Her focus was on the adventure that lay ahead. What's more, she had little time to dwell on feelings. There were wedding arrangements to make and then her new life in Alexandria to plan for.

Henry wanted to give Janet jewellery to mark the marriage, but she preferred books. After consulting Meredith she went to the bookseller and publisher Willis and Sotheran and ordered a huge number of them to be packed and sent to Alexandria — novels and histories and plays as well as adventures and tales of travels, in French, German or English. To her grandmother she made a similar request. Sarah Austin recounted that 'Janet has bracelets enough to cover her arms up to her shoulder, and she wishes for a good edition of Molière which her father has seen and admired. I shall get it for her'.

Finally she had her photograph taken and copies sent to both Meredith and Kinglake. Like all photographs of her, she thought it bore little likeness. Meredith was pleased by the gesture, though when he wrote to thank her for it he described it as 'a good and fitting present at this awful instant … Looking on it, I see the corpse of the maiden Janet. Just what she may henceforth give of herself, and no more. It isn't bad, it's pleasant enough to have, but its Janet washed out and decorated with soot'. He also suggested that she write about her expectations and deliver to him under seal so that he might compare them with the reality in a year's time. This time, his mocking tone barely disguises the resentment he harbours about her decision.

The wedding took place on December 5, 1860 in the town of Ventnor on the Isle of Wight where Lucie was resting and trying to get well for the ceremony. On the day, however, Lucie was too ill to attend. Sarah Austin travelled to Ventnor for the wedding, but spent most of her time sitting with her sick daughter. George Meredith arrived and, along with Alexander and Tom Taylor, signed the marriage certificate. Alexander arranged for a marriage settlement to be drawn up and put aside some money in his daughter's name. It was hardly a great celebration, although Janet at least, must have enjoyed a sense of anticipation. Before the wedding, Henry suggested that Lucie might benefit from joining them in Egypt, but for now her doctors wanted her to stay where she was. Finally, the newlyweds set off alone for Egypt via Malta and Paris in lieu of a honeymoon. Ross was forty years old and Janet was eighteen.

A LIFE OF HER OWN

In January 1861, the steamer with Mr and Mrs Ross aboard berthed at Alexandria. A carriage was at the port to meet them, and they were driven home through the local bazaars, which Janet thought wonderful. Further on however, when they got to the European Quarter, her excitement receded. It reminded Janet of a 'tenth-rate' French provincial town, devoid of all interest and colour. Fortunately, the house was attractive and very comfortable. Set near the harbour, it was large and airy and Henry — a keen gardener — had made a beautiful garden on the roof.

By the nineteenth century Alexandria, founded by Alexander the Great in 331 BC, had become a bustling city of commerce and trade. After the capital Cairo — 225 kilometres (140 miles) inland up the Nile — Alexandria was the second biggest city in Egypt. Its busy harbour was the centre of the country's fast-growing export trade to Europe. By the time Janet arrived the population was moving towards a quarter of a million people.

The next day an important bank client, Halim Pasha, uncle of the Viceroy, called Henry away to Cairo. Janet was left alone with a Greek cook, an old Maltese housemaid and a young waiter called Mohammed. They spoke only Arabic and Italian, of which Janet did not know one word. Henry spoke Turkish and Arabic fluently and in his absence she saw an opportunity to learn herself. Mohammed was about fifteen and reminded her of Hatty. They got on well and he was happy to be her teacher and friend. She walked around the house touching objects that he would name. She methodically wrote everything down and committed it to memory.

After a few weeks she felt confident enough to venture some basic requests. One of the first was to go to the stable and ask for Henry's horse to be saddled — a beautiful beast he had brought down from Mosul. Mohammed took another horse, and together they set off outside the city walls.

> Once outside the walls of the town the country struck me as wonderfully beautiful in a peculiar way. The never-ending stretches of sand, the waving palm trees, then statuesque, graceful people who smiled at me, and the glorious sunset, were intoxicating.

On Henry's return, she was obliged to accompany him visiting other English residents. Henry was well regarded among their European neighbours and unfailingly polite. Janet was welcomed as Henry's wife and was courteous in return, but with few exceptions, she found them dull. Over the coming years she attended all the parties and major events of the English community and, while she came to enjoy them more, most of the excitement for her lay elsewhere.

After a short stay at home with his new wife, Henry had to return to Cairo on business and asked Janet to join him. They would be away for some time. The bank had an old Turkish house there close to the fashionable Ezbekiya Square, so they did not have to stay in a hotel. Cairo, 'jewel of the orient' with its minarets and bewildering chaos of colours that she recognized from Flaubert's descriptions, fulfilled all Janet's expectations. She felt herself transported bodily into *The Arabian Nights*. Intending to furnish her house with carpets, she went to the sprawling bazaar, rummaging up alleys and peering in the stalls, utilizing her Arabic as best as she could.

She was taken to visit the important client, Halim Pasha, who gave her a magnificent bay horse as a wedding present. He showed her his beautiful gardens and then directed her to the harem to meet his current wife and his daughter by a former wife. This was the first of many invitations into women's quarters — a privilege that allowed Janet an understanding of their lives, off-limits to most foreigners.

On another day, she was invited by an Armenian friend to whom she had been given a letter of introduction, to join the wedding party of a young Turkish boy (the son of a friend of the Armenian's) and an older girl of about twenty. Janet was enthralled by the event and wrote of it years later in her memoirs.

> [The bride] was deadly pale with eyes which, thanks to the deep border of kohl, seemed larger and more brilliant than they really were, her hair in countless plaits interwoven with strings of pearls, which fell from under a jaunty little takeeyeh, or tarboosh, entirely covered with precious stones, she realized my dreams of the wonderful princesses in the Arabian Nights...

Girls dancing and singing and dwarfs telling bawdy stories, entertained the party. Then came dinner, eaten cross-legged on the floor. Janet sat close to the little inlaid table so as not to spill food. For the first time she ate with her fingers an excellent dinner. 'I wonder', she thought, 'Turkish and Arab cooks have not taken the place of French chefs. According to our ideas the dinner was somewhat of a jumble, the dishes seemed to come up whenever they were ready, puddings and creams mixed up with meat and vegetables, and the rapidity with which they were served was extraordinary'. This is one of the earliest of Janet's written observations of food. Her interest is in food as part of a larger social context, an interest developed in her later writing.

Visits to tombs, invitations to festivals and special celebrations, learning local stories and legends; everything she saw was new and wonderfully different. She was living the Victorian ideal of the exotic East in a way that she could hardly have dreamed of in rural England.

When she had the time, she liked to be on a horse, preferably riding in the desert as she had with Mohammed. Other times she would race or go hunting for gazelles. One day she beat Halim Pasha in a race and won a gold Arab bracelet that she wore for the rest of her life. The Arab men she spent time with had no difficulty accepting her skill and energy. She had the advantage of being foreign and so was not obliged to lead the sheltered existence of the local women. Her outgoing forthright manner was acceptable because she was European.

On returning to Alexandria, she was invited to accompany the great French engineer and father of the Suez Canal, Ferdinand de Lesseps, on a tour of his partly completed masterwork. De Lesseps had known John Austin in Paris and became a frequent guest at the Rosses' house. Eventually he asked if she would like to join him on a field trip up the canal. The party travelled along the canal by day, sometimes on horseback and sometimes riding camels. This was Janet's first attempt atop the dromedary and she managed one three-hour stint across the desert. Further along the canal they went by a boat towed by two camels and on the same day came across a plague of hideous large brown-green grasshoppers. Finally, they reached Port Said where Janet celebrated her twentieth birthday on the roof terrace of the house belonging to one of the French engineers. Two days later, at sunrise, they set off in an Arab boat out across the vast Lake Menzaleh on which Port Said is built. There Janet was amazed at the sight of so much wildlife; fish of every kind and masses of birds; pelicans, flamingos, herons, wild geese, ducks, swans and many others besides.

It was clear from her letters home that she was very happy. Henry gave her all the freedom she wanted. The couple were well suited not only in their shared interests but also by temperament. He made no effort at all to constrain her, indeed, he seemed to take considerable pride in her enthusiasm. Her independence fitted well with the demands made on him by work at the bank.

In the meantime, family and friends including Meredith, kept her informed of news from home. Meredith wrote of his planned novels and recent travels to Italy. The country had affected him deeply and he hoped to set his next two novels around the theme of the Italian struggle for freedom from foreign rule and unification. Despite Janet's departure, Meredith remained friendly with the Duff Gordons and he wrote of little Urania and how he wished for his son to 'conquer a fair position in the world and lead her away' as her older sister was led. Janet had recently sent little Arthur a pair of Egyptian slippers and Meredith told her in a letter about new friends he had made, one in particular impressed him as 'one of the rare women who don't find it necessary to fluster their sex under your nose eternally, in order to make you like them'. He added, 'I give her private's rank in Janet's Amazonian regiment, with a chance of promotion'.

Meredith was still in a quandary about what to give her as a wedding present. She had received so many books and he did not like jewels. His suggestion was a magnified photograph of Alexander, Lucie, Maurice and Rainy (which was the pet name that Urania was given). His idea was that Lucie could sit for the picture when she was better. But time would tell that this touching suggestion was overly optimistic; Lucie was not improving.

In the second year of her marriage, Janet became pregnant. Not an unusual event for a young married woman, but not one she relished. She claimed later that she could not imagine how it happened, that she must have been drugged! Flippant or not, the comment makes it plain that sex was not the most enjoyable part of her relationship with Henry and that having a child was not a great desire for her. Her family, however, was delighted by the news and Janet and Henry returned to England in anticipation of the birth.

Lucie had sailed for the Cape of Good Hope the previous year and after much agonizing, little Urania was left behind with Charlotte Austin, her unmarried great-aunt and a woman well known to the little girl. The tuberculosis was so persistent that Lucie was now advised not to stay in England for another winter. Alexandria had been suggested, but it was too damp. The upper reaches of the Nile were a possibility but thought too expensive to reach, so she had settled on the Cape.

She had set out hopeful of a recovery so that she might return to her husband and youngest daughter. One month before the arrival of Janet's baby, Lucie came back to Escher but was still far from

Janet in a Turkish costume given to her by an Egyptian friend.

A LIFE OF HER OWN

Janet's mother, Lucie Duff Gordon, painted by Henry
Wyndham Phillips shortly before the move to
the Gordon Arms.

well. For one last time the family was reunited, but Lucie was advised not to stay long. This time she sailed for Egypt regardless of the costs involved. Janet was pleased, having encouraged her by letter some time before, 'O! how you will love Egypt, my dear mother, it is exactly like our dear Arabian Nights, only the Europeans spoil it'.

In England, just before the delivery there was another drama. Henry became seriously ill with typhoid fever. Sarah Austin witnessed Janet, within a few days of her confinement standing by her husband's bed, doing everything for him, 'this young woman, apparently so giddy, seemingly caring for no one, only thinking of her own amusement, shows a devotion and a courage which astonishes everyone. Never a word of complaint, never an illusion [sic] to her own condition'. This little story was a cameo of the family dynamic that would evolve. Janet's first loyalty was to Henry.

On September 8th, 1862 Janet had her baby — a boy they named Alick, in honour of Alexander. Lady Layard, wife of Henry Layard became the little boy's godmother, and Layard became the godfather. The newborn was soon sent off to a wet nurse named Mrs Walsh in Godalming in Surrey and he stayed there when his parents sailed back to Egypt the following January. Janet and Henry were of the view that England was a safer place than Alexandria for a young baby. As difficult as it is for our modern sensibilities to reconcile such a decision, there was no doubting that the English countryside posed less threat of disease to the newborn baby than the Eastern metropolis. Less obvious was Janet's determination to stay close to her husband rather then her child. However, the family took news of her return to Egypt in its stride, suggesting nothing unusual in the path chosen by Janet.

With his family dispersed, Alexander returned to London and back into his mother's house in Mayfair. He had been staying there while Lucie was in the Cape, now he made it his permanent residence. The Gordon Arms was emptied of family belongings and put up for sale. Sarah Austin wrote sadly of Alexander's situation, 'His household has been costly discomfort, and poor Lucie's wanderings absorb a great deal of money ... All proofs of her admirable taste are stripped down and stowed away; nor do I expect ever to see them again'.

Back in Alexandria, Janet resumed her Egyptian life with renewed enthusiasm. She was invited by a Frenchman Jules Guichard — a colleague of de Lesseps — to an important Bedouin religious festival near Tel-el-Kebir located in the desert between the Suez Canal, Cairo and Alexandria. The plan was to camp. Again she travelled without Henry who was on bank business. She rode side-saddle, out across the desert wearing a Bedouin *abayeh* or cloak and a bright striped Arabic *kuffieh* scarf wound around her hat with one end hanging over her face to give protection against the sun. Her stamina and horsemanship made such an impression that one sheikh rode up to her and teasingly complimented her, saying she rode like ten Bedouin, and adding that he had heard it said her conversation was so enlivening that her husband had no need to go to the coffee shop for entertainment or knowledge. After a day's hard riding and festival displays, they sat down to a dinner of whole roasted sheep stuffed with pistachio nuts and raisins followed by baklava, which Janet described as 'excellent'.

Her pursuit of life outside the confines of the expatriate community led to her gaining a reputation as a knowledgeable source of information on Egypt. Even so, she was surprised and delighted when a couple of months after returning from England she received an unexpected proposal from the manager of *The Times*, Mowbray Morris, to become a correspondent for the paper. For 100 pounds a year, she put her powers of observation and capacity to write to useful purpose. As well as colour pieces, there was interest among readers in Egyptian politics and commerce. Janet was well placed to produce what was required.

Over the forthcoming years, there were a couple of trips back to England to see friends and family, including, surely, little Alick who was now with Urania at Charlotte Austin's house. We can only presume she saw her young son because Janet left no account of any visits. From the time of Alick's birth, Janet had been clear that she wanted no more children. One incident suggests, however, that she may have become pregnant again. In March 1863, Janet and Lucie were due to meet in Cairo, but Henry sent a letter saying that Janet was seriously ill and would not be able to travel. Lucie thought she might have miscarried, but another possible cause was that an abortion had made her so sick.

This aside, Janet flourished in Egypt. By contrast, Lucie was terminally ill. She was now settled at Luxor, the cultural capital of Upper Egypt, where she lived quite simply among local people. It was in Luxor that she wrote her finest work, *Letters from Egypt,* published in 1865, an account of her life in Luxor, which became very popular and remains one of the few books written by a westerner to be read by Egyptians. The book made her a celebrity. This followed her earlier book, *Letters from the Cape*, edited by Sarah Austin.

Due to her ill health and the difficulty of travel, Lucie and Janet saw little of each other. She disliked Alexandria for its climate and European influence and Janet did not find the time required to travel up the Nile. Alexander came once to meet his wife in Cairo, but never made the more arduous trip south to Luxor. Congenial as he was, he found it difficult to appreciate his wife's new life and much preferred to see her in more familiar surroundings where he felt comfortable. At the end of his visit Janet felt 'almost glad when he left for England in spite of the delight of having him with me'.

Janet's Egyptian life was agreeable and might have gone on for some years before the long planned move back to England was contemplated. But as it turned out events conspired to hasten the decision. March of 1866 saw Henry Ross very sick with some sort of inflammation of the lungs. When he was well enough, he and Janet went to Sicily so he could recuperate in the dry climate. In their absence, a crisis in the Egyptian economy was gathering momentum.

With the end of the Civil War in America the previous year, Egyptian cotton producers lost their monopoly of supply to the Manchester mills and the price of cotton fell. A number of banks and trading houses that had lent great sums of money for local business expansion were now on the brink of collapse. Henry's bank was among them. This was very bad news for the Rosses, who had most of their savings invested in bank shares.

Janet left Henry to recuperate and went to London to do whatever she could to retrieve the situation. She did not alarm him with any bad news, but put her energy into contacting friends with influence to try to recover some of the repayments due to the Bank. In the case of the Egyptian Commercial and Trading Company, the Egyptian Viceroy, the largest landowner in the country, owed much of the debt. Through her efforts, some of the money owed was repaid, but not enough. The Rosses finances were in ruin.

When Henry was recovered and his wife revealed the extent of the situation, they returned to Alexandria. They planned to stay only long enough to clear up their affairs and gather their belongings. There was no future in Egypt for them now.

During these last months, they did finally make the long overdue trek up the Nile to see Lucie at Luxor. This was to be Janet's last reunion with her mother. Prior to their arrival, Lucie was anxious lest Henry and Janet not appreciate her new home and friends. She need not have worried. In letters to Alexander, Janet describes the feeling of the local people for Lucie, who enjoyed almost saintly status among her neighbours. The same warmth and generosity were extended to Janet and Henry.

Janet found her mother happy but noticeably changed by her illness. She reported to Alexander that Lucie looked well, 'but I find her a good deal aged. You have no idea what power she is in the land. Henry who knows the East, is astonished'. She described an elaborate dinner of many courses, 'during which we made no end of pretty speeches to each other, and then we had pipes and coffee'. All three then went further south to Philae, from where Janet wrote of the indescribable sights and the statuesque beauty of the people.

> But what words can describe Philae. I can't even attempt to speak of its loveliness. There is a colonnade from whence one looks far, far up the river towards Ethiopia. Such a view I never saw, it made one long to go on and on up the mighty river.

She was given beautiful things from ancient tombs, and from a man who had been taught English by Lucie, an alabaster jar which had belonged to a woman hundreds of years earlier and still had faint traces of kohl inside. Though the trip had an air of finality about it, it was a great success for Lucie and Janet. At the end of the visit, Janet and Henry returned on the steamer to Alexandria. Janet spent her last days sorting through belongings. Some furniture was set aside for shipment to London and the remainder was auctioned off.

Though not penniless, they were shocked by the loss of so much of Henry's capital in what were now worthless Egyptian investments, and the debacle was not over yet. There would be months ahead of sorting through debris from what looked like a financial house of cards. In the final wash up, Henry was to loose about 70,000 pounds. They realized as they faced the future that significant adjustments would have to be made to the way they lived.

Once she had overseen the packing, Janet set sail for Italy. She was going to Florence as the guest of her cousin by marriage and dear family friend, the British Ambassador Sir Henry Elliot. She would meet Henry there in two weeks' time. Then they would travel together home to England. In England, among friends and family, they would try to re-establish themselves.

A Place to Live

IT was good to be back with family and friends again; to see how five-year-old Alick had grown, and how beautiful and sweet-natured was his playmate and little aunt, Urania. Both children were still living under the watchful eye of their spinster great aunt Charlotte Austin and Janet had no intention of taking over from her. There was joy at being reunited with Alexander again and great comfort in catching up with old friends too. Apart from having no clear plans, the Rosses had no fixed address. For weeks they seemed comfortable dividing their time between the country and the city, staying with friends and family.

Hardly had Janet arrived, when she was approached by the publishers Richard Bentley and Son to undertake a translation of a work by a Belgian writer, Jules Van Praet. The work was published under the title *Essays of the Political History of the XV, XVI and XVII Centuries* in 1868. The translation had earlier been offered to Sarah Austin, but she was unwell and felt she could not do the job without

Janet in 1867 by Lord Frederic Leighton, just after her
first visit to Florence.

assistance. She suggested her granddaughter do the bulk of the work and she would do the final edit. Janet agreed, even though the translation would come out under her grandmother's name, just as in earlier years her mother's first work had been attributed to the better-known name of Sarah Austin.

In between hours of translation, Janet somehow managed to squeeze in time to sit for the renowned Victorian painter Frederic (later Lord) Leighton in his studio in Kensington. Next door to Leighton, lived Janet's old friend, the other great artist of the period, Frederic Watts, whom she had posed for as an adolescent as his Patroclus. He enjoyed visiting her at Leighton's studio while Janet was sitting. He liked to reminisce about the countryside at Escher and the 'old days'.

Having been in England less than two months, Henry, probably still not completely recovered from the chest infection of the previous year, and with the strain of his business affairs, felt run down and in need of rest. He had no particular illness, but lacked his usual vigour. His symptoms may have been exacerbated by the fact this usually energetic man effectively had no employment. Always loyal to Henry, Janet made the time to accompany him to the German spa town of Homburg. While they were there, however, they learnt that Sarah Austin had died. Unwell for some time, she succumbed to heart and kidney failure on August 8. She was seventy-four. In her will she left a legacy to Maurice but nothing to Janet or Urania.

The death of this extraordinary woman was not wholly unexpected. All the same, her passing was a great loss to Janet. When Janet returned to England shortly afterwards, she set about editing the translation of essays that her grandmother had been unable to finish, a job made all the more gratifying for the many letters and tributes written in Sarah's honour.

Not long after Henry's illness and her grandmother's death, Janet suffered a very bad bout of bronchitis. Only too aware of the dangers of respiratory infections, the Rosses decided to head south to a warmer, dryer climate. The decision to move may also have been influenced by the money situation. After a few months back in England, it must have become obvious that they faced a reduced lifestyle if they were to settle there as originally intended.

Janet and Henry headed back to Italy. There were no fixed plans beyond the idea of living there for a while. Rather than uproot Alick, they decided that he would be better off staying where he was comfortable and happy. If the departure of his parents was a disappointment to the little boy, there is no evidence of it. For most of his life so far, he had managed without them.

Given the success of Janet's holiday in Florence, it was little surprise that they retraced their steps back to the old city. Before her visit in the spring, she had not considered settling in Florence — or she would not have shipped their belongings to London — but once there, its merits as a place to live must have became obvious. Florence had much to offer.

A PLACE TO LIVE

Part of the attraction of Italy to foreigners was the low cost of living. An expatriate could live in comfort and style on considerably less than in England. One person who knew the value of the place was Elizabeth Barrett Browning. 'I love Florence', she wrote, 'the place looks exquisitely beautiful in its garden ground of vine yards and olive trees, sung around by nightingales day and night. If you take one thing with another, there is no place to live in – cheap, tranquil, cheerful, beautiful, within the limits of civilization, yet out of the crush of it' than Florence.

This time, rather than stay with the Elliots, Janet and Henry took a short-term lease on a furnished apartment by the Arno river, on the Lungarno degli Acciaiuoli, the street running alongside the water between the Ponte a Santa Trinità and the Ponte Vecchio. Art galleries, churches, Café Doney and the Via Tornabuoni — Henry had the chance to explore the city his wife now knew quite well.

A couple of months later the Rosses were still in Florence, despite Henry having to return in the meantime to Egypt to wind up business affairs and Janet taking a short trip in France with her father. By September they had decided to commit to a longer-term arrangement in an apartment on the other side of the river, on the Lungarno Torrigiani. The sun-filled windows of the new apartment had long sideway views back across the Arno to the Uffizi. The apartment was spacious and comfortable enough that Janet decided to send for the furniture that had been shipped from Alexandria to London. It was the first sign that she and Henry had made up their minds. They intended to establish themselves in Florence rather than return to England, though the implications for six-year-old Alick remained unclear. Was he to leave all that was familiar to him, to join his parents, or would he remain in England with little hope of being reunited with them?

In the meantime, Janet and Henry took advantage of the warmer climate and lower cost of living. They discovered a city agreeably less conventional and more relaxed than nineteenth-century England. There were enough interesting people living there and passing through to make the place lively. The British painter William Holman Hunt, a founding member of the Pre-Raphaelite Brotherhood, came to dinner often and introduced them to other artists, and locals too were quick to include the former banker and his charming young wife on their guest lists.

Their social success was assisted no doubt by the connection with Sir Henry Elliot and the Embassy. As in Alexandria, both the English-speaking community and old local families welcomed them. There were balls and concerts and dinners aplenty and many nights of dancing till the early hours. Beautiful horses were put at their disposal for riding in the Cascine and invitations arrived from Court.

Consciously or otherwise, Janet enjoyed having some distance between herself and England. It renewed her sense of independence. The plan was that, for the foreseeable future, she and Henry would live in Florence, with trips to England in the summer. The one thing missing was Alick, and finally his parents resolved to have him join them. For the first time in his life the young boy was to sleep in his parents' house. It is highly unlikely that anyone consulted Alick on this decision, but for the moment at least he could get to know more of his mother and father.

One person who was pleased by this development was Lucie, who had previously expressed concern about the way Janet dealt with her young child. On hearing Janet express some irritation about Alick, Lucie criticized her daughter thus, 'I am sorry you are wroth with my grandson, I fancy you hardly know what children are and how they all do make a horrid row'. As if to assure her mother that all was well with Alick, Janet sent Lucie a photograph of him taken in Florence.

Living in Italy meant that their altered financial circumstances had little effect on the Rosses daily lives. What they had lost was a large proportion of Henry's savings, what remained was enough to live on comfortably, especially here. Quite fortuitously, Janet had recently received some money from a small family inheritance. It had come directly to her after Lucie urged Alexander not to hand it over to Henry — thus Lucie may have had doubts about the durability of the Rosses' finances even before the bank collapsed. Welcome as this money was, it was nothing compared to the lost thousands.

Despite marrying Henry in part for financial security, Janet was not materialistic. That he had now essentially retired and she was less secure made little difference to her enjoyment of the everyday. As she grew older she would have periodic moments of anxiety about money, but she never complained publicly. The examples of her mother and grandmother had demonstrated how a life might be lived large, even on a restricted budget.

Henry had a few last-minute business affairs requiring him to travel back again to Alexandria but, in reality, the chapter of their life in the East was over. The conclusion came with news of Lucie's death. Just before taking the lease on the Lungarno Torrigiani apartment, Janet had left for London, intending to meet her father and travel with him to Egypt to visit her mother.

Lucie's most recent family visitor had been her son Maurice. After leaving Eton he had spent time studying languages with a tutor in Brussels in preparation for what his parents hoped would be a diplomatic career. Since he was a boy he had always wanted to join the Navy, but Alexander did not encourage him in this. Maurice was no academic but he was good with languages. Brussels was considered preferable to Paris because it held fewer distractions and was less expensive. Maurice, however, was less focused on his career than on women and pleasure.

Now in his early twenties, Lucie thought he might complete his education with a tutor in Egypt. However, the tutor employed to accompany him was far from satisfactory and only encouraged Maurice to stay out late visiting bars and probably brothels. Maurice made up for much of his behaviour with the charm and attention he lavished on his mother. Despite the frustration and anxiety he caused her, the two were close, all the more since he seemed to embrace her new life and the ways and customs of her adopted country. Despite his lack of seriousness, Lucie enjoyed having him so near. When he left to return to England, Lucie was already aware that she would not live much longer. Indeed, it was because of this that she gave up her plan of educating her son in Egypt. It was Lucie who brought forward his departure. She did not want her family to witness her last days. Her haemorrhages and attacks of coughing and sweating were becoming more frequent and violent. With each one, her body became weaker. Knowing how close her death was, Lucie had written to Alexander and Janet urging them not to come. Undeterred, they stuck to their plans but, just before their ship set sail, news came that they were too late — Lucie had died. She was forty-eight years old.

She was buried in the City of the Dead on what was the outskirts of Cairo — a vast ancient necropolis, possibly the world's most elaborate and extensive burial ground. In many ways, it was a tragic, lonely end to a magnificent life. Lucie had been forced to leave her husband and children and live alone in a foreign country. Her happy marriage of earlier years had suffered under the heavy strain of separation and ill health. Circumstances had sent Lucie and Alexander in different directions that were often difficult to reconcile. Her deep attachment to the Arab world had little resonance for him.

On the other hand, her adversity had brought wonderful and unforeseen rewards. Those years in Egypt were arguably the high point of a life well lived; a life full of foreign pleasures she could never have imagined had she remained healthy and content in England. Janet collected the many heartfelt obituaries and arranged them in a cuttings folder. Within two years Janet had lost the two towering female figures in her life. She did not dwell on the fact but she was aware of all she had inherited from these women. Years later, in the introduction to *Letters From Egypt*, Meredith produced a beautiful written portrait of Lucie, one that Janet was particularly proud of:

> She preferred the society of men, on the plain ground that they discuss matters of weight, and are — the pick of them — of open speech, more liberal, more genial, better comrades... In England in her day, while health was with her, there was one house where men and women conversed. When that house was perforce closed, a light had gone out in our country...

> But the grief of her poor neighbours at Luxor was even greater. Her almost passionate pity for all oppressed creatures, her kindness and ready sympathy, had won their hearts. When she left, for the last time, a man burst into tears and said 'Poor I, poor my children, poor all the people'.

Returning to Florence from England, Janet continued to be social, but also spent time alone writing, reading and riding. She also took up her old habit of foraging around markets and back alleys to see what she might pick up for the house. The redevelopment of the old medieval centre that came with Florence's new status as the capital saw the loss of many artisans' workshops. Despite this, the city remained a city of craftsmen. Many workshops were pushed onto the other side of the river, the district

A CASTLE IN TUSCANY

known as Oltrarno — the area where Janet now lived. The workshops opened directly onto the street, forming part of neighbourhood life — much as they still do today. Passing by, the observant pedestrian could watch men chisel the elaborate detail of a picture frame, or forge a piece of metal into a useful implement. Furniture and paintings were restored with minute attention, and silk threads were woven into lengths of beautifully patterned material.

In the evenings, the streets reverberated with songs clearly audible to Janet upstairs in the apartment. There was a playful rivalry between singers from the different *quartieri* and in her area of San Niccolò a certain Ulisse was one of the finest. Janet invited Ulisse up to the apartment and asked him to teach her some of his tunes. She discovered that the words were available in print but the tunes she had to decipher by ear. Her musical ability was accomplished rather than first rate, but she took pleasure in music and became renowned among her friends for her guitar playing of Tuscan folk songs. Transcribing Ulisse's tunes began as a sort of personal challenge, and a fascination that resulted years later in her publishing a little collection of Tuscan popular songs and music.

Far sharper than her ears were her eyes. Janet possessed a sophisticated visual aesthetic. She began seeking out pictures, looking for affordable works by Old Masters. She broadened her knowledge of Florentine artists, filling scrapbooks with cut-out images of great and beautiful works by Renaissance Masters, often taken from magazines and postcards. There were pages devoted to Donatello, Fra Angelico, Michelangelo, Signorelli, Masaccio and other pictures, neatly laid out and glued in. Armed with this research, Janet set about looking for pieces that would increase in value. She enjoyed the process of buying and selling and looked forward, without any false modesty, to taking a profit. What's more, she was bold enough in her judgement to take risks with paintings that a less assured person would not. She became familiar with various dealers and managed to collect a number of fine small drawings and paintings.

Among these was a little drawing by the High Renaissance painter Andrea del Sarto. The drawing was a study for the much larger and more significant painting of the *Deposition from the Cross* in the Pitti Palace Museum in Florence. Henry and Janet bought the drawing for 230 pounds from an old engineer, del Sarto, who Janet believed to be the last in the family line. The price they paid was equivalent to five times the annual salary of a cook working in England in 1865. Not an inconsequential amount of money, but there was clear potential to make it back. What's more, they could live with the beautiful drawing in the meantime. Over the coming few years they bought a number of smaller interesting pieces at reasonable prices.

They also made a chance purchase of a magnificent major work by one of the great painters of the Renaissance, *The School of Pan* by Luca Signorelli. An old picture-framer who Janet knew had mentioned a 'great' painting for sale at a very reasonable price. Eagerly following the lead, Janet persuaded Henry to join her in viewing the mystery painting. They clambered up to a studio a stone's throw from the great neo-gothic façade of the church of Santa Croce. The studio in Via de' Benci,

Janet's greatest art purchase *The School of Pan* by Renaissance artist Luca Signorelli.

belonged to a distinguished picture restorer by the name of Signor Tricca. In pride of place was a huge picture over 1.8 metres wide and 2.4 metres tall (6 x 8 feet). The painting was by Luca Signorelli, and was probably painted for Lorenzo de Medici.

The history of the painting was a complicated one. It had come into the possession of the Corsi family as part of the dowry of a bride from another old Florentine family who in turn had inherited it as part of a dowry from one of the Medicis. It hung in the Corsi palace until the eighteenth century when a Cardinal Corsi, shocked by its nudity, had white drapes painted over the figures. This so disfigured the work that it was relegated to the attic.

Years later, another Cardinal Corsi inherited the same palace and its contents, and employed Tricca to clean several sacred paintings and check the attic for other works that might be cleaned and hung. Tricca found the big painting and quickly saw the difference between the refined heads and crude white draperies. He carefully cleaned a small portion of the painting and realized that underneath the awful garbs were Signorelli's beautiful figures.

But the revealed masterpiece was not to the taste of this Cardinal either and he had asked Tricca to find someone who might want it. Working on a commission basis, the restorer took the picture along with ten others to his studio where he made detailed drawings to send to prospective buyers. Originally he had in mind Prince Napoleon who could place it in the Louvre. But the French were understandably distracted by the Franco-Prussian War of 1870–71. Wealthy Americans were not yet interested in Italian Old Masters and the local market looked weak until the old frame maker thought of Janet as a possible buyer. It was an inspired idea. The impact of the painting on Janet and Henry when they saw it was immediate. Henry turned to Janet and, in Arabic, said that they must try to buy it. The Cardinal wanted 20,000 francs but was so keen to rid himself of the painting he was prepared to accept less. The Rosses offered 15,000 francs to be paid in gold napoleons — this amounted to about 600 pounds. They also agreed to pay Tricca 10 per cent of the asking price if they subsequently sold the painting. *The School of Pan* was theirs.

The painting was, essentially, a study of beautiful nude and semi-nude figures. In the painting, the goat-footed body of the god Pan sits in the sunset with a crescent moon resting on his head. Olympus stands next to him, piping, and another young man lies at his feet playing on a reed. A female figure stands slightly removed in the left foreground.

Signorelli was almost obsessive in his studies of the human body and in *The School of Pan* the figures have a godlike quality. Signorelli was born about 1441, a kinsman of the painter and writer Georgio Vasari, who described him as an excellent painter. According to Vasari, Signorelli was considered one of the most famous artists working in Italy and his works were more highly valued than almost any other master's, because he showed the way to represent nude figures in painting so as to make them appear alive.

The work the Rosses acquired is a celebration of the dignity of nature, especially the nude human form. The effect is religious even if not strictly to the taste of the Church. Renaissance expert and later friend of the Rosses Bernard Berenson described it as one of the most fascinating works of art in our heritage.

Even before they had paid for the painting their intention was to sell it, preferably to a public gallery. Proud as they were of their acquisition, Janet and Henry could not afford to have that amount of money tied up indefinitely. Nor did the size of the work easily fit the domestic scale of their apartment. They had purchased the painting on impulse because they recognized its greatness and the price was very reasonable. Until they found the right buyer, they would treasure it. The masterpiece was hung on the longest wall in the dining room of the apartment, the only space big enough to take it.

A short time later, the director of The National Gallery in London, William Boxall, came to visit. Janet liked to tell a story that had him sitting opposite the painting. The poor man was so caught up in conversation with her that it was some time before he noticed it. He had previously heard that the painting had been rediscovered in Florence, but was under the impression it was already sold and taken elsewhere. He had heard that the buyer was a Hungarian gentleman with a long moustache — possibly this identification was a Florentine take on Henry's own appearance at the time. Eventually, to his astonishment, Boxall recognized the painting in front of him. At this point in the meal, Henry in a moment of spontaneous patriotism offered it to the Gallery for the price he had paid. This was a steal for the Gallery and with the promised commission to Tricca, Henry and Janet would have been severely out of pocket. Henry's generous gesture was not what Janet had intended at all. Though no less patriotic than Henry, her pragmatic nature was in the ascendency and she was very relieved when Boxall, erring on the side of prudery, finally decided that the figures were 'rather undressed' for the British public and declined the offer.

Still keen to find an institutional home for the painting and realize his percentage, Tricca quietly sought out would-be buyers. Finally, he managed to interest the Kaiser Frederick Museum in Berlin. It immediately committed to buy the piece and Janet and Henry were very pleased to accept an offer of 66,000 francs. This represented a profit of more than 400 per cent in less than two years! Everyone was delighted with the windfall, although Janet and Henry had some regrets seeing the painting come down from the dining room wall. Over the forthcoming years many visitors to the museum enjoyed the painting until it fell victim to allied bombs in World War II.

In the summer of 1870, the Rosses were invited to spend the summer at a villa seven miles south-west of Florence, near the town of Lastra a Signa. The villa was called Castagnolo and was home to a friend, Marchese Lotteringo della Stufa, known as Lotti to his intimates. They had been introduced to Lotti when they were new to the city and greatly enjoyed his company. They were so delighted by the stay at his villa that they began to talk about moving to the country full time. Henry enjoyed the space and

Janet found the rhythm of the rural life refreshing. A young boy like Alick would also enjoy the freedom offered by such a place. Janet had fond memories of her own childhood in the English countryside — the Tuscan countryside was a very appealing prospect.

A world away from the lively society of Florence, that summer Janet found herself inspired by the simple pleasures observed on outings to villages and farmhouses, and enthusiastically described how:

> Immense golden pumpkins, melons, watermelons, and scarlet tomatoes were being picked, and on some farms the women and children were busily employed in making round cakes of the latter fruit, and drying them in the sun for winter consumption. Outside the windows hung branches of the Acacia horrida, of which the crown of thorns is said to have been made; each long thorn bearing a crop of skinned figs, the gelatinous, sweet drops of juice oozing out and congealing in the sun's rays. On the low walls surrounding the threshing floors were flat baskets, boards, and plates, all covered with split peaches and figs drying in the sun, for the children to eat in winter with their bread.

She discovered a beauty and dignity in these rural labours, quite different to the city. The fact that the lives of these people were so different to anything she had previously known added to the appeal.

Meanwhile, Florence was changing. That year, King Victor Emmanuel had moved on to Rome and claimed it the new capital. Among Italians generally there had been much anticipation about the prospect and even the Florentines who stood to lose so much by the move, generally understood the inevitability of it. The following year the King would relocate his Court and Parliament. This meant that the large numbers of people in the bureaucracy and royal retinue would move on too. An estimated 30,000 people left Florence at this time. With them went much of the gaiety associated with the city. The social whirl that Janet had enjoyed for the last few years was largely finished. Realizing that it was the end of an era, a move to the country looked even more appealing.

Lotteringo della Stufa was Court Chamberlain to King Victor Emmanuel, and with the Parliament's move to Rome, his villa would for the most part be unoccupied. The Rosses saw this as their opportunity to move from the city and arranged to take a wing of the old villa on a yearly basis. The agreement was that Lotti would live in another section of the house when he was in Florence. Although it was probably Henry and his love of gardens and nature that led the way into this new life, Janet had few qualms about giving up the apartment in Lungarno Torrigiani. Indeed, she began to see that the change presented new opportunities.

Why they rented rather than bought is not clear. With such an exodus of people from the city, there was a glut of affordable villas and grand houses, but still the Rosses chose to move into Castagnolo with Lotti. It may have begun as a temporary arrangement that continued without much thought because it suited all parties. Whatever the reason, the decision incited some local intrigue and wild gossip.

The exact nature of Janet's early relationship with Lotti is unclear, but it is true that during the years Janet and Henry lived in his house, Janet and her landlord became very close. At the time the Rosses moved in, Lotti was forty-one and unmarried, Janet was twenty-eight and Henry, fifty. Lotteringo's descendents recall the gossip around their great-uncle, 'Even if nobody has seen Janet Ross and Uncle Lotto (sic) in the same bed … [they had] no doubt the love affair existed'. In the main, Janet was oblivious or impervious to such loose talk.

Aside from his role as Court Chamberlain, Lotti was a knowledgeable agriculturist, inventor of various mechanical devices, and had been an elected Member of Parliament for Lastra a Signa. He had also spent some time in Burma, supervising the building of the railway from Rangoon to Mandalay, an episode that would no doubt have appealed to Janet's taste for adventure. She appreciated the breadth of his experience, intelligence and charm.

Janet described the villa, which had been in the Stufa family since 1462, in a sketch she wrote on vintaging in Tuscany:

> In the lower Val d'Arno overlooking the fruitful plain which extends from Florence to Empoli, stands an old villa, a long, low, roomy house, anciently belonging to the Arte della Lana, [wool producers' guild] whose lamb bearing a banner over one shoulder is sculptured on various parts of its walls. In the twelfth century it was only a roof resting on high arches for drying the wool; then our host's ancestors bought it, filled up the arches, built a first floor, and gradually added wing after wing. The rooms are large and lofty, the staircase handsome, and the ceiling of one of the rooms is frescoed with Raphaelesque designs like the loggia in the Vatican. The house is full of old furniture, old china, and various Roman and Etruscan statues, and there is a splendid sarcophagus which was found on the property, for we are near Signa, the old Signa Romanorum of the legions. The villa, slightly raised above the plain, and about two miles from the Arno, is opposite Monte Morello, the weather-teller of the country round.

For many years, their wing of the house had remained uninhabited except by the bailiff who oversaw the farms and the house. The outside was decayed but, ignoring this, Janet set about putting their wing of the interior right. She turned the washhouse into a sitting room for herself in which she placed a beautiful writing table that had belonged to Lucie — the desk at which her mother had penned her books and letters. The large room next to it, where the clothes were hung to dry, became a drawing room. The terrace she arranged with huge pots of lilies and tulips. This opened onto a garden with pergolas and large orange trees in tubs.

Once the house was organized, she had time to become acquainted with local people and local customs. She did not miss the city. She had had the best of it for nearly four years and was happy to change. She began to enjoy the seasonal routine of farm life and became interested in some agricultural processes like the grape vintage and olive oil making. She went to Florence when necessary, but by and large she was just as happy to stay at the villa and receive visitors there. Friends came to stay and Janet took them on excursions to nearby towns and farms.

It seemed that the Rosses were finally establishing some roots. She was proud of the life they were creating, and Janet was keen for her father to come and see for himself how lovely it all was — the beautiful old house were she lived with her small family, and her growing circle of interesting friends. It was a world that resembled her childhood at the Gordon Arms in many ways. Alexander came at the end of August 1871 and passed a few mostly enjoyable weeks at the villa, but Janet thought he was sometimes depressed and uncomfortable. She thought of accompanying him home but was dissuaded by Henry's concern that a London autumn might bring on an attack of her bronchitis.

Shortly after Alexander left came the shocking news that he had developed cancer of the tongue. Over the next twelve months he optimistically sought out remedies, including travelling to America with Maurice in pursuit of a miraculous cure. But there was nothing that could be done. Janet travelled to England to nurse him for the last five and a half months of his life. At the time of her father's decline, Urania was just fourteen years old and continued to be looked after by her aunt. For the last few years, Alexander had based himself with them in the Austin's old cottage at Weybridge. When Janet arrived she was as devoted to her father as she had ever been — they were the 'inseparables' again one last time.

It was an appalling experience for Janet to see his pain and physical decline. He became so reduced, unable to speak or eat, that she decided to keep almost everyone away. She wanted him remembered as the handsome, witty man he had been. With his death in 1872, she lost the person she loved most. In contrast to the number of obituaries written after Lucie had died three years earlier, Alexander's departure went barely noticed. There is just one small obituary among Janet's cuttings. It describes a man of charm and integrity, better appreciated by his close friends than by the public at large. This was perhaps a reference to Alexander's nagging lack of remarkable achievement in public life. He never reached the heights of his potential.

Meanwhile, Urania had grown into a beautiful and sweet-natured adolescent, but she was not physically robust. Unbeknown to her family, she was incubating tuberculosis, most likely caught from her mother, and would survive only another five years. Just a few months before Alexander's death, the charming Maurice had married a wealthy widow, Fanny Ball Hughes, and now he inherited his father's baronetcy. A career in the diplomacy had not eventuated, instead he would venture into the world of stockbroking.

Alick by this time was again living in England. How long he had stayed in Florence is not clear, but at ten years of age his education was becoming an issue of consideration for Janet and Henry. Henceforth he would return to the pattern of earlier years and see his parents on visits to Italy or when they were in England.

When Janet finally returned to Castagnolo, and without a small boy to take up her time, she threw herself into the work that was to dominate her life. Quite possibly, she was looking to distract

Janet, formidable in riding kit.

herself from the loss of her father. She became increasingly involved in the farms and spent more time writing. What she discovered in herself was a natural flair for agriculture. The move out of the city and the death of Alexander seemed to emphasize a more serious aspect of her character.

During this time, her relationship with Lotti also became closer. When he could, he came up from Rome and stayed at Castagnolo. Henry, unfailingly polite and himself close to Lotti, removed himself to the background. Perhaps he did not want to see what others saw or perhaps he was pleased enough to have the time and space to devote to a burgeoning collection of orchids. In any case, he had always allowed his wife freedom to do as she pleased. Janet enjoyed Lotti's company when he was around and he was pleased by her interest in the farms. Sometimes they went together to the city but more often they spent time at the villa where friends became used to seeing the three of them together. The relationship was so close that, when Maurice and his new wife had a baby, Lotti was invited to become her godfather. The little girl, named Caroline but known as Lina, was anointed with water from the River Jordan that Henry had collected nearly twenty years before.

Such was the relationship that, although everyone knew Janet was married, visitors could be forgiven for construing that Lotti and Janet were master and mistress of the house. In reality the nature of their relationship was probably more complex. Most Florentines, like the della Stufa family, felt sure that the relationship was physical, and that Henry was gentlemanly about the situation rather than ignorant. Descendants of the Stufa family still believe that she hid the true nature of her relationship with Lotti, 'If a woman has a lover, [the] last ones to know it are people of her family and when a love affair is quite ardent, an intelligent woman, to avoid [exposing] herself to criticism, must convince the family that she is frigid and that her love affair is [platonic]'.

Despite this popular belief, it is more likely that the relationship between Janet and Lotti was not romantic in nature, and that Janet had no overt sexual interest in him. Similarly, if Lotti were homosexual as some have suggested (art connoisseur Bernard Berenson was of this opinion) then his physical lack of interest in women would have appealed to Janet. A handsome man, intelligent and attentive but no sexual threat, he made an ideal companion.

One who saw none of these subtleties was the Victorian popular writer Ouida. Born Maria Louise Ramé to an English mother and French father, she later elaborated her name to Louise de la Ramée. She is barely known today, but in her time was a hugely successful English romance writer whose novels challenged much of the common morality in Victorian literature. Queen Victoria was a devoted reader of her books. From 1860 she spent a great deal of time in Italy, and in 1874 she settled in Florence.

She was a colourful character, socially astute but prone to dramatics. For a while after she and Janet first met — Ouida had come with a letter of introduction from Alexander before his death — the two women enjoyed a casual friendship until Ouida fell in love with the Marchese della Stufa and determined to marry him. In her mind, the only obstacle in the way was Janet who, Ouida believed, was holding Lotti against his wishes.

Ouida's desire to marry the object of her affections quickly became the subject of local intrigue. Stories abounded of her slavishly following Lotti about from place to place in the city. According to the talk, one day she waited for him to step out from his club on the Via Tornabuoni, threw her arms around him and in vain demanded he marry her.

He did not overtly encourage her fantasy and may well have felt embarrassed by it, but he never did, or said, enough to put her off. Janet thought her former friend was making an unseemly spectacle of herself and could barely disguise her hauteur. But Ouida devised a ruse. In 1878 she published a barely disguised revenge novel called *Friendship*, in which she penned unflattering portraits of the residents of Castagnolo.

Janet was Lady Joan Chandler, a scheming, controlling woman unwilling to let the hero follow his true love. In the novel, Ouida wrote, 'Go and see dear Joan, she is a faggot of contradictions; extraordinarily ignorant, but naturally intelligent; audacious yet timid; a bully but a coward; full of hot passions, but with cold fits of prudence'. Lotti is Prince Joris, who loves the heroine but is too cowardly to leave the clutches of Lady Joan. Lady Joan blackmails him over a crooked business transaction that he unwittingly made with Lady Joan's husband — an equally thinly disguised Henry. When the book came out, there were wild rumours that Janet had rushed over to Ouida's villa and horsewhipped the author.

The whole episode was ridiculous, and ultimately rather pathetic for Ouida. Of course Lotti had no intention of marrying her or anyone else. If he was indeed homosexual his current arrangement suited him very well. And in any case he was deeply attached to Janet and would never want to hurt her. Janet, in usual form, refused to show any emotion she may have felt. Though for years afterwards she did keep a copy of the book, without its binding, in the lavatory for guests to read. This was her quiet triumph.

Aside from a close and enduring friendship, Lotti's great legacy to Janet was an education in the practices of Tuscan agriculture. He was an acknowledged specialist on the subject. Not simply a theorist, he worked, when he was able, in the fields assisting in the endless round of tasks that are the stuff of farm life. With his encouragement and assistance, Janet became an authority too. As one of her visitors, Augustus Hare, the English travel writer and biographer recalled some years later:

> The Marchese is charming, living in the hearts of his people, sharing their interests, working with them — taking off his coat and tucking up his sleeves to join in the sheep shearing, gathering the grapes in the vintage. But the presiding genius of the place ... [it is she, Janet] who has redeemed lands, planted vineyards, introduced new plans for pressing grapes — whose whole heart and soul are in the work here.

When visitors came to Castagnolo they were often invited to attend local festivals and help with the vintage. English visitors and locals would join Henry, Janet and Lotti for excellent meals, cooked simply with the best local produce. When the weather was good these would be taken into the fields. At other times, Janet would devise entertaining excursions to a nearby town to join a festival or seek out some particularly beautiful fresco or painting. The English found the whole experience enchanting, relaxed and somewhat bohemian, though behind the scenes, Janet was a first rate planner. In Florence too, she was regarded as a generous and energetic hostess whose invitations were keenly accepted. There were old friends, like Tom Taylor, a favourite from her childhood, who came with his family to Castagnolo. There were distinguished guests too. Four times British Prime Minister William Gladstone and his wife came once and, on another occasion, the Duke and Duchess of Teck with Princess May and her brother, Alexander. They were all interested to see what this Englishwoman had achieved in the Tuscan countryside.

It was during the years at Castagnolo that Janet employed the cook Giuseppe Volpi. (In years to come she would collaborate with him on her recipe book, *Leaves from Our Tuscan Kitchen*.) In the mornings in late summer, Volpi prepared delicious lunches in the kitchen, while a party of friends and visitors led by Janet would set off to assist in picking the grapes. The workers sang at their tasks and at lunchtime Janet continued the singing accompanied by her guitar. These were happy, even idyllic days.

Janet soon realized that the life she found so captivating would also make appealing subject material for people in England. Her own enthusiasm and the immediate response she saw on the faces of English visitors suggested there might be a ready market of English readers who would enjoy her descriptions of Tuscan life, so removed from their own. What's more, if she were successful, she would make some welcome extra cash. So began Janet's writing on rural Tuscany.

In this piece from 1874 originally written for the literary *Macmillan's Magazine*, she describes a typical expedition (she was the *padrona* – mistress or boss, describing herself in the third person). She recalls picking the famous vintage of that year, a year that saw the most abundant harvest since the outbreak of iodium, a disease that had devastated the vines twenty-six years earlier. It was a harvest worth celebrating:

On a fine September morning we started, Italian and English, men and women, masters and mistresses, and servants laden with innumerable baskets, big and little, each armed with a rough pair of scissors, and our 'padrona' leading the way, with her guitar, pouring out as she went an endless flow of 'stornelli', 'rispetti', and 'canzoni', in which Tuscany is as rich as in any of the country products, maize or figs, pumpkins or tomatoes, oil or wine, or grain, the Italians amongst us improvising words to the well-known airs. The vintage is always a happy time; everyone works with a will, and is contented and light-hearted. As Modesto, one of our men, said, 'buon vino fa buon sangu' (Good wine makes good blood)…

Twelve o'clock brought a welcome arrival — lunch from the villa. Grape picking is a capital sharpener of the appetite. We were soon reclining — 'sub tegmine fagi' — round a steaming dish of risotto con funghi, and a knightly sirloin of roast beef, which would have done honour to old England. A big fiasco (a large bottle bound round with reeds or straw, and holding three ordinary bottles) of last year's red wine was soon emptied, well tempered, I should say, with water from the neighboring well. At a little distance the labourers in the vineyard were enjoying the unwonted luxury of a big wooden bowl full of white beans crowned with 'polpette', little sausages of minced meat and rice.

Our happy holiday vintaging lasted for five days, and then we went to help the vintaging of one of the 'contadini' [farm labourers] of the 'padrone' [landlord], a family that had been on the estate for two hundred and eighty years. All their vines were trained Tuscan fashion on maples, and we had the help of ladders and steps to gather the grapes. Half the grapes, and indeed half of all the produce of the land — grain, pumpkins, flax, fruit, or wine — belongs to the 'padrone', who pays all the taxes and buys the cattle. The 'contadino' pays no rent for his house, which the 'padrone' keeps in repair. The peasant gives the labour, and the master finds the capital.

The arrangement that Janet describes is known as the *mezzadria* or *metrayer* system of land tenure and was universal in Tuscany at the time. The system was simple in concept, but subtle in its detail. It underpinned a way of life that has now vanished, but was essential to enterprises like Castagnolo. It had ancient origins in which the *contadini* saw themselves as the *gente* or 'people' of the *padrone*. In some places, families had been on the same land for several hundred years and felt themselves to almost belong to the landlord. In addition to providing houses, the landlord also paid all the taxes and provided money for the purchase of cattle and the area of land necessary to support a family, the usual calculation for this being five acres for each able-bodied man. Women and children were factored in too, but the calculation on them varies according to locality.

The workers gave all their labour free. If a beast died, the farm worker and the proprietor shared the loss. Likewise they shared in any profit, and everything produced on the farm was divided between them equally. This profit sharing agreement between the landowner and the labouring family was outlined in a contract. The first contract was traditionally signed on February 1 — the beginning of the agricultural year — and ran for one year; but it could continue tacitly for centuries.

The produce divided between owner and workers came under three headings. First, the actual produce in kind — crops of corn, oil and wine, divided at the harvest and stored at home. Then, the division of money taken for wholesale produce sold, such as beetroot (beets) for sugar and tomatoes for preserve. There may also have been the sale of tobacco. Thirdly, the current account of

A PLACE TO LIVE

A vintage is loaded onto the ox cart.

Harvesters showing off the fruit of their labours.

The large white oxen common in rural Tuscany.

produce, such as livestock and dairy, as well as money received for surplus hay, straw, oats and so on, not needed on the farms.

The *contadini* often repaid loans in kind or by labour. There was always a certain amount of capital outlaid on a farm, for such things as digging new trenches for vines or planting fruit trees. This work was done by the workers and paid for at local rates. These extra sums were useful for a worker's personal expenses.

Janet understood that a knowledgeable proprietor represented by a decent bailiff could make the system work well for everyone. As a rule, the *contadini* were good, hard-working men. Dishonesty would result in being sent away with little alternative but to become a lowly day labourer. Every month, the *capoccia*, or head of each family, went to the bailiff to have his account book written up. Janet became used to the sight of often-illiterate men remembering the details of the whole month's work without the aid of notes. This observation convinced her that knowledge of reading and writing, while she valued both, enfeebled memory.

Skilful application of the *mezzadria* was essential to her success on the farms. With Lotti often in Rome it was she, rather than Henry, who took the role of *padrone*, or in her case *padrona*. This was an unusual role for a woman, but she found that her ability to work the system to mutual satisfaction, and her preparedness to labour alongside the workers, delivered her considerable respect from men and women alike.

⁂

The more Janet observed and read, the more obvious it became that agriculture in Tuscany had changed little since the time of Virgil, to such an extent that his descriptions would pass muster with anyone working at Castagnolo in Janet's day. Tools, for example, were made according to the ancient ways. Men went into the woods to find suitable timber to season and fashion in the style used by their forbears. Some of the olive types had changed, but the method of cultivation remained the same.

Similarly, the old poet's advice on cattle husbandry was familiar to Janet. Virgil's recommendation to leave all the cow's milk to young calves rather than taking some for the house was still the practice. It was understood that the large white oxen favoured in Tuscan farming were poor milkers and have only enough for their offspring. Moreover, Italian peasant households had no great demand for milk and butter.

Cheese was a different matter, and sheep's milk was used most often for this. Just as Virgil described, Janet saw the sheep milked and the milk then slightly warmed over a fire. To the warm liquid was added a mixture of rennet and the beard of a wild artichoke. After four hours the milk was set and ready to be laid out on a piece of basketwork. It was then gently pressed by hand into its final form.

A PLACE TO LIVE

Wine-making had also changed very little since ancient times. There were more grape types, but otherwise the vintage process was the same. Grapes were picked and filled into a large vat that was loaded onto the back of a heavy red cart pulled by two of the ever-present white oxen. The grapes were taken to the villa and transferred into large vats to ferment. Then the business of extraction began. Janet looked on as workers with purple stained legs sang *stornelli* at the top of their voices while they trod the grapes.

Virgil's advice about thoroughly seasoning and breaking up the land before planting vines was carried out to the letter at Castagnolo. A trench was dug 1 metre (3 feet) deep and 1 metre wide and left open to the elements for six months or a year. Then all available stones were pitched into its bottom, to provide good drainage and finally it was filled in again. Finally, two shoot cuttings, or better still, a couple of two-year-old rooted plants, were placed on each of four sides in a square around a young maple tree, which was used to provide support. The layout of the grapevines was based on the 'quincunx system' recommended by Virgil, that is, four couplings planted to form a square, in the centre of which is the fifth central planting.

(One of the few significant differences from Virgil's time was the horse. Far from the beautiful horses he described, the present-day descendent was a poor specimen. To Janet's opinionated mind, the modern Italian horse was a wretched animal. Small, ill-made, overworked and under-fed, broken in and made to work at too young an age.)

In all, Janet flourished in the country. She was completely at home and within a short time hit her stride as a farmer. What began as a friendly arrangement to rent part of Lotti's old family villa proved so satisfactory it continued for seventeen years. Each year she learned more about the land — the best ways of working it — and each year she enjoyed greater regard and devotion from the farmers. But in all the years at Castagnolo her greatest admirers were Lotti and Henry.

Sketching the Landscape

To English eyes the wealth of grapes appeared incredible,
and the colours marvellous. From maple to maple hung
long garlands of vines in fantastic shapes, the Buon Amico,
or 'good friend', with large loose bunches of purple-black grapes,
the Trebbiano, brilliant yellow, with the sunny side
stained a deep brown, the Uva Grassa, a dull yellow-green,
and the lovely Occhio di Pernice, or 'partridge's eye',
of a light pink with ruby lines meandering about in every grape,
the flavour of which was quite equal to its beauty.

JANET ROSS
ITALIAN SKETCHES (1887)

WHEN Janet offered her pieces on Tuscan life to publishers in England, *Macmillan's Magazine*, *Frazer's Magazine* and *The English Illustrated Magazine* all took her work. Straight away, her writing proved popular with readers. And while there were many others attempting to cover similar ground, her authoritative knowledge of the Tuscan countryside and its habits set her writing apart from most examples of the genre. Janet's sketches of Tuscan life proved to be some of the most durable written in English in the late-nineteenth century and arguably well beyond. Indeed these were the pieces that would go on to capture the imagination of Elizabeth David in her exploration of Italian food nearly a hundred years later. David admired Janet's *Italian Sketches* for their clarity of description and evocation of the sun, light and earth of the Tuscan countryside. She trusted Janet as an authority on the vintage and the making of olive oil and she admired the style of her observations; the Trebbiano grape 'brilliant yellow, with the sunny side stained a deep brown'.

The popularity of Janet's magazine pieces had her old mentor Alexander Kinglake urging her to write a full-length book based on her life in Italy. He even suggested a working title, 'Farm Life on the Arno', to be accompanied by illustrations. Though she had recently finished re-editing Lucie's *Letters from Egypt* (a few years later she would translate it into French), she was not ready to write a book of her own. She had a definite preference for writing shorter pieces. These snapshots gave her free reign to move readily across subjects. The shorter length also had the practical advantage of fitting in with the demands of farming.

Janet's success as a writer was the result of a clear descriptive style and an eye for detail. Just as she had an innate appreciation for good painting, she possessed acute powers of observation and the ability to describe exactly what she saw. The style conveyed her admiration and enthusiasm for the places and customs of Tuscany. The detail she included resulted in her accounts becoming historical documents in their own right.

One such piece was a description of oil making in Tuscany, outlining the entire process of producing virgin green olive oil from harvest to pressing. In the early-nineteenth century, olives for oil production became a lucrative commodity and over the following decades, sprawling acreage was turned over to the planting of trees. Until then, olive growing in Tuscany had been largely confined to districts near Lucca and the hills around Siena. For centuries, Italians had treasured the sweet fresh oil for its health-giving properties, but most people could not afford to use it in great abundance. Contrary to popular notions of a traditional Italian diet based on olive oil, much Tuscan cooking had hitherto relied on animal fat, especially pork fat, rather than oil.

The pig was important and when it was killed, every part was put to use. There were all sorts of old Tuscan dishes that called for fat: pork livers cooked in their own fat, frittata with pancetta, braises and stews based on the frying of pork fat with finely diced onion, celery, carrot, garlic and rosemary and little fritters bound together with pork blood and fried in fat. Pork was also salted and made into salamis and the like for eating in winter. For centuries, it was more economical to have a couple of pigs scratching around and cleaning up household scrapes throughout the year and then killing them for meat and fat, than it was to have row upon row of olive trees.

The great surge in the planting of olive trees began at the very end of the eighteenth century and continued on until the end of World War Two. Popular varieties were Moraiolo, Leccino, Frantoio and Morchiaro. Over time Pendolino, Maurino, Olivastro and Saggianese were added in significant numbers (though today Frantoio trees account for about forty-eight per cent of the Tuscan crop). The increased demand for olive oil from the growing Italian middle class in the cities and the export market meant that most production was sold off rather than used at home on the farms. Indeed, everyday use remained something of a luxury in the kitchens of rural labourers until well into the twentieth century. Moreover, the expansion of groves onto land traditionally used to grow cereal crops brought its own problems. Farmers had to make do with less land to grow grains needed to feed themselves and their animals.

When Janet took over the supervision of the olive harvest at Castagnolo there was a well-established practice of separating the first grade, harvested olives from those that fell on the ground and became bruised. In earlier times, the olives had been mixed in together with little regard to the impact on the quality of the oil. But the premium now paid for first-quality oil over second-quality made the effort worthwhile.

In the cold and windy last months of the year, men carried their ladders down to the trees, angled them inwards against the trunk and climbed up to pick the fruit. Each filled a neat crescent shaped basket that sat snugly on the side of the body attached to his belt. To keep warm the men would come down from the trees and stamp around and blow on their fingers. Janet described this process for *Macmillan's Magazine*. Accompanied by a local farmer, Bencino, she witnessed the hard day's work needed to yield the beautifully flavoured oil:

> The black shining olives hung thick on the slender branches, which bent low under the weight. The crop was abundant, 'una vera grazia di Dio' (a real bounty of God), as Bencino said. All the 'contadini' of this 'fattoria', whose 'podere' was situated on the slopes of the hills, where the ground is stony, and therefore suitable for the cultivation of olive trees, were busily engaged gathering the fruit; the men up in the trees and on ladders, the women and children picking up those which fell to the ground. The bruised berries are kept apart, to make the second quality of oil. The trees are most carefully and severely pruned, hollow in the middle, to form a cup-shaped tree. 'Agli olivi, un pazzo sopra e u savio sotto' (A mad man at the top of the olive tree, and a wise one at the roots) says the proverb.
>
> Enough fruit had been picked for the day's pressing, so we climbed up the bare bit of steep road which led to Bencino's house … The house stood on the brow of a hill, and was built round two sides of a square courtyard paved with bricks; on the third side rose a high wall, with an arched gateway over which was an old escutcheon, carved in stone, of the fifteenth century, with a lily and 'S.M.' entwined. A covered staircase outside the house led into a large room, with huge beams and rafters browned with age and smoke. The fireplace was immense, with seats in the corners …
>
> With the picking complete the business of pressing gets underway. The fruit is transported to the nearest press. Next it is picked over and any leaves or twigs removed. Only then are the olives delivered onto the press.

In the centre was an immense stone basin, in which revolved a solid millstone about five feet in diameter, technically called, I believe, an edge-runner, turned by a splendid white ox, which, to our astonishment, was not blindfolded. Our host told us that it was difficult to get oxen to do this work; it takes time and patience to accustom them to it. The millstone was set up on edge and rolled round in the stone basin, secured to a big column of wood that reached to the ceiling. The whole machine was most old-fashioned and clumsy, and the padrone said, laughing, evidently as old as Noah's ark.

Into the stone basin, as clean as a dairymaid's pan, five sacks of olives were emptied, which, in a short time, were reduced to a mass of dark greenish-brown, thick pulp. Stones and all were mashed with but little noise, save the occasional lowing of the ox when his tasselled and ornamented nosebag was empty. When Bencino judged that the olives were sufficiently crushed, the pulp was taken out from the mill, with clean new wooden shovels, and put into a circular shallow basket with a large hole through the middle, made of thick cord fabricated from rushes grown in the Pisan marshes, and looking very much like open coconut matting.

As fast as these 'gabbie', or cages, were filled, two men carried them on a handbarrow to the press in the corner of the room, and piled one on the top of the other under the press. Then began the hard work. Two huge posts clamped with iron support a colossal beam, through which goes the screw, finishing below in a large square block of wood with two square holes right through it. Into one of these Carlo [one of Bencino's kinsmen] stuck a long beam, to which he hooked a rope, the other end of which was secured round a turning pillar of wood some six or eight feet distant, with a handle against which the men threw their whole weight.

With many groans and squeaks the big block of wood revolved to the right until all the rope was twisted round the pillar; then it was unhooked, the beam was lifted out of its hole in the block and carried on Carlo's stalwart shoulder to be inserted into the next hole, and the rope again hooked round the end of the beam; this process continued until not a drop more oil could be extracted. The press was then screwed back, the 'gabbie' carried on the handbarrow to the mill, where they were emptied, and their contents again ground; then they were filled, and put under the press for the second time, when more oil came dripping out, but of inferior quality. The refuse that remains, called 'sansa', is almost black, and quite dry and gritty. This is sold for threepence or fourpence a 'bigoncia' full, about fifty-five pounds in weight, for making soap … La prima oliva e oro, la seconda argento, la terza non val niente goes the Tuscan proverb which translates as the first olive is golden, the second silver, and the third is worthless.

Olives contain two-thirds of water and one-third of oil, which naturally floats on the top of the water, and Carlo Bencino was busily engaged in skimming it delicately off with a big

The millstone crushing the olives and a 'conca' or terracotta urn for storing oil. Etching by Carlo Orsi.

The vintage being unloaded from an ox cart. Etching by Carlo Orsi.

tin scoop. He poured it through a funnel into a clean wooden 'barile' (a small barrel with narrow ends held together by large, flat, wooden hoops, holding about thirty-six quarts); and when this was full he shouldered it, carried it off to the 'chiaritojo', or oil-clearing room, and emptied it into a large 'conca', a terra-cotta case well glazed inside. The room, like everything else, was scrupulously clean, and paved with red bricks sloping towards the middle, where there was an underground marble receptacle, in case of an accident, such as the breaking of a 'conca'. The temperature is kept as equable as possible, and in cold winter weather a brazier is lighted at night. Nothing spoils the look, though not the flavour, of oil so much as getting frozen; it becomes thick, and seldom quite regains its golden limpidity, even when treated by people who thoroughly understand it …

The jollity and fun of the 'battitura' (thrashing), or of the vintage was wanting; the days were short and the wind cold … however, we make up for it at night when we have 'pan unto' (oiled bread). We asked what this was, and he explained that during the process of pressing the 'contadini' who made the oil always invited their friends to eat pan' unto or toasted bread dipped in the new oil.

Our host insisted on our tasting the new oil, and to our surprise it was delicious, like a decoction of very aromatic herbs, and entirely free from the rank, nasty taste we generally associate with oil. We now understood why Italian salads are so different from ours, and how a 'fritto', or dish of fried meat and vegetables, comes to be so excellent in Tuscany.

Though mechanized, the process of extracting olive oil continues much as Janet described it in the 1870s. So too, the tradition of dipping a thick slice of unsalted Tuscan bread into the fresh green liquid. At the end of such hard work on a cold winter's day, this treat is a welcome reward.

Janet readily conceded she wrote for payment rather than honour and glory, and could not understand why the subject of money was so odious to many people. Money, she thought, was a delightful thing to possess, 'the wont is it runs away as soon as one has it'. But some of her other efforts to earn income left people puzzled. Henry James was one. During a sojourn in Florence — where he spent his time observing local society and writing — he was invited out to Castagnolo. He was immediately struck by Janet's presence and her penetrating gaze. For the rest he was less sure. In a letter to a friend, he wrote that he had seen a good deal of the English writer Vernon Lee (Viola Paget):

who though very ugly, disputatious and awkwardly situated comme famille … possesses the only mind I could discover in the place — unless the famous Mrs Ross, with whom I spent three days at her picturesque old villa (or rather the Marchese Stufa's) at Castagnolo, may be said to have another. But I am not so sure of Mrs Ross's mind as of her eyes, her guitar and her desire to sell

you 'bric-a-brac'. She is awfully handsome, in a utilitarian kind of way — an odd mixture of
the British female and the dangerous woman — a Bohemian with rules and accounts.

In the realm of 'bric-a-brac' were the painted fans that Janet produced. She hoped these pretty fans decorated with musical notes and flowers would bring in some extra money. She sold quite a number of these privately, but was keen to find a shop that would take more. With the fans and the writing, Janet could make, by her own estimation, about 80 pounds in a year, 10 pounds less than an English estate gardener would be paid annually — a reasonable sum given that no income tax was payable on it. Money from writing was used for personal expenses but money earned from fans and similar items was usually given to a needy farm family or a struggling local artist.

It is hardly surprising that Henry James found Janet difficult to classify, the result of her unconventional education and an energetic and able mind. Vernon Lee, younger than Janet by some fourteen years, was an obvious counterpoint. She was the author of many books, both fiction and non-fiction. She lived in Florence and her circle of friends and acquaintances overlapped Janet's, as in the case of Henry James. Vernon Lee was a feminist with a preference for bobbed hair and neckties who established herself as a public critic keen to stake her intellectual claim in contemporary debate. During her life she had a number of unsuccessful love affairs with women. By contrast Janet felt no urgency to prove her intellect, she took it for granted. Where Lee was an emotional extrovert, Janet was emotionally restrained. It was hardly a surprise they were not close.

Throughout her life, Janet remained quite uninhibited in her interests. She might have been mistaken for a sophisticated dilettante, but that was to misread her. However far flung her interests, she applied herself thoroughly to whatever subjects caught her attention. She refused to follow fashion or the dictates of scholarly discipline. Instead, she followed her instincts and sense of taste. She was as comfortable working on the farms as she was deciphering manuscripts in the archives, as happy to strum Tuscan folk songs on her guitar as she was immersed in a complex work of translation.

After some years writing journal articles about Florence and the surrounding countryside, Janet became acknowledged as an authority. The colour pieces were proving so popular that in 1887 publishers Kegan Paul proposed combining several of them into a collection to be called *Italian Sketches*. The book would be illustrated by a young friend of Janet's who lived nearby. He was Carlo Orsi, one of three brothers who became friendly with the Rosses early on when Janet discovered them as close neighbours just down the road in the Villa Orsi. All three brothers sang beautifully and often came over to join Janet in singing folk songs. Carlo became one of her closest friends.

Carlo was originally a sculptor, but turned to painting when unable to afford the cost of stone. Shortly after Janet and Henry moved to Castagnolo, he began work on a large discreetly naked picture of Janet, after the style of Velasquez's *The Rokeby Venus*. Like the prototype, Orsi's picture is overtly erotic, showing a rear view of Janet in recline, her lower body draped in heavily folded material. Unlike Velasquez's Venus who is washing herself and looking into a mirror held for her by her son Cupid, Orsi

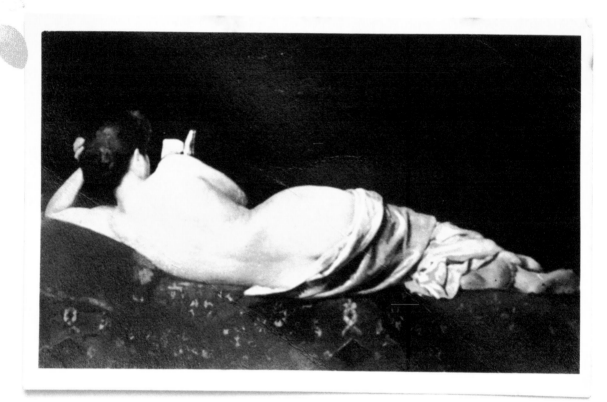

Carlo Orsi's beautiful picture of Janet as few would have seen her.

has Janet reading a book, much more in character with the sitter. Janet was very happy with the result and hung the picture prominently above her bed. The relationship with Carlo was close enough to excite some speculation that they too were lovers. What is certain is that they were firm collaborators.

Italian Sketches contained some previously unpublished articles including the beautiful lamentation on 'The Ghetto in Florence'. There was a history and description of the picturesque towered town of 'San Gimignano' and a piece on the 'Freemasons in Eighteenth Century Florence'. Janet's perfectly pitched tone and broad sweep of subject matter made it a critical and commercial success.

Janet put most of the money she earned from writing towards the considerable cost of Alick's education. Since returning to England he had completed his school education, spending time with his parents during holidays. Sometimes, he would see them in England where they often travelled in the summer. Sometimes, he would make the trip south.

Alick was intelligent and, like his mother, showed signs of being a very good linguist. When he finally completed his schooling, he went up to Balliol College. Now in his early twenties, his time at university was drawing to a close, and his parents were anxious for him to find a job and become self-supporting.

A friend suggested that Alick should sit examinations for a clerkship in the House of Lords. So Henry approached his well-connected old friend Henry Layard to make arrangements for his son to sit the exam. Layard also suggested Alick consider a position in the British Museum where he was himself still influential. Unfortunately, Alick narrowly missed out on both the clerkship and the museum job. Layard then suggested a position in Japan, but Janet was reluctant for her son to live so far away.

In 1887 having completed his degree, Alick came to Castagnolo, his future still undecided. This was an extended stay and a rare opportunity for him and his parents to spend a good amount of time together. It was an indication of how little they knew each other that Henry only now discovered that his son was a poor speller. Henry was incredulous that in all this time tutors or crammers did not pick up the problem. That the issue came to light so late also suggests there had been little correspondence between Alick and his parents over the years, quite extraordinary given Janet's habitual letter writing. Henry took it upon himself to dictate to Alick everyday in English, German and French. To his delight, Henry discovered that the young man had a tenacious memory and never made a mistake twice. Moreover, he had an excellent grasp of history. There is no evidence that Alick resented his father's efforts, so perhaps he enjoyed the parental interest though subsequent events would suggest that any close bond between them was fragile.

Alick was with his parents again in the winter of 1888, though this time Janet's response was mostly to find his presence a noisy intrusion, especially his violin playing. Perhaps he was new to the instrument or perhaps Janet was simply unaccustomed to the sound echoing through the wide halls of the villa. She wrote to a friend that she could hardly think clearly with the noise he made. With Alick around, she complained of having no time at all to put pen to paper. Even if Janet was writing in jest, there is a suggestion that she was unused to interruptions to the rhythm of her day.

In August of the same year Janet wrote triumphantly to Layard that Alick had received an offer from Canada of a professorship at Kingston College at a salary of 420 pounds a year and immediately afterwards an offer had arrived to join G. Schiff stockbrokers in the city of London. Then just a few days after that, Balliol wrote to say they had selected him for a professorship in Australia at 700 pounds a year!

In the end, Alick chose the City. Mr Schiff paid for his entry into the stock exchange and gave him a good commission. Janet was delighted even though her own brother Maurice had unsuccessfully taken up stockbroking a couple of years into his marriage to Fanny.

This is one of the last definitive images we have of Alick. In the following years, his presence becomes reduced to the faintest outline. He comes and goes but there is little tangible evidence of his existence. He becomes a familiar stranger in his family's life.

After *Italian Sketches*, Janet at last felt ready to attempt a full-length work. She conceived a biographical survey of her maternal forebears — Lucie, Sarah Austin and her great grandmother, Susannah Taylor. Called *Three Generations of Englishwomen*, it too proved a success. Based largely on letters written and received by the women, the work did not take Janet long to complete and it came out in 1888. By putting the lives of these remarkable women together, Janet created a context in which their talents and achievements could be displayed to advantage. The book delivered an insight into the intelligence and capacity of the three individuals, but it also allowed Janet to portray her family for posterity and for surviving family members, as she felt appropriate. Consequently, some problematic details were omitted altogether.

Janet's emphasis on the positive, and denial of the difficult, reflected her general view to life. There are only hints of the despair of Sarah Austin's marriage and no mention at all of the compromising and passionate correspondence with Pückler. Similarly, parts of Lucie's story are avoided, especially the last strained years of her marriage

Of course such omissions were not obvious to the general reader and bar some criticism of her over-use of commas, reviews were good. *The Pall Mall Gazette* wrote, 'The power of heredity is strikingly revealed. The ability varies, but there are three common qualities — courage, insight and enthusiasm. The volumes will be a stimulus to women and a rebuke to all men who scoff at learned ladies'. One review that did hint at the emotional restraint of the work was *The Melbourne Argus*, whose reviewer thought the book a very creditable piece, 'though we should have liked to hear more of the personal characters and the inner lives of these distinguished Englishwomen'.

The book sold well and was republished in an extended version in 1892. Janet's somewhat hagiographic style had produced a sort of popular feminist biography.

Buoyed by the response, Janet began thinking about another book on Italy. This time she decided to venture beyond the familiar landscape of Tuscany. She had long wanted to explore and write about the great southern region of the Italian peninsula. The idea had been in her mind since a visit to an estate called Leucaspide in Puglia in 1884. Janet and Henry had been invited there to stay with a friend they had met through Lotti. His name was Sir James Lacaita, a prominent Anglo-Italian, Dante scholar and a member of the first Italian Parliament. He was born in Naples and educated there as a lawyer, later migrating to England for political reasons. After Italian unification, he returned to live on his estate near Taranto, the regional town at the top of the 'instep' of the 'heel' of Italy. The town faces out onto the gulf of Taranto.

It was a long way from Florence and before the Rosses had set off on that visit, there was no shortage of warnings about the perils and difficulties of venturing south. They were told to beware of bandits, thieves and murderers. Janet was advised to leave earrings and her gold watch at home. Much of this came from people who had never been south themselves. In the minds of northern Italians, the south was another world — primitive, dangerous and suspect.

Janet's first impression of Puglia was of a wild untamed place. Everything her northern neighbours feared seemed to unfold when Janet and Henry were met at the station by an armed guard sent to accompany them to the Lacatia house. The burly guardsman carried a pistol in his belt and a gun over his shoulder. The visitors travelled in a carriage with the guard trotting alongside. It was an inauspicious start, but suddenly, and thankfully, the atmosphere changed. As they approached the house they were greeted with a massed ringing of bells; cowbells, sheep bells and hand bells, people everywhere were wielding bells. It was the most splendid and generous welcome. From this moment on Janet developed an intense love of the place, its people and its history. She wrote:

> A wild curious, melancholy country, beautiful in its way, and a very paradise for the botanist. In March the short turf is starred all over with the lovely yellow and purple Romulia Columnoe, sometimes all purple, sometimes nearly white, with a most delicious smell, like violets, only more so. The untilled parts of the country are a soft blue-grey colour from the rosemary, which grows in immense bushes and is used for firewood.

She loved the immense space, reminiscent of the Egyptian desert. Here, though there was wonderful vegetation — hedges of rosemary in full flower, mastic trees, myrtle, pink and white rockroses, and masses of small iris. Janet discovered that she could tell the time just by looking at these flowers, because they opened at midday and faded with the setting sun. The air smelled of lemon and orange trees, thick with blossom, and there were heavily scented Parma violets and stocks. The fields were planted with miles of olive trees and young corn. Shepherds dressed in goatskin waistcoats and trousers and played tunes on their reed pipes while tending the sheep. In contrast to the cultivated slopes of the Tuscan hills this was a vast and rugged land, possessed of its own traditions, legends and songs.

What Janet now had in mind would be one part history and one part travelogue. The history would cover the reigns of the medieval Hohenstaufen kings, Frederick II and his illegitimate son Manfred. Frederick II lived in the first half of the thirteenth century and was a great, though unorthodox emperor of Germany and Sicily. His father, Henry VI, heir to the German Empire, married Constance, daughter of Roger II of Sicily. Sicily in those days included the island and everything south of Naples on the mainland. At the time, Sicily enjoyed a cosmopolitan culture and Frederick's court became known for its Islamic scholars and artists, astrologers and exotic animals. While Frederick is remembered for bringing order to the lands under his control, his attempts to impose imperial rights on the northern and central towns of Italy put him on a lifelong collision course with the papacy. Rome felt increasingly hemmed in by his imperial aspirations and came to depict Frederick as an Antichrist figure. His intentions to the north remained frustrated throughout his reign. Three sons, including the illegitimate Manfred, survived him. It was Manfred, who continued the fight to consolidate territories in the north until he was killed in battle in 1266.

In the following years Janet undertook further field trips south to research the subject. She returned in 1886 and again in 1888. On the last of these, she travelled with Carlo Orsi who, after the success of *Italian Sketches*, was to do the illustrations. Janet's maid, Maria, and the young son of an English friend, Ambrose Poynter, accompanied them. (Henry remained at home with Lotti, who was now retired and living more or less permanently at Castagnolo.) What assistance Poynter offered is unclear, although his presence would have added some respectability to the group. Even so, there was some confusion about the relationships. One innkeeper thought Carlo and Maria were husband and wife and Janet and Ambrose were mother and son. Travelling was difficult and the conditions often primitive, but Janet's vision for the project propelled them on. She was at pains to travel in the historical footsteps of Frederick, visiting all the forts and towns he had built. They moved around by carriage and sometimes, where roads were inaccessible, they stepped down and walked along the potholed dusty tracks on foot. The determined English woman and her entourage foraging around the back roads must have been an unusual sight to behold.

They went to small out of the way places as well as bigger centres like the port city of Bari and the beautiful Baroque town of Lecce, known as the 'Florence of the south', because better Italian is spoken there than anywhere else in the region. Usually the inns were dirty, though Janet was impressed with the Puglian custom of bringing in sheets and blankets folded on a tray to show they

Janet in one of the wide-rimmed hats she favoured.

A photograph of one of Henry's orchids.

were clean and the beds reliable. Janet also came equipped with a travelling bath, which was a marvel to all who saw it.

All in all, Janet and Carlo judged the trip successful and when they returned home after the weeks away, Janet began to map out the manuscript. She usually worked in the evenings after dinner when she was free of the demands of the farms and house. As central as writing was in her life, it had to fit in with everything else she took on.

There were always daily distractions or pre-existing commitments taking up time. One of these was a long-standing undertaking to paint Henry's orchid collection. Janet had been encouraged in this by an English friend, Marianne North, an intrepid traveller and painter of exotic botanicals that she showed in her gallery at Kew. Janet had invited her to Castagnolo for the vintage and while she was there Marianne made sketches of the different kinds of grapes. She also spent a lot of time with Henry in the glasshouses he had built for his ever-increasing number of orchids. The range of his collection was so impressive that Marianne suggested Janet paint them. Taking up the task, every week she set aside hours to sit with her watercolours and paint the likeness of the plants and their exotic flowers. When the work began no one — least of all Janet — imagined it would run to 900 detailed specimen paintings. So complete was her survey that it ended up in the illustrations collection at Kew Gardens.

Another worrying distraction was Lotti's health. He was now nearly sixty years old. The specific nature of his illness is not clear, but it produced a gradual decline accompanied by pain and weakness. Possibly, it was cancer. He was ill enough that a good deal of Janet's time was spent nursing and keeping him company.

When she could, she worked on the book. For additional research she went into Florence where she was on friendly terms with the head librarian at the National Library. He was happy to assist her. This meant that often as not, she was relieved of dealing with the cumbersome library catalogues. She merely described her area of interest and the obliging librarian would produce the books.

Even so, as the manuscript progressed, she realized she needed more material than was available in Florence. She decided to go to London to seek out more material on the Hohenstaufen kings in the British Library. Having made arrangements for someone to look after Lotti, she travelled north with Henry. In the reading room of the British Library, without the personal service of an experienced librarian, she was on less familiar ground, but the effort was worthwhile. She makes no mention of seeing Alick during this visit although he was in close proximity. She did spend time with some friends during the couple of months spent there in 1888 but her real focus was on the research job at hand.

Her book, *The Land of Manfred*, published by John Murray, came out the following year and was generally well received by the reviewers, 'Mrs Ross, through her intimate acquaintance not only with the Italian tongue but with some of the most distinguished Apulians [sic], is able to enter into the life, manners and beliefs of the people, and in describing all this lies her chief charm'.

Unhappily for Janet, *Manfred* failed to engage the book-buying public. Just half of the first edition of 500 copies was sold. It was a huge disappointment.

Murray thought the title had been a mistake because it failed to explain what the book was about and he thought that some people had mistaken the hero for Byron's Manfred. However, Janet's publisher in Puglia sought permission to have the book translated, which was some small consolation.

Before the book was published, while Janet and Henry were still in London, news arrived of a further decline in Lotti's health. Janet and Henry returned to Florence as quickly as they could. Janet took on the role of full-time carer for him and, in her inimitable style, oversaw every detail of the patient's wellbeing.

The intensity of these final months became a sort of confirmation of the attachment between Janet and Lotti. All through late autumn and the winter months she turned her back on the outside world and focused only on him. Though very ill, he lost none of the generosity, intelligence and elegance that had first attracted Janet. Despite her attention, however, the friend around whom Janet and Henry had arranged their lives would be gone before spring.

Lotti's condition meant that the Rosses were forced to think about their future and consider looking for a new place to live. On and off over recent years, they had discussed the possibility of moving — now it was imperative. Their tenure at Castagnolo would not survive once Lotti's family inherited the place. Although the middle-aged ménage attracted little of the gossip and intrigue of earlier years, there was not much warmth between the Rosses and Lotti's extended family. And anyway, Henry and Janet were now of the view that it would be better to own a house of their own than spend more time and money on a leasehold.

To own their own house would require huge effort and the outlay of significant capital assets, but it would be secure. They had lived with Lotti for nearly eighteen years and while the inevitable end of that happy relationship was difficult for them, the Rosses were enthusiastic enough to look forward. At this point, there was no question of returning to live in England. They were both resolved to live in Italy for the rest of their lives.

A Castle in the Country

The spot in question was some distance away from any road,
on a small hill that was agreeable to behold for its abundance
of shrubs and trees, all bedecked in green leaves.

GIOVANNI BOCCACCIO
THE DECAMERON (1350)

OVER a period of a couple of months, Janet and Henry had looked at several villas but were left uninspired by what they saw. One cool autumn day, they set off in the carriage to the district of Settignano in the hills to the south-east of Florence, below the Etruscan hilltop town of Fiesole. Their intention was to inspect another villa in the area, this one near the village of Ponte a Mensola.

On the way they chanced to pass an old castle set back among the trees. It was an imposing square structure with a tower on one side, built in the thirteenth century. With its abrupt battlements it looked more forbidding than the villas commonly found in the Florentine hills. This was a medieval castle, imperious and strong, a landmark that had seen battles won and flags raised in victory. It was surrounded by fine old trees and had wonderful views back towards the city and out towards distant mountains. Janet immediately imagined herself chatelaine of this noble and majestic edifice; its scale suited her aspirations. The only problem was that it did not appear to be for sale.

The castle was called Poggio Gherardo. It was built as one of a line of fortresses intended to defend Florence against an ancient enemy. That was in the days when the great Florentine families lived in their strong-houses like robber chieftains, a time when they waged incessant war on each other and on adjacent villages and towns. It sat on the side of a gently sloping valley dominated on its upper reaches by another in the line of medieval castles, Vincigliata.

That great pile had been bought by the British merchant J. Temple Leader in 1855 and completely restored and reconstructed into a gothic wonderland. Temple Leader also held large tracts of forest and agricultural land around his castle and on nearby holdings.

Although only a few kilometres from Florence, the atmosphere was far from the bustle and noise of city life. The valley had cultivated fields, olive trees and crops of maize and wheat, with villas here and there. On a clear day, walking on the byroads and lanes through deep ploughed fields, the only constant sound was the burbling stream running into the village; occasionally the song of small birds rang out. This little scene of pastoral perfection was — and remains even today — one of the most pleasant parts beyond the city walls.

Making some preliminary enquiries, Janet discovered that the castle belonged to three unmarried sisters by the name of Gherardi, an old and esteemed name in Florence. The family had lived there for centuries. Their forbear, Gherardo Gherardi had bought Poggio Gherardo — or Palagio del Poggio as it was originally known — from the patrician Zati family in 1433. At various times since, it had been in the hands of other well-known families, including the Baroncelli, the Albizi, and the Baldesi and Magaldi families. When Gherardo bought the place he changed its name and it had remained home to his descendents until now.

To her joy, Janet heard that the old castle and adjoining three *poderi* or farms were in fact about to come onto the market. The farms comprised about 30 hectares (70 acres) of valuable agricultural land given to growing vines, olive trees, cornfields and fruit trees.

What a piece of luck! Although realistic enough to know the castle would be a substantial commitment to purchase and maintain, Janet remained undeterred. She began by convincing both herself and Henry (who would be outlaying the money) that it had potential to be economically viable. Once they were agreed, she was cautious to avoid any inflation in the price on account of being a foreign buyer. With this uppermost in mind, she asked an Italian friend to arrange the purchase on Henry's behalf. (Among experienced expatriates this was not uncommon.) Henry must have been confident that if anyone could make the place work it was Janet.

Poggio Gherardo from the eighteenth-century fresco by Tommaso Gheradini and others in the Palazzo del Circola dell' Unione in Florence.

The Decameron codex of Poggio Gherardo.

Both the village of Ponte a Mensola and Poggio Gherardo enjoy a literary association, thanks to Giovanni Boccaccio's great medieval work *The Decameron*, the bawdy, entertaining epic set in fourteenth-century Florence. Boccaccio's tale takes place in the summer of 1348 when a terrible plague ravages the city and ten young Florentines flee to the hills seeking refuge. For the first two days of their odyssey they establish themselves in a patrician villa nestled below Fiesole. They pass their time by telling each other 100 stories of love, adventure and fortune. From Renaissance times to the present the villa has often been identified as Poggio Gherardo. Boccaccio described the villa as:

> Some distance from any road, on a small hill that was agreeable to behold for its abundance of shrubs and trees, all bedecked in green leaves. Perched on its summit was a palace, built round a fine, spacious courtyard, containing loggias, halls, and sleeping apartments, which were excellently proportioned but richly embellished with paintings depicting scenes of gaiety. Delectable gardens and meadows lay all around, and there were wells of cool, refreshing water. The cellars were stocked with precious wines, more suited to the palates of connoisseurs than to sedate and respectable ladies. And on their arrival the company discovered, to their no small pleasure, that the place had been cleaned from top to bottom, the beds in the rooms were made up, and the whole house was adorned with seasonable flowers of every description, and the floors had been carpeted with rushes.

Janet embraced the connection and in subsequent years enthusiastically promoted the romantic association to her English readers.

Although large-scale land clearing on the hills around the city had changed the landscape since Boccaccio's time, Janet could still identify some of his landmarks. In *The Decameron*, Boccaccio described, 'the queen, accompanied and followed by her ladies and the three yong men, and led by the song of maybe twenty nightingales and other birds, walked westward by an unfrequented lane carpeted with grass and flowers whose petals were just opening to the rising sun'. Janet walked the same lane, still unfrequented and found it 'fragrant with wild violets and narcissi, leading through cornfields, bright with sweet-scented yellow tulips and scarlet anemones ... The hedges tangled with eglantine and honeysuckle, and here and there an old oak recalls the forest that once was'.

The old castle appeared in other local legends and tales too. There was the story of a siege at Poggio, and the destruction of the eastern facade in the fourteenth century by the notorious English mercenary, Sir John Hawkwood. Hawkwood, the son of an Essex landowner had fought in France as well as Italy. He achieved notoriety as commander of a band of several hundred freelancers known as the White Company, a marauding force of cavalry and infantry. Essentially a band of hoons and thugs, Hawkwood and his men specialized in terrorizing innocent people. They clambered over town fortifications by night to kill, rape and loot until ransoms were paid. In Tuscany and elsewhere, Hawkwood's White Company was dreaded. (This is the same White Company that inspired author Conan Doyle to pen his historical thriller of that name. It appeared in serial form in 1891 and was hugely popular.)

In a pragmatic twist, Hawkwood later gained respectability when he was invited by city elders to become Captain General of Florence. The shrewd Florentines saw the benefit of having such a man on side and agreed to pay him a large salary to protect the city.

Janet claimed an idiosyncratic affection for Hawkwood, whose proud likeness dominates the inside north wall of Florence's Duomo. There he is represented in a splendid equestrian-style fresco painted by the Renaissance artist Uccello. Undaunted by Hawkwood's more dubious accomplishments, Janet — like Doyle — was drawn to his feats and daring. To her, his larger-than-life character was the personification of adventure. The association with Poggio Gherardo brought him to life for Janet and she happily overlooked the fact that at the time he attacked Poggio he was fighting for the Pisans against the Florentines.

The Rosses successfully bought the property in November 1888, although settlement took a further two months. Janet and Henry had their belongings moved from Castagnolo in January, one month before Lotti died. While goods and chattels were being moved out, Janet spent time with her sick friend in his part of the old villa. She busied herself nursing him and keeping him comfortable.

Janet was forty-six years old. Henry was sixty-eight. They had been married for twenty-eight years, living for most of that time in or around Florence in rented accommodation. Poggio Gherardo was the first house they actually owned. It needed a considerable amount of money and an enormous amount of work. The work may well have served as a distraction from the sorrow of Lotti's death as it had after Alexander's death. With so much to do, she had no time to dwell on her loss.

Though Janet and Henry lived well in Italy, by English standards they were not rich and could scarcely have afforded a comparable place in England. In all their years in Italy, their main source of income was revenue from investments, supplemented by Janet's writing. Buying Poggio Gherardo was a major capital expense. Moreover, once bought, it would require additional investment in the first years to bring the house and the farms up to standard. Only then could they hope of making the whole thing viable over the longer term. In this sense, it was a gamble.

Poggio Gherardo was to be Janet's great project, which Henry, even if he had doubts, agreeably supported. The arrangement at Castagnolo, where she had been free to run the house and farms as the *padrona*, had suited them well but was inherently limited. Here, on this great blank canvas, Janet could work to her own design. Everything she learnt at Castagnolo under the tutelage of Lotti she could practise on her own account. Now she was hoping that her accumulated agricultural knowledge would transform the farms, making them models of Tuscan agricultural practice.

Like Castagnolo, these farms worked on the *mezzadria* system of share farming, with three extended families living on them. This was still the prevalent form of agricultural tenure in Tuscany,

A CASTLE IN TUSCANY

although for the first time some agricultural collectives were being established without a *padrone*. This was a radical shift.

One of Janet's great pleasures in Italian country life was the farming traditions that, through practise and observation, she had become an authority on. She had long ago discovered satisfaction in the simple physicality of working with the men, and in organizing their labour to achieve her plans. Some locals and expatriates thought it strange she spent so much time outdoors, but she found it invigorating to work alongside skilled men — heirs to ancient practices and customs.

⁂

During this period of settling in she wrote to Kinglake, 'I wish you could see this place, it is worthy to belong to some very great personage, all battlemented round and standing on its hill right into the plain … a great rich plain all dotted with villas and farm houses, and then tier upon tier of rolling hills as far as one can see, each crowned by some church or monastery'.

Grand and romantic as it was, there was a huge amount of work ahead restoring comfort to the house and productivity to the farms. Boccaccio's description of Poggio Gherardo as a well-stocked refuge inspired Janet's vision, but the immediate reality was that she and Henry were living in a draughty old castle in urgent need of attention. Of the marvellous gardens described by Boccaccio nothing remained except a few bits of old masonry that could have belonged to anything — walls, arbours, pedestals for statues; it was hard to tell.

The beautiful 'scenes of gaiety' decorating the walls that Boccaccio wrote about had long gone. A few decorations from later years remained, but most rooms just featured ugly wallpaper; the decorations underneath were irretrievable. Janet had the walls washed in the customary light grey stone colour. To undertake the task and the masses of other renovations needed, she took on local casual workers; men who lived on site and were paid in cash. Even with the relatively low rates of pay it was a costly business.

The list of improvements grew as Janet uncovered more and more pockets of neglect. She was shocked for instance at the condition of the worker's houses. For a start, there was no glass in the windows. It had obviously never been considered necessary. She dryly commented, 'I have just discovered that the former owners of this place imagined that gentlefolk and peasants are made of different clay'. How could she establish good relationships with families that were so poorly housed? Although Janet had not seen this at Castagnolo, rural poverty and inadequate housing were commonplace throughout Italy, but she would not be party to it.

The scale of the work required at Poggio Gherardo might have dwarfed a less determined woman, but the new *padrona* was not discouraged. Bringing order and functionality were Janet's preoccupations and to this end she immersed herself in all manner of domestic detail. Overseeing repairs

Poggio Gherardo's poodle room and hall
beyond after restoration.
Photographed by Vittorio Jacquier.

and painting, removing walls to make bigger, lighter spaces, placing doors where there had been none and measuring rooms and cutting up the old carpets to fit them. Among the remaining wall decorations was one *trompe-l'oeil* showing a favourite poodle of the old Gherardi family, and the stylized pooch dominated what became known as 'the poodle room'. She converted the old chapel into a bathroom. The leaky roofs were mended and when that was done, she developed plans for new cottages for the *contadini* and their families.

Janet set out her 'boudoir' — as she called it — or sitting room, arranging it in a similar fashion to her sitting room at Castagnolo; the walls were crammed with pictures, sketches and portraits of friends and relatives. Against one wall, she placed the old writing table she had inherited from Lucie. She put a bust of her father on the same wall so that every time she looked up from her work she would come almost face to face with his likeness. To friends who had visited both houses, the look and feel of the rooms was almost identical. The house was beginning to feel comfortable. Her sitting room, was one of the cosiest rooms in the house and was a treasured, private retreat. Here she worked on farm accounts by day and sat down to her correspondence and manuscripts in the evenings.

In the quiet of night, after others had gone to bed, she would get to work on research and writing. Before long, she began preliminary work on a slim autobiographical book, *Early Days Recalled*. It captured some of the well-known names of her youth and early-married life in Egypt. Seated at her mother's desk among the clutter of family keepsakes, it was easy for her to evoke the stories of people and events from her past.

Out of doors, she worked under a scorching sun all through that first summer. Every day after lunch she took her white linen and muslin hat and walked outside sometimes accompanied by one of her large Maremma sheep dogs. She was teaching the farmers the art of pruning vines in the Burgundian style — otherwise known as cane pruning — a technique, she considered, that produced a superior fruit than that achieved by the local faster method of spur pruning. Later she turned her attention to the olives. With these she encouraged the men to zealously follow her time-honoured dictum to prune hard and manure heavily. While she was notoriously intolerant of social bores and fools she displayed infinite patience with labourers.

To her secret delight she saw that her local friends, both English and Italian, were surprised by her habits. In a letter to Kinglake in 1899, she boasted proudly that:

> All my English acquaintances here are open mouthed at the amount of work I get done. The other day it threatened to rain and we have just built a cistern for rainwater. I lamented that the drain which would take a large body of water into the cistern was not finished and that as it was six o'clock, and work stops at sunset, it would be sure to pour all night and we should lose the water we so much needed, so six men actually worked till 8:15 and finished the drain.

To demonstrate her appreciation she stayed with them until the job was finished. This kind of gesture led to her growing influence. Another factor too, must have been the inspiring novelty for the men in having a determined and striking Englishwoman as their *padrona*. As one visitor observed, in a country where personal beauty is a talisman, her looks ensured the devotion of all who were dependent on her at Poggio Gherardo.

Throughout the first year she wrote often to Kinglake, keeping him abreast of progress and local news. She wrote of the need for rain, progress on the farms and the enjoyment she took in the beauty of the place. She was proud of what they were achieving and enjoyed the role of farmer, 'I have been doing farmer all day, settling where asparagus is to go and where tomatoes will bear fruit earliest'.

By August, Janet and Henry saw the first early rewards for their efforts in the form of a surplus of perfect, ripe fruit ready for sale. Melons were sent fifty or sixty at a time to the city market. Also dispatched each morning were three or four hundred figs, carefully packed in baskets, although these were barely profitable once the labour of picking and packing was accounted for. But even with the small return, the pleasure of having produced them was worth the effort.

September brought further earthworks in the field. Deep ditches were dug up for new vines and large holes made for olive trees. Casual labourers drained ditches and lined them with loose stones set on end, a method that improved the drainage. Once the fields were sown, the space between trees and vines was utilized for the growing of smaller plants. On the sloping fields of olives Janet put in purple artichokes. Under the grapevines, wheat was planted. The soil benefited and at harvest, the wheat provided good mulch.

By the end of the month, Janet proudly oversaw her first vintage. Alarming the farmers somewhat, she introduced new methods of wine-making developed at Castagnolo. Sensing their disbelief that such a deviation from tradition might possibly produce anything drinkable, she diplomatically suggested that in this first year they should make their share of wine their way and her share in the new way. At the end they would see whose wine was best. To men used to making wine by the ancient methods, her experiment appeared eccentric at best, but of course they went along with it. Once bottled, the wine was stored in large cellars that ran half the length of the house. Janet was very pleased with the results and considered the experiment a success. She served some of the wine in the house and sold the rest.

Also cellared under the house were the bottles of special Poggio Gherardo vermouth. This was made to a secret recipe given to Janet from a friend, the Marchese Ridolfi Perizzi, on the strict understanding that it not be divulged to anyone outside the family. This too was served in the house and the remainder sold.

Come October, and Janet's enthusiasm turned to experimenting with wheat types. 'Are your brothers great farming people?', she inquired of Kinglake, 'If they are, do ask them to send me

A CASTLE IN THE COUNTRY

a sample packet of their best wheat by post'. She proposed comparing this wheat with samples she had received from Australia and America to see which responded best to local conditions.

By autumn the wet weather set in and work in the fields came to a halt. Now was a good time to turn attention to the garden. Hours and hours were spent cutting down dead trees and digging in manure. In one month alone, some one hundred trees where planted. By November after ten months of hard work, the farms and gardens were taking shape.

Even to the modern reader with a busy schedule, the extent of Janet's activity and output is hugely impressive. Not withstanding the support of the farmers and plenty of household help at her disposal, the improvements at Poggio Gherardo were admirable. Part of her success was that she made little distinction between work and leisure. In an average day there was precious little time for self-reflection. Her focus remained on the work to be done and the results were quite remarkable.

Janet spent considerable time and effort in accounting for the farms. (She was good at adding up columns of figures but she had never learnt multiplication, so her sums are all based on additions.) Her correspondence is peppered with costs incurred and prices achieved. But despite the careful tracking of cash flow, there were times when she felt genuinely short of money. An anxiety more often imagined than real, and probably a hangover from the Egyptian fiasco.

However effective her accounting practice, Janet was by nature prudent. She only felt at ease when she was across all the detail: the flowers to be planted, the rotation of the crops, the market prices for this and that, the vintage and the making of oil and wine, discussions about menus and the needs of guests and so on. She was the mastermind of the operation, keeping a tally of the myriad tasks to be undertaken on the farms, in the gardens, the house and kitchen. All this detail she committed to memory and dispensed effortlessly as required.

While life at Poggio Gherardo was settling into a harmonious and industrious rhythm, the family situation was about to change in an unexpected way. Alick was twenty-eight years old and now working in London. Though he visited, nothing had changed in the distant relationship he shared with his mother. She had formed easier relationships with the farm workers and her dogs than she had with her son. Although capable of enormous tenderness, she had never pretended to have any maternal instincts or to hide the fact that she and her only child were not close. Throughout Alick's childhood, even among his extended family in England with whom he spent his formative years, close personal bonds seemed to have eluded him.

For parents so obviously uninterested in children, it was surely a surprise to Alick when Janet and Henry invited his cousin, Lina Duff Gordon, to live with them at Poggio Gherardo. Sixteen years old, Lina was the only child of Maurice and his estranged and recently deceased first wife, Fanny.

Maurice, though popular and handsome, had made little of the opportunities that came to him. His godfather, Lord Lansdowne, who had financed his education, also left money to Maurice in his will and as a young man, he had received the small inheritance from Sarah Austin. Without a compelling vocation, Maurice, financed by his cousins, joined the stock exchange, but all the time he seemed more interested in hunting, fishing and women.

When he inherited his father's baronetcy in 1872 he became Sir Maurice, and then in 1884 he inherited the vast turreted Fyvie Castle in Aberdeenshire. It had come to him from his father's cousin Captain Alexander Gordon, who died without children of his own. After separating from Fanny and her subsequent death, he went on to marry a second time. Again he wed a wealthy woman whose fortune he managed to squander. Eventually his debts accumulated to the point that he was he forced to sell Fyvie. Since his youth he had lived a life of pleasure, undisciplined and lacking in achievement.

At some time in his youth Maurice picked up syphilis, one of the great health blights of the late part of the nineteenth century. As a young man his parents had been concerned about his use of prostitutes. When he visited Lucie in Egypt before her death she was alarmed by what she thought was a case of gonorrhea and insisted he seek treatment. The more serious symptoms of syphilis would not reveal themselves for some time.

After Lina's parents separated when she was still a young girl, Lina and her mother moved to France and the little girl was placed in a convent. A short time later Fanny became seriously ill and died. At the news of his wife's death, Maurice revealed to Lina his plans to marry Sophie Mary Steer, placing his daughter in a terrible predicament. She did not want to live with her father and a new stepmother who she knew had displaced her own mother before her parents separation, nor was she enthusiastic about convent life. Suspicious that there might be plans afoot for her to embrace the veil on a more permanent basis, she took things into her own hands. Lina decided to spend her next holiday break, with her maid Félicie at Poggio Gherardo and not return to the convent.

When they arrived, to Lina's relief, they received the warmest welcome. As she walked through the lofty hall with its vaulted ceiling, a door opened and there stood her aunt, a magnificent figure dressed in a plain white dress. Around her waist she wore a black leather belt, from which hung her watch, a silver key to the front and side gates and a leather bound notebook. Standing behind his wife was Henry, with a bunch of his hothouse flowers for Lina. The Rosses had always been fond of their niece in a way that they were not of their son. From this first moment, the stay was a success and after a short time Janet was only too happy to persuade Maurice to let her and Henry adopt his daughter. Maurice knew Lina did not want to live with his new wife, and with her aunt she would be well provided for. Lina was tall and slim with a long face and straight blond hair. She liked books and writing and was intelligent and determined – perhaps a quality that endeared her to Janet.

As it turned out, before her death Fanny had already broached the idea of Lina's adoption with Janet and Henry. Fanny must have been aware of Janet's troubled relationship with Alick. Regardless, she recognized qualities in her sister-in-law that convinced her she was the best person to take care of her adored daughter. Janet's enthusiastic response to the proposal was even more surprising than Fanny's faith in the idea. What moved Janet to take on such a responsibility given her avowed lack of interest in mothering is not clear.

From the time of Lina's move to Poggio Gherardo, references to Alick in Janet's correspondence become even fewer. Whatever aspirations Janet harboured for the next generation she now directed towards her niece.

For Lina, the new arrangement with her indomitable aunt and dear uncle in their wonderful castle was a lifeline. She embraced the place. Janet saw that Lina's education was rounded out with a strong dose of Italian political and cultural history. She found specialist tutors in Florence and much was acquired from visitors and friends. Lina spent a lot of time by herself, though she did find companionship among the children of some of Janet's friends, especially the daughters of Italophile and scholar, John Addington Symonds, Madge and Katherine. These two lived with their parents in Davos, Switzerland but spent quite a lot of time in Italy. They shared Lina's love of books and ideas and her enthusiasm for history and writing and were as enchanted by the place and way of life as Lina was. Lina also met some local children but none were as important to her as the Symonds girls.

The three girls would sit in the large drawing room to listen to Janet play the piano, sometimes accompanied by Carlo Orsi singing local love songs. On the walls were statuettes of Lansdowne and Sir James Lacaita, Janet's friend from Puglia, drawings by Watts, Lear and Thackeray and objects brought from the East. The floors were strewn with carpets brought from Egypt, and the chairs, large and comfortable, were covered in embroidered designs stitched by Janet. Ornate cages of exotic birds were dotted about and the whole effect was eclectic high Victorian. Madge described it as a place inhabited by people who had reached a certain point of aristocratic splendour, though the grandeur never spilt over to extravagance or pretension.

On Sunday afternoons, Lina and her friends would join the open house gatherings that Janet liked to host. Friends and visitors would come to these informal affairs. Sometimes Janet would play her guitar, occasionally a visiting musician might perform. Good food was sent out from the kitchen and there was stimulating conversation. The girls mingled easily among the guests who sat and talked inside the house or on the terrace and in the garden.

When her friends returned to Davos, Lina was left to her own devices. Regardless of the paucity of young company and despite Janet's love of timetable and pre-occupation with the farms and garden, self-reliant Lina was happy. She admired the way her aunt planned her life and stuck to it with clockwork regularity, although on later reflecting for her own autobiography, Lina thought Janet lost a lot of pleasure by her incessant activity.

Janet's brother Maurice.

A CASTLE IN THE COUNTRY

Carlo Orsi in Janet's sitting room.

Sometimes Lina would accompany Janet on excursions into Florence for shopping or to visit a library or occasionally to call on a friend. They would take off in an open pony carriage driven by her aunt. Other times she was left free to read, look at pictures and sight-see. She loved the airy spaciousness of the castle, its contents and their stories, its position on the hill and the wide view. Simply sitting in Janet's boudoir and contemplating the landscape was a favourite activity. So was wandering through the garden in the warmer months.

The garden was not formally laid out, but was arranged with plants that appealed to Janet — many rare and exotic — clumped together in informal beds and terraces. When it came to gardens, Janet was motivated by botanical interest rather than structure and design. In any case the castle, with its medieval lineage, did not suit the formality of the Renaissance-style gardens that were popular with the owners of many villas in the neighbourhood.

At Poggio, there were masses of roses of all kinds and at the rear of the house, azaleas and citrus. Large terracotta pots filled with hydrangeas, plumbago and lemon trees were dotted around the place and oleanders, mock orange, balsam, tree peonies and banksia roses filled the beds. On one side of the garden was an immense camphor tree and in another part stood a tall magnolia. There was also, as in most Italian gardens, a persimmon tree delivering its lantern shaped fruit in the late autumn.

The long driveway that swept up the hill from the front gates was bordered with flowering fruit trees and little pink roses. Augustus Hare, the travel writer, recalled in his autobiography, *The Story of My Life*, published in 1900, the marvellous effect of approaching the house through half a mile of these roses in bloom. On the large terrace in the front of the house was a fishpond with a central fountain. It was home to a rare species of Burmese goldfish, gorgeous creatures with double tails. Henry, who fed and looked after them, had introduced them to Poggio.

More than his fish though, Henry's overriding passion was for the orchids. He transferred them from Castagnolo and continued to add to the collection, now one of the most extensive in Italy. Refined and mysterious, the elegant specimens suited him well. They were housed on the southern side of the garden in new large purpose-built conservatories. The glasshouses contained long pools of water to provide the requisite humidity for the plants, doubling as holding pools for more Burmese fish. Both Henry and Janet were assisted by the gardener, Beppe, and the under-gardener, Petrino (who did tasks such as gather kindling wood for the boilers in each bathroom and the iron stoves in each bedroom).

Also in the garden was a poultry yard. Being Janet's, however, this was no ordinary poultry yard. There were great cages of golden pheasants and other rare and wondrous birds as well as more ordinary fowl. There were hens and chickens and lots of guinea pigs. Huge cypress trees provided shade and there were roses trailing and falling on the roofs of the pens. Further on was a little forest of ilex trees and umbrella pines, cypresses and sweet bays where nightingales sang through the spring nights. In the middle was a small arch surrounded by stone seats and tiny sarcophagi containing the ashes of the dogs that had died in the villa in the eighteenth century. Poggio Gherardo seemed enchanted.

     This was partly the nature of the place itself and partly the aura of its new owners. Within a couple of years, Janet had the house and farms in reasonable order. The project would be a lifetime's work but she had established a firm footing. The farms had been rejuvenated and looked sustainable. Over the coming years, Poggio Gherardo was to become something of an icon among locals and visitors alike. To stay there was to enter a special world.

Friends and Visitors

POGGIO Gherardo embodied Janet's aesthetic. The way she arranged the house, her love of nature and her pleasure in intellectual pursuits bore testament to her taste and values. Developing the farms, writing, and enjoying the company of friends filled her days. Among the Anglo-Italians of Florence, Poggio achieved almost iconic status. Visitors from near and far found their way out of the city to Ponte a Mensola. Some she specially invited, others would arrive with letters of introduction.

By the early 1890s the reputation of Janet and her castle had spread, so that almost anybody of note visiting the city came out to call. Other than houseguests though, weekdays saw few visitors. Instead, people were asked to come up to Poggio for the regular Sunday afternoon open house receptions. Janet never begrudged showing off the house and farms and countryside, but she definitely preferred to see people on Sunday, when she gave a warm welcome to friends and others with letters.

On these occasions, numbers of locals and foreigners mingled in the drawing and sitting rooms, in the warmer months spilling out onto the terrace. Lina recalled the fascination of first-time visitors with

Janet's early-Victorian sitting room filled with the faces of interesting and well-known people. Florentine grandees, foreign writers, escapees from colder climates and friends from Janet's past, came to enjoy the company and the view, all the more pleasant for the good food sent out from the kitchen. Janet, commanding in presence, and the unfailingly courteous Henry, were natural hosts, happily mingling among their guests, sharing stories and introducing people. If the mood took her, Janet sometimes reached for her guitar and gave an impromptu performance of folk songs. This treasured instrument with its coloured ribbons tied to the end was always near at hand, laid on the piano or sofa. Sometimes it seemed that the singing would never stop. Such entertainment was surely not to everyone's taste (Henry James for one, seemed ambivalent) but the gatherings became an institution.

Neighbours came regularly. Lina remembered Pen, the son of Elizabeth Barrett Browning and Robert Browning, who came with his American wife. They had the lease on a villa not far away, as had the then Poet Laureate, Alfred Austin who had succeeded Alfred Lord Tennyson in the role. His Sunday visits, however, were less successful because Janet kept forgetting he was a poet. Carlo Orsi came often.

The city might come up to the villa on Sunday afternoons, but Janet did not have the time or inclination to go too often to Florence. She found the crowds of blank-faced tourists with their Baedeker guidebooks intrusive and preferred to avoid them if possible. Outings to the city were rare, remembered Madge Symonds:

> except to visit churches and its picture galleries and to hurry home with some rushed shopping ... We would go into the embroidery shop and pull over the bundles and search amongst the mountainous heaps of that glorious Florentine filosel with which she always embroidered ... or we would drive through the Corso — the public gardens, greeting and greeted by a host of unknown personages.

There were exceptions, invitations that even Janet could not refuse. In 1896 Princess Corsini, matriarch of an old Florentine family and friend of Janet's, hosted a ball for the occasion of the marriage of Crown Prince Victor Emmanuel — grandson of King Victor Emmanuel II — and Princess Elena of Montenegro. On a mid-winter night, twelve hundred finely dressed and bejewelled guests arrived at the vast, candlelit Corsini palace. On such an occasion, Janet couldn't resist the opportunity to make a spectacular entrance, harking back to her days in Egypt, and had dressed in a splendid emerald green Indian dress embroidered all over with peacock feathers — a gift from her friend the writer and painter Marianne North. Henry had extended the rare offer to Madge and Lina of allowing them to choose any orchid they liked to pin to their dresses. Such a grand event was a special occasion for residents of Poggio, especially for Lina and Madge.

Although such invitations were few and keenly awaited, the girls did not generally hanker after more sophisticated entertainments than were on offer at Poggio. Like other visitors, what Madge liked most was the rhythm of the castle and farms and the company of Janet, Henry and Lina.

The main entrance to Poggio Gherardo. The busts
represent the four seasons.

The pond on the terrace in front of the castle.

Henry, Lina and Janet on the front terrace.

A CASTLE IN TUSCANY

Janet would wake early and begin the day with her habitual light breakfast of coffee and toast. Then she would sit down at her easel and turn her mind to painting an orchid chosen for the purpose by Henry. For a couple of hours she worked away with her watercolours and brushes, mixing exact colours and adding tiny flourishes of detail to achieve the most perfect botanical likeness she could manage. Even though she was good at the work — Bernard Berenson thought the results were not only exact, but that they reproduced the movement and beauty of the flowers — she claimed not to enjoy it much. She really did it for Henry. It gave him a great deal of pleasure and she knew that his collection was extraordinary.

By mid-morning she was well settled at her desk and immersed in accounts. She also allocated farm tasks and, with the cook Giuseppe, planned meals for family and guests. At lunch she joined Henry, Lina and any houseguests in the dinning room. After the meal, Janet, like clockwork, withdrew to the balcony — or to the fireplace in winter — and smoked her ritual half cigarette; a pleasure she repeated in the evening.

In the afternoon, grabbing her hat as she went (a felt one with exotic plumage in winter and the white linen one in summer) she strode off to see what was happening on the farms. If there were weeds to be pulled as she passed or fallen olives to be salvaged, she bent over and did the work.

The sheer scale of the house meant that guests had plenty of space. If all they wanted was to read all day or sit and take in the panorama, that was fine. Thankfully for those close to her, Janet did not demand everyone else be productive and busy. Her only expectation — and it was a very real one — was punctuality at meals. Otherwise, she was relaxed about what people did with the rest of their time.

The guest bedrooms were light and airy and decorated with garden flowers that Janet, having a natural dislike of artifice, simply clumped into the vase without regard for arrangement. In winter the fires glowed with the perfumed wood of olive trees and the beds were made with linens that had been hung with dried lavender and herbs from the garden. In her own room she preferred to sleep on a mattress of Indian corn leaves rather than one filled with wool. She was convinced it was more hygienic. (Originally all the mattresses had been filled with corn leaves, but when it became clear that visitors found them noisy, she changed them over.)

Such quirkiness in her personal habits didn't prevent the house being beautiful and comfortable for visitors. Madge expressed the impression all this made on guests, 'To live under her roof was to be carried back to the rule of some lady in the Cinquecento ... Her standard of service being so high, it may well be imagined to what a pitch of horrified indignation her mind would be excited by the vision of an English household even at its best'.

In the evening everyone was expected to change for dinner. For a family meal, the food was simple but always delicious. When guests joined the family something more elaborate would be prepared. The wine was from Poggio farms and the bread was made in the kitchen oven. Servants brought in dishes and the room was alive with conversation.

In the drawing room, the post-dinner conversation roamed freely across subjects. The guest most appreciated by Janet was one with good conversation. She never tired of hearing lively stories or of listening to an expert expounding on his — for it was usually his — subject. Mostly though, it was Janet who dominated the lively talk while Henry immersed himself in newspapers and orchid lists. Scattered all around her were splendid coloured silks she used for embroidering great squares of a flame pattern she had taken from an old Italian design. Always productive, she happily worked her needle and thread while she entertained. As well as covering chairs, this embroidery found its way onto curtain borders, stools and cushions. Quietly stitching as she talked, night after night, she must have embroidered miles rather than yards in her time. When she wasn't talking, she listened, as Henry 'the old traveller', looked up from his reading and recounted some fantastic past adventure. He was as good a raconteur as when Janet had first met him.

Throughout the years of their marriage there had always been a great degree of respect and regard for each other. By temperament they were well suited and together they were well liked. He was considered and thoughtful and she more outgoing. Most who came to Poggio could see the important, if somewhat subtle, role played by Henry in the enterprise.

Madge passed many evenings in the amiable company of Janet, Henry and Lina in the drawing room after dinner. She remembers Janet as a somewhat dogmatic talker, bold and emphatic in her argument. Men were particularly comfortable with her tone. If present, they were invariably drawn to her for conversation.

One of these was Madge's father, John Addington Symonds. Madge remembered the first time she accompanied her father to Poggio:

> We had come through the crowed streets of Florence out into the open country and up through the carefully tended olives and vineyards of Poggio Gherardo, to the huge wooden door of the villa; this was flung open to us by the hospitable butler of those days, Fortunato, and we had passed through the lofty entrance halls with their vaulted ceilings and scagliola floors and come to the big drawing room where Mrs Ross was waiting for us, her arms flung open in welcome … Those clear and seeing eyes now fixed themselves upon myself; they realised without one moment's doubt, that what the rather frightened (and very small) stranger wanted was a bed, and not flowers or terraces or new sights or people. So to bed I immediately went: and it was in that particularly white bed — Aunt Janet's linen was the softest and the whitest and the sweetest, too, that I have ever met with …

In the meantime, Symonds would be made comfortable and shown his own bedroom and a place he could sit and write. He is best known today for his works on Michelangelo and the pamphlets he published privately on homosexuality. He was the son of an eminent physician from Bristol, and was educated at Harrow and Balliol College, Oxford. Although homosexual, he married Janet Catherine North — sister of Marianne North — and had three daughters, Lotta, Madge and Katherine. He suffered from tuberculosis and as a consequence had moved his family to Davos, Switzerland where the air was dry and fresh.

In the field of gay and lesbian studies he has become something of a hero of nineteenth-century homosexual consciousness. Because of homosexuality's illegality at the time, Symonds' work on the subject had to remain private. His poems — while not generally considered to be great literature, are among the most frankly sexual of the Victorian period — he distributed privately to friends. Likewise, his pamphlets in defence of homosexuality and calling for legal reform, were quietly passed from friend to friend.

He and Janet first met in England in the early 1880s over a meal with mutual friends. After dinner Janet was asked to play her guitar and sing to the assembled gathering which, unfortunately, proved horribly unresponsive. The only person in the entire room giving any sign of life was a good-looking man with a clipped beard standing at the back of the crowd. His uninhibited cheering in this company intrigued Janet, who sought him out.

It was her Italian folk songs, or *Tuscan Volks Lieder* as Symonds called them, that first drew them together, but it was soon obvious that they shared a lot more. After listening to his brilliant talk, Janet remembered feeling the cobwebs had been brushed away from her brain. Straight away, Symonds encouraged Janet to publish some of the popular Italian songs that she had been collecting since she first heard Ulisse sing in the streets of Oltrarno in her early days in Florence. The book, *Italian Popular Songs* was published in 1893.

Janet invited Symonds to visit her in Italy at Castagnolo where she was then living; but now he was a regular at Poggio Gherardo. He often brought his daughters, especially the younger two. After Lina moved in, either Katherine and Madge or both usually accompanied their father, and before long they were staying on their own account to spend time with Lina. Madge and Lina, encouraged by Janet, even began writing together. They turned their energies to researching and writing the stories of nearby towns.

'The historian', as Janet called Symonds, was acutely aware of his physical vulnerability due to consumption. He knew he had limited time to accomplish all he hoped. So what time he had, he spent productively. Janet no doubt admired his focus and determination. Until his early death in 1893, whenever he was working and studying in Florence, most famously on Michelangelo, he used Poggio as his base.

Symonds was interested in the classical notions of platonic love that appeared in Michelangelo's work. He believed that much of the great artist's work — poetry sculpture, architecture and painting — was deeply influenced by his homosexuality. In his study of Michelangelo, which was to become a classic piece of scholarship, he made a compelling connection between the artist's sexuality and his aesthetic. Although broadly accepted today, this was breaking new ground when Symonds argued the case.

He spent hours each day immersed in the Florentine archives and then more time drafting his thesis. Much of the writing he did at Poggio. What time was left, he devoted to family and friends. He was fond of his wife — although they were no longer physically intimate — and adored his daughters. He took a great interest in their education and achievements and enjoyed their company on his travels.

The great complication was his homosexuality. At this point in his life, his sexuality expressed itself in a long-standing relationship with a Venetian boatman, Angelo Fusato. Though both were married with children, Fusato and Symonds maintained their relationship for twelve years until Symonds' death. Symonds kept a house in the lagoon city and employed Fusato as boatman. Each year Symonds and some or all of his family spent time in Venice. Between visits, Fusato would sometimes travel with Symonds, although he never stayed at Poggio.

Symonds' life was complex, but Janet seemed to understand and take it all in her stride in a way she did not with lesbians like Vernon Lee. Social rivalry between these two prominent women might have prohibited much understanding. But more likely, given what we know of Janet's own sexuality, Vernon's Lee's lesbianism may well have been too close to home for Janet's comfort. By contrast, homosexual men were much safer. Nonetheless, Lina and Madge developed a fascination with Lee who they sometimes saw while they were out walking, in her old hooded cart drawn by a very thin white horse that Janet referred to as 'Apocalypse'.

For her friend Symonds, Janet offered support and affection, and Poggio Gherardo became a refuge to think and write. After a hard day of work they would take gentle walks along the lanes or through wooded pathways or make expeditions to towns or nearby churches in search of some painting or statue or other point of interest. If he did not feel strong enough, he could rest on the terrace. He appreciated the civilized world that Janet had established, 'the presence of the Arno valley and the hills is always felt inside the house, adding a dignity and charm, not ours, to what we say'.

Poggio Gerardo was a perfect base from which to pursue his work and Janet was pleased to have him stay. He would come to Florence and work as much as he could then return to the dry mountain air of Davos. As his health forced him to take extended breaks from work, Janet increasingly undertook research for him in the Florentine archives and libraries. He admired Janet's uncommon attitude and energy and regarded her to be one of the handful of women who had influenced his life.

In early 1891 Janet helped Symonds find material for the Michelangelo study, and when he finally finished he paid her the compliment of asking her to read his proofs and make suggestions. Symonds' admiration for his subject amounted to a passion. He declared that Michelangelo 'beat every artist quite clean out of the field'. By comparison he thought Raphael insipid and felt that the painter's rooms in the Vatican were like milk and gruel after Michelangelo's Sistine Chapel. When the work *The Life of Michelangelo Buonarroti* finally came out, Janet took great pleasure in reviewing it enthusiastically for the English monthly review *Nineteenth Century*.

Janet's sitting room. Her treasured guitar sits on the
chaise longue.

The encouragement and support was not all one-sided. Symonds always gave Janet helpful feedback on her writing. If she asked for help or clarification on a subject familiar to him, he was quick to respond. He had given such assistance on a number of books including her autobiographical account of her youth, *Early Days Recalled*, sequel to the popular *Three Generations of Englishwomen,* which was published mid-1891. (Sadly for Janet, the man who had first suggested she write about herself, Kinglake, had died just a few months earlier at the age of eighty-two.) She was finishing *Early Days Recalled* when she began helping Symonds with *Michelangelo.* Symonds also encouraged her to consider re-editing her mother's *Letters From Egypt,* which had been out of print for some time. (This edition would finally come out in 1902.)

When Symonds was not in Florence the two continued an affectionate and frequent correspondence. They shared ideas and snippets about Florentine history and art, and of course news and gossip. In October 1891 from Rome he wrote:

> the Sistina [chapel] has exhausted me to-day; and I visit a German artist of great skill in painting nudes. I am going to make him pose models in the impossible positions discovered by M.A.B [Michelangelo Bounarroti] ... M.A.B is my vampire at present. If only the work would come out worth the pains I take about it ...

Not infrequently, he sought her assistance in finding a document or image from one of the libraries and Janet being on good terms with most of the city's librarians, loved the challenge. Earlier in the same year he wrote to thank her for the photographs of all Michelangelo's works that she had arranged to be sent from Florence to Davos.

The last project she worked on for her friend was a paper on Michelangelo to be delivered in the spring of 1893 in Florence. As it turned out, Symonds was double-booked for the day the lecture was to be delivered. He had another speaking engagement in Rome. As he considered his dilemma, the absurdity of delivering a lecture on Michelangelo in English to an Italian audience began to dawn on him. Hoping she might have a solution to both problems, he turned to Janet. Her answer was to translate Symonds' paper into Italian herself and ask a local critic and professor to deliver it in the author's absence. Janet went down to the city to hear the lecture and while she had a strange sense of anxiety throughout, she was relieved and delighted with the enthusiastic response it received.

The last she had heard from Symonds and Madge was their intention to come to Poggio the following week, but in the meantime unbeknown to Janet, Symonds had fallen very ill. His health had deteriorated so quickly that just after the conclusion of the lecture in Florence, Janet got the shocking news from Rome that her friend had died with Madge by his side. He was fifty-three years old. They had been close for over a decade. By her estimation he had probably died just before the Florentine audience

Lina and her great friend Madge Addington Symonds on the front steps.

applauded his paper. Her 'perfect friendship' had come to an end. Remembering him years later, she wrote of her 'admiration for the frail, delicate man whose indomitable power of will and brain conquered bodily weakness and suffering which would have prostrated anyone else'.

In the weeks after her father's death, Madge received heartfelt love and support from Janet. In later years she recalled that time:

> In the most shattering sorrow of my young days, namely after my Father's death in Rome, I was brought by a friend one hot May night back to Aunt Janet's villa. A small and wretched human wreck — shattered broken and forlorn, thrown up upon that generous beach for comfort. Mrs Ross had clearly loved my Father, whose life, perhaps always too frail, had now gone out in early splendour. She understood him and revered him, and I was glad to go to her, for my own distress amounted to a physical illness. She took me in. She helped to heal the wound which at its very best, would be but a deep white scar. The world will remember Janet Ross as a rather domineering and commanding figure in the literary and social circles of her day. But some there are, who like myself, will bless this great Victorian lady because of her hidden tenderness, and because of that deeper and serener charity which reaches the heart of its affliction.

From her first years at the castle, Janet was regarded locally as a practical problem solver, a fixer. It was not uncommon for new arrivals to Florence, looking for help, to be directed to Poggio Gherardo. In 1892 an American neighbour — Professor Daniel Willard Fiske — who lived near Fiesole, brought over an American man who was visiting with his family. He was introduced to her as Mr Samuel Clemens, otherwise known as Mark Twain.

Clemens had left his home in Hartford, Connecticut and travelled to Europe in an attempt to offset financial difficulties. When Janet first met him he was fifty-seven years old and already the most popular writer in America, having had his greatest success with *The Adventures of Huckleberry Finn* eight years before. Despite his own success and his marriage to an independently wealthy wife, he was saddled with huge debts. In addition to the expansive Clemens' lifestyle, he had heavily financed the ill fated 'Paige Compositor' — an automatic typesetting machine. The failure of this innovation drew him to the brink of ruin. Moreover, he had financed the machine with money from the successful publishing company he had set up to publish his own work and the work of others. When his investment in the typesetting machine collapsed, everything else went with it.

Florence, with its affordable cost of living, cultural heritage and reputation for attracting literary expatriates, suited his current circumstances very well. Clemens came to Janet seeking assistance to find a suitable house for his family to lease. His wife, Olivia — known as Livy — suffered from neurasthenia, a condition with similar symptoms to modern day Chronic Fatigue Syndrome. She was not well enough to organize domestic arrangements, so it was left to Sam to arrange everything for his wife and three teenage daughters, Suzy, Clara and Jean. What he was looking for was someone who had local knowledge and knew how to get things done. This was Janet's stock in trade.

At first meeting he struck Janet as quaint, kindly, shrewd and amusing. Happily for him, she was able to sort out the house problem, finding a suitable place nearby. Known as the Villa Viviani, it stood between Poggio Gherardo and Settignano, the hilltop district to the south-east of Florence, and had a lovely outlook across the valley. The Clemens planned to go to Germany for the summer and then return to Florence to take up residence.

When they came back, they went out to the villa to find that Janet had made sure everything was prepared for them, including dinner ready and on the table. Clemens appreciated his neighbour's kind gesture, 'It takes but a sentence to state that, but it makes an indolent person tired to think of the planning and work and trouble that lie concealed in it'.

Clemens was delighted with the place:

The situation of this villa is perfect. It is three miles from Florence, on the side of a hill. Beyond some spurs is Fiesole perched upon its steep terraces; in the immediate foreground is the imposing mass of the Ross castle, its walls and turrets rich with the mellow weather stains of forgotten centuries; in the distant plain lies Florence, pink and grey and brown, with the ruddy huge dome of the cathedral dominating its centre like a captive balloon ... I still think, as I thought in the beginning, that this is the fairest picture on our planet, the most enchanting to look upon, the most satisfying to the eye and spirit. To see the sun sink down, downed in his pink and purple and golden floods, and overwhelm Florence with tides of color that make all the sharp lines dim and faint and turn a solid city into a city of dreams, is a sight to sit the coldest nature and make a sympathetic one drunk with ecstasy.

This was a happy omen for a writer who habitually set his desk outside to work. Against this backdrop he worked on the short story *Tom Sawyer Abroad* and on *The Tragedy of Pudd'nhead Wilson* (both released in 1894). When both these manuscripts were sent off to America for publication, he began and mostly completed the *Personal Recollections of Joan of Arc,* which would be published two years later.

From the time he and his family moved in, Clemens was a frequent visitor at Poggio Gherardo. Often he or one of the girls wandered over to ask for something that was not in their own villa and Janet would always oblige. With Livy mostly resting, Sam would set out on his own, wandering across fields and down the lanes. He might appear at any hour of the day or night because, he said, Poggio Gherardo was on the way to anywhere he wanted to go. The Rosses did not mind. Janet could see a clear distinction between the personas of the amusing Mark Twain and the 'keen sighted, sensible and large-hearted Mr Clemens'. She was also greatly impressed by the devotion and almost 'womanly' tenderness with which Clemens looked after his wife.

FRIENDS AND VISITORS

Sometimes he would come to dinner, usually without Livy. Unlike Symonds, he was no scholar of the Florentine Renaissance but he was enthusiastic about the city and Italian life and learnt a great deal from Janet and the people she introduced him to. What he knew best was the American south and to Janet and anyone staying at Poggio, his stories were wonderful. One evening he was persuaded to sing some 'Negro' songs, as he called them. For Janet they were a revelation.

Sometimes Clemens walked over to the Sunday afternoon gatherings and Janet made sure that he met people who might interest him. On other days admirers and friends would go to the Villa Viviani. Clemens soon settled in to the idyllic world:

> *This carefree life in a Florentine villa is an ideal existence. The weather is divine, the outside aspects lovely, the days and nights tranquil and reposeful, the seclusion from the world and its worries as satisfactory as a dream. Late in the afternoons friends come out from the city and drink tea in the open air and tell what is happening in the world; and when the great sun sinks down upon Florence and the daily miracle begins they hold their breath and look. It is not a time to talk.*

Apart from his great storytelling, Janet was flattered that her American friend showed serious interest in the farms. He listened attentively when she showed him the achievements of her first years and talked him through her adventures in agronomy — she had now set aside a few acres for experimentation and employed a couple of labourers on wages to work the projects. He even managed to engage her in a scheme of his own. Clemens was of the view that no proper corn was grown in Italy and so promised to have some seeds sent over when he was next in America.

A short time later Janet sent an invitation across to Villa Viviani asking the Clemens to dinner with her cousins who were visiting from England. In response she received this note:

> *It was my purpose to run in and indulge my great pleasure in the society of Sir William and my Lady a little more, and I count it a loss that I failed of the chance; but my time has been taken up in clearing the decks for America. I shall go over and pay my dinner-call the moment I get back from America. This seems unprompt; but I have a trained conscience, and I quiet it by telling it I am on my road to pay it now, merely going by way of New York and Chicago for the sake of variety, and because it is more creditable to go 8,000 miles to pay a dinner-call than it is to go a mere matter of 600 yards.*
>
> *Auf wiedersehen*
>
> *S.L. Clemens*

Some time later a parcel arrived containing the corn seed and a note from Clemens. He told her how flattered the seed supplier had been to become an agent for the introduction of corn among the Italians. 'It is to be hoped', quipped Clemens quoting the supplier, 'that by a vigorous effort on the part of the English lady who is to cultivate the cornfield and a strong appetite upon your part when the corn shall have been grown and boiled, that this delicious food may be popularised among the deluded consumers of macaroni'.

Clemens did not, however, return to eat the corn. Events compelled him to give up the villa and go on the lecture circuit and focus more on the needs of his family. In the meantime, the corn grew well and was thought to be sturdy and sweet tasting. By contrast some watermelon seed that he had also included in the package was less successful and did not compare well with local varieties.

Some years later, in 1904, Clemens returned to Florence, but his stay lacked the warmth and beauty he remembered from the first trip. The first wintry days were full of fog and rain. It was not easy to find suitable accommodation and when he did, his landlord was unhelpful. The weather did improve and Clemens managed to get some writing done, but it was not the magical place he remembered. This time there was no one to smooth out the difficulties because Janet was away most of the time he was there.

But Clemens always held fond memories of Poggio Gherardo and the time he spent in the hills above Ponte a Mensola.

On May 19, 1895, a severe earthquake hit Florence and the surrounding areas. It struck in the evening just after nine o'clock and before most people had gone to bed. There was an ominous, horrible rumble that rose up from deep underground and the old castle rocked and swayed on its foundations. Within seconds, the walls cracked, pictures fell and china came crashing down. Janet, Henry and Lina were sitting in the drawing room. Lina had been to Pistoia that day and was tired, so she had already said goodnight but had been called back by Henry asking her some question, and this probably saved her life. When they realized what was happening, all three rushed for the back door, along with Giuseppe and other staff who came tumbling downstairs from the kitchen. Everyone raced out into the pitch-black night, terrified.

If the quake had hit when more people were asleep, casualties would have been far higher. As it was, the number of deaths in the area was quite low, but the physical damage was widespread and severe.

When day broke, the devastation was obvious. The tower was in ruins. Although it had fallen mostly outwards, some large chunks of masonry had collapsed through four stories, destroying the pigeon house, the fruit room, Giuseppe's room and then smashing through the vaulting of Lina's bedroom, crushing her bed. Many of the doorways were split from the top of the door to the ceiling. On the farms, the aftermath was even worse; all the houses had been badly damaged. One house had a wall that had come away all together and was left tilting out at an angle so that the landscape could be seen through the gap.

The tremors continued for some months, Janet counted another fifty-two of them, but none as ferocious as the first. Many of the repairs required urgent attention — that meant finding extra money quickly. The Government offered some financial assistance to those hardest hit, but it was paltry compared to the actual costs involved. After all the progress of the last five years, this unforeseen event was a major setback.

The tower would have to be rebuilt although slightly lower to make it less vulnerable in any future earthquake. For the same reason iron tiles would replace the terracotta on the roof. As well as the damage to the main house, there was an urgency to put right the workers' houses and farm buildings. Work began while Janet and Henry were still looking for ways of raising enough money to pay for it all.

To bridge the shortfall, Janet turned to a couple of pictures she had bought in her early years in Florence. If there was any hesitation in parting company with these companions of the last twenty years, it was eclipsed by the current reality. There was rubble all about the castle and the farm workers were struggling to keep their families dry and warm; the pictures should be sold at once. While Janet was a lover of beautiful things, she had a pragmatic attitude to all but a very few personal belongings. She would not, for instance, have parted with Lucie's writing desk so easily.

(Usually she only decided to sell an object if she could be guaranteed a profit on the sale. But there had been one occasion when the need for money had forced her to sell a picture at a small loss. While still at Castagnolo in the 1880s and supporting Alick at university, Janet had put on sale in London the little tempura drawing by Andrea del Sarto that she and Henry had bought when they lived on the Lungarno Torrigiani. Such was her eagerness at the time to raise some money to enable herself and Henry to take a holiday in England, she offered and sold the drawing for a little less than she had originally paid.)

This time with bills for earthquake repairs piling up, Janet turned to another two pictures. The two paintings were particular favourites of Janet's and she was sure that they would prove to be valuable. She turned to her friends to see if any of them could raise interest in the works. One of these was a recent aquantance, an American, Charles Dudley Warner, who was visiting Florence. He was a writer from Hartford, Connecticut and an old friend of Samuel Clemens. He was staying with the Rosses' neighbour Professor Fiske at Villa Landor in Fiesole and had gone with Lina to Pistoia on the day of the earthquake. When he was told that Janet was looking for an expert to value her pictures, Warner recommended a young American art scholar currently studying in Florence. His name was Bernard Berenson. Warner organized Janet's first meeting with Berenson — or BB as he became known — and thereby began a friendship that endured for the rest of Janet's life.

Berenson was then a relatively unknown art scholar of thirty, but among connoisseurs and collectors he was fast gaining a formidable reputation for his knowledge of Italian painting. He was still some way from achieving the fame that later attached to him, but even at this early stage in his career, this fine-boned man with his studied appearance, trimmed beard and well-cut suit, carried an air of

Repairs being carried out a Poggio Gherardo after
the earthquake.

distinction. With his civilized intellect and attentive manners, he immediately won the affections of Janet and Henry.

He studied the pictures and confirmed Janet's thoughts about their value. He told the Rosses of his passion for the Florentine painters of the Renaissance and his intention to publish a book on the subject. He was convinced that one of the paintings that Janet was selling was a *Madonna and Child* by the Florentine Alessio Baldovinetti.

Although Berenson was not a great admirer of the late-fifteenth-century painter Baldovinetti, his authoritative authentication of the work almost guaranteed a good sale. The pictures (the identity of the second painting remains unknown) were sent to the studio of Janet's old friend Watts in London and sold. They made several hundred pounds, about 15 to 20 times the annual wage of an English housemaid at the time. This was enough to pay for the new tiles. Janet and Henry were relieved and pleased by the sale. They were also delighted with their new friends, Berenson and his witty, unconventional Anglo-American companion, Mary Costello.

The cultivated style of Berenson's adult life was in marked contrast to his beginnings. He was born in Lithuania into a poor Jewish family. At the age of ten, he migrated with his mother and siblings to join his father in Boston. Bernard exhibited a prodigious intellect at an early age.

With huge effort, enough money was found to send the boy to Harvard where he continued to develop his ideas, aspirations and style. He studied Oriental languages — Sanskrit, Hebrew and Aramaic, and in the 1880s some Harvard colleagues led by Charles Loeser put together funds to enable Berenson to travel to Europe. Assistance for the trip also came from the patronage of a leading light of Boston society, Isabella Stewart Gardner. She was amassing a collection of old masters and Bernard agreed to keep a discerning eye open for her while he was away. It was this travel that transformed him from a student of comparative languages to a student of the visual arts.

When he came to look more closely at Italian painting he found a degree of confusion in the methods of attribution, unthinkable in other disciplines. Using his eyes, he could see that paintings thought to be by a certain artist were in fact by someone else. How could such mistakes be avoided? He realized there was little in the way of empirical testing that had long been current in the study of language. Seeing the opportunity to develop his own theory he took the major decision to turn his focus to art and to develop a method of saying who painted what picture.

His approach sounds straightforward enough but it was novel at the time. By studying an artist's approach to the detail of, for example, one part of the human form or some piece of topography (the turn of the feet or the details of tiny leaves on a tree), Berenson could identify minute but tell-tale styles of different painters. To do this, over his lifetime he methodically collected and categorized thousands of photographs. He organized them by school — such as Florence, Siena or Northern Italy. The photographs, which he continued to collect and organize until his death, formed the basis of an archive that today contains 300,000 images. His 'lists' developed a reputation for being infallible and brought a level of rigor to the identification of artists hitherto missing.

Berenson met his future wife Mary when he was twenty-six and she was twenty-seven and married with two adored daughters. Mary's background was one of social reform and progressive liberalism. She was a highly intelligent and attractive woman, naturally drawn to ideas and people. Passionate and forthright, she had been raised to pursue her interests as she pleased.

The year after her first meeting with Berenson she left her husband and children and moved to Florence. When her husband died in 1899 ten years after she had left him, Mary was finally free to marry again. In the intervening period Mary and Bernard had kept independent lodgings but they spent much of their time together.

Mary and Bernard were intellectually compatible although she produced little in her own name because most of her effort went into supporting his work. Being a prolific note taker, she helped develop the encyclopaedic 'lists'. *Venetian Painters*, Berenson's first book published in 1894, and one that made his reputation, was really a rewrite of Mary's detailed notes. Domestically, they were far less suited. Mary's lack of exactitude and unconventional approach to housekeeping did not sit well with her husband's aspirations and sense of order.

In the period immediately prior to his marriage, Janet asked Bernard to stay at Poggio where he was attended to with the usual high standard of care. In fact, he was so well looked after that he voiced misgivings about moving into a household run by the less fastidious Mary. On the eve of the wedding, Janet gave Berenson a moonstone ring to see him through the civil and religious ceremonies.

After the wedding, the Berensons settled in a villa called I Tatti just down the hill. It was literally a stone's throw from Poggio and was leased from the Vincigliata estate of Temple Leader. When they first moved in, the house, which dated back to the sixteenth century, was a simple rectangular three-storied building with gardens, surrounded by farms, vineyards and olive groves. Berenson found the place snug and warm. He very much liked its position, 'at the very entrance to the most beautiful strip of rock and forest country that we have near Florence'. Only later, after much money had been lavished on masterful renovations, would it become the revered place where Berenson dispensed bons mots to a court of attendant admirers.

Janet became an indispensable point of reference for her new neighbours. Like others before them, they were the happy beneficiaries of her generosity and thoughtfulness. She introduced them to friends and always made them welcome at her Sunday afternoon receptions, although in the early years of their marriage, Bernard and Mary were just as happy spending their Sunday afternoons walking in the hills, discussing ideas.

FRIENDS AND VISITORS

Leaves from Our Tuscan Kitchen

The innate love of change in man is visible even in the kitchen.
Not so very long ago soup was the exception in English houses — almost a
luxury. A dish of vegetables — as a dish and not as an adjunct to meat —
was a still greater rarity; and even now plain-boiled potatoes, peas,
cabbages, etc., are the rule.

JANET ROSS
LEAVES FROM OUR TUSCAN KITCHEN (1899)

IN the spring of 1899, a London publisher visited Poggio Gherardo. He was Joseph Dent and the reason for his coming was to meet with Lina who had recently co-authored a book for him. Lina, now twenty-four, and her friend Madge Symonds had collaborated in writing *The Story of Perugia*, one of a series on Italian cities. This first effort had been well received and Dent was keen to follow progress on a second book she was working on, *The Story of Assisi*.

Seeing the opportunity offered by his visit, Janet put a proposal of her own to Dent. After years of writing out recipes for English visitors who found vegetables served at her table a revelation, she struck on the idea of putting the recipes into print. Always looking for new ways to use her skills to make money, she was convinced the book would be popular enough to bring in some additional revenue.

The English cook had little stimulus or guidance in the area of cooking and preparing fresh vegetables, which were all but ignored by the mainstream manuals found in the British kitchen. Janet's idea was a simple response to a perceived gap in the market. There was no equivalent book available and she hoped that the book would touch a cord.

No doubt encouraged by a good lunch, Dent warmed to the proposal and suggested adding a literary introduction to be written by Janet. This stroke of publishing cleverness would transform the book from a practical manual into something altogether more appealing, a glimpse into the private kitchen of an Anglo-Tuscan household. Janet's short preface would provide a little history and a sense of place.

Janet had originally thought Lina would help compile the recipes, but writing up recipes is a time-consuming business and the research for *The Story of Assisi* was filling Lina's days. Janet then decided to do all the research herself with assistance from her talented cook Giuseppe Volpi. After all, it was his cooking that originally inspired the project. To fill the book out, they decided to allow additional recipes that Giuseppe would test before considering for inclusion.

The tricky part was to write up Giuseppe's recipes. More than simple translation was needed, because methods that Giuseppe knew instinctively were often not written down. Techniques had to be explained and the quantities formalized. Janet spent hours at her desk deconstructing his dishes and reassembling his methods in plain English. To complicate matters, Janet herself had the barest knowledge of kitchen technique. Typical of her upper-class background with its reliance on domestic servants and cooks, she had never so much as boiled the proverbial egg.

Unlikely as this may sound today, her lack of practice was not the result of a lack of interest or neglect and in no way diminished her appreciation of good food. She knew exactly what made a well-flavoured dish and she had clear views about how food was best cooked. Moreover, she understood the delicate art of achieving balance in a meal. It was no accident that Poggio Gherardo enjoyed a reputation for excellent food, for she went to great lengths to ensure she had a first-rate cook and that he was provided with the best produce.

Giuseppe and Janet would meet regularly in her study to plan menus for the family, for dinner parties and for Sunday afternoon gatherings. If Janet knew a guest's special likes or dislikes, Giuseppe was able to accommodate these in his preparations. His approach to cooking was essentially Italian with some French influence. He was comfortable producing something homely and delicious with a handful of perfectly ripe, sweet tomatoes as he was making an esoteric Victorian dish of truffles in champagne. His starting point was always the produce available and the context of the meal.

Giuseppe Volpi had cooked for the Rosses for over twenty years and had moved with them from Castagnolo to Poggio Gherardo. He was a professional cook. This meant he had served an apprenticeship under another professional cook. It also meant that he was trained in classical French methods as well as local Italian traditions. Such men, and they were always men, were employed in the city's grand houses and in smart hotels. In a tourist town like Florence, some of these cooks were actually foreigners — French, German or Englishmen who acquired their local knowledge only after their arrival. Some professional cooks would later go on to manage or even open their own restaurants. This male-dominated world was in contrast to the feminised *casalinga* or home cooking of the less grand house and local trattorias.

At the time, the central place of the cook in a well-run house is hard to overstate. A good cook was much admired, respected, and often considered irreplaceable. Losing a cook could spell catastrophe to domestic equilibrium. Such was the anxiety of many a mistress who enjoyed good food but didn't have the skill to produce it herself. The lengths that Janet took to ensure she wouldn't fall victim to such a fate are testament to the dread of such disruption. She took her food and kitchen seriously and left nothing to chance.

Later, in Giuseppe's final years at Poggio Gherardo, Janet thought of a plan that would ensure a smooth transition after his retirement. It was devised with neighbours and close friends Bernard and Mary Berenson. Although this was Mary's second marriage, she was new to the business of setting up a house in Italy. Eager to have her home run smoothly, Mary often turned to Janet for advice. When Mary walked up the hill to ask for help in hiring a good cook, Janet saw her chance. She could simultaneously help her friends and fix her own longer-term problem of finding a suitable replacement for Giuseppe.

Janet consulted Giuseppe on his possible successor and he recommended Agostino, a former apprentice of his. Janet then suggested to the Berensons that they employ the younger cook now, on the understanding that he move to Poggio Gherardo once Giuseppe retired.

As Janet's solution gave immediate relief to the void in the Berenson's kitchen, they were very happy to accept her proposal. For the following four years, Agostino became the linchpin in the Berensons' kitchen. Mary Berenson came to rely on him absolutely and gave little thought to preparing for the day when Janet would call in her cards, as she surely would. That day came in 1907 when Giuseppe confirmed his intention to retire. Mary Berenson was horrified and referred to it as 'a most appalling situation', admitting that she had all but forgotten the original arrangement. 'I got into feeling that it was a fixed thing and that the bother was off my housekeeping shoulders.' It was a testament to the relationship between the two women that Janet's call on Agostino did not permanently affect the friendship between them.

Cooks like Giuseppe and Agostino were trained locally and knew how to prepare typical Tuscan dishes, staples of hearty bean soups, perfectly roasted meats, delicately fried vegetables and salads of field greens. But they also used ingredients and methods reflecting new influences spreading across the recently united Italy. Their great skill was the interpretation and incorporation of local dishes into a broadly based style of Italian cooking.

In fact, the political unification of the country, though a relatively recent event, was changing the eating habits of Italians up and down the peninsula. The best-known example of the phenomena was Pellegrino Artusi's famous *The Science of Cookery and the Art of Eating Well*, published in 1891. Artusi's collection was aimed at the growing number of middle-class housewives in Italy. His recipes were not regional, although they were influenced by his native Emilia-Romagna and his adopted Tuscany. In addition to those recipes he collected himself, later editions included others sent in from all parts of Italy. The resulting collection reflected cooking across the whole country. Readers now had the opportunity to attempt and experiment with dishes from other regions. The immense popularity of the book had a significant impact on Italian eating.

In the kitchen at Poggio Gherardo, Giuseppe, and later Agostino, referred to a well-established repertoire of favourites, with Giuseppe passing his recipes and techniques on to the younger chef. One of their trademark dishes was a very grand and theatrical roast pheasant, from a recipe dating back to the fifteenth century. The bird was seasoned and spit roasted over an open fire, with careful attention given to basting. When cooked and rested, it was sliced and dressed in a pelt of feathers. Finally, the magnificent bird was placed on an appropriately large dish and sent to the table to great applause.

Apart from ingenious and thrilling dishes like the pheasant, cooking at Poggio Gherardo was founded on Giuseppe's ability to delight family and guests with dishes that enhanced the best produce available, much of it from the Poggio Gherardo farms. Katherine Symonds who was visiting during this period remembered, 'strange new dishes — little meat, no puddings, but lots of vegetables of all sorts — tiny cucumbers an inch long and baby artichokes and fungi of all sorts, and all cooked better than anywhere else I know'. She was also delighted with the wonderful combination of fresh ricotta eaten with Marsala and sugar that was served as a dessert.

Giuseppe's laboratory was the kitchen, well described by Janet's great-niece, Lina's daughter, Kinta Beevor. Her memoir, *A Tuscan Childhood*, covers the time she spent at Poggio during the First World War and again in the 1920s. She writes about the kitchen in some detail. It was located on the first floor adjacent to a cold store and larder, these two being connected by a service lift to the pantry on the floor below. The same lift was used to transport prepared dishes from the kitchen to the dining room, also on the floor below.

What looks like cumbersome placement of the kitchen on an upper floor was a common feature in big Florentine houses. The idea was to reduce cooking smells in the reception rooms below. In fact, it was usual in the old Florentine palaces for the kitchen to be at the top of the building, perhaps four or five levels above the street. Sometimes it was set behind a wide airy loggia, allowing breezes to flow

Agostino, Giuseppe's successor, in the kitchen at
Poggio Gherardo.

in and reduce the stifling temperatures of open fires. Cooking on the upper level of the house also reduced the risk of the whole house catching fire if there was an accident in the kitchen.

The kitchen at Poggio was a long large room, ordered and well managed. Against the outside wall stood a fireplace and two little *fornelli* or charcoal-fired barbecues, their temperature controlled by waving a straw fan. There was also a cast-iron range that incorporated a hot water tank and an open fire with a mechanised spit under a huge hooded chimney. Next to the spit sat a container of olive oil and some goose feathers that were used for basting roasting meat, like the pheasant.

High up on the walls a ledge ran around the perimeter. Up here Giuseppe kept his various shaped moulds and a range of different sized copper saucepans. In the centre of the room was a huge kitchen table with a wooden top several inches thick. On a side table were several sets of mortars and pestles. One was used only for making the *battuto*, the pounded or whacked mixture of chopped onion, carrot, celery and aromatics, commonly used as a starting point for Italian sauces and braised dishes. Another was reserved for crushing hazelnuts and other ingredients for *dolci* or desserts. The adjacent larder was full of store essentials. Kinta remembered dried tomatoes, tomatoes and artichokes in oil, pickled vegetables, capers, pine nuts, breadcrumbs, juniper berries and saffron for risotto and a large terracotta jar of olives.

Most of the produce came from the farms and the *orto*, the Italian equivalent of a vegetable or kitchen garden. The hardier crops like artichokes thrived in random plantings between and underneath vines and olive trees on the farms. Nearer the house, the *orto* was the place for delicate plantings. Fine lettuce leaves, fragile herbs and sweet young peas and beans, were sheltered and tended by the gardener.

The *orto* was common in Italy. At its most basic, it comprised a few pots of herbs on a windowsill. Where more space was available, it was an elaborate layout of beds with rows of vegetables. A well-planned *orto* could produce vegetables ready for picking one after the other in seasonal progression. It might also include potted fruit trees, especially citrus, hungry for sun after spending the cold months indoors. Vegetable beds were close enough to the house for Giuseppe to stroll out and pick what he needed.

What he didn't have at hand he sourced from the markets in Florence. Coffee, tea, salt, sugar and spices were regularly on his list. At other times he might look for fish or a particular cut of meat not available from the farms. Or he might buy oranges and lemons transported from the south when they were not available from his own garden.

Cooks like Giuseppe would rise early to make the trip down into the city and after the market would meet up with their peers from the other big houses for a coffee. Chatting and exchanging gossip, they also shared recipes. These sorts of informal meetings were a well-established tradition.

LEAVES FROM OUR TUSCAN KITCHEN

Pictures of the vintage at Poggio Gherardo with
Janet supervising.

With Giuseppe's assistance, Janet began to research and test the recipes. She immersed herself in recipe books wherever she stumbled on them. Not confined to Italian sources, she also became well acquainted with English, American and German cookbooks. If she found something that might be suitable, she gave it to Giuseppe to trial. Given his training, he had no qualms adapting ideas from elsewhere. Even so, the great inspiration for *Leaves from Our Tuscan Kitchen* was Italian cookery. There were a number of books written in Italian and devoted wholly to vegetables, as well as the relevant chapters within general books of Italian cookery like Artusi's. His chapter on cooking vegetables provided recipes to accompany meat dishes as well as suggestions for stand-alone dishes of stuffed vegetables, tarts and moulds. There were nourishing vegetable stews and vegetables prepared in the ancient sweet-sour manner known as *agro dolce*. He also included methods of cooking such local varieties of vegetable as cavolo nero, the dark green leafy vegetable essential to the Tuscan *ribollita*, a hearty bean and bread soup commonly served in winter.

Of books solely devoted to vegetables, Janet particularly liked *Come si Cucinano i Legumi* (*How to Cook Vegetables*), compiled by the famous Italian seed suppliers, Fratelli Ingegnoli. Started as a family business in the eighteenth century, Fratelli Ingegnoli has long been dedicated to growing and importing seeds and today their seeds are sold worldwide. The little book they published that so delighted Janet came out in Milan in 1895. Its purpose was to encourage the eating and, no doubt, the growing of vegetables.

Included at the back of the book is a price list of available seeds, interesting to modern cooks for its range. It offers five varieties each of asparagus and artichokes, seven varieties of cauliflower, five different types of eggplant (aubergine), ten varieties of sweet capsicum (peppers), and eight types of celery. From this book a number of recipes found their way into *Leaves from Our Tuscan Kitchen*, together with an acknowledgement from Janet in her introduction.

Another specialist vegetable cookbook of the genre is *100 Maniere di Cucinare i Legumi* (*100 Ways to Cook Vegetables*), which came out a little later in 1906, after the first edition of Janet's book. Like the Ingegnoli book, this small tome was not primarily concerned with regionality. Although happily including such recipes as *Funghi Genovesi* and *Funghi Peimontesi* — mushrooms cooked in the styles of Genoa and Piedmont respectively — it described a broad sweep of appealing dishes, attractive to the newly emergent middle-class Italian housewife. Janet's objective was to provide a similar aid to the English housewife.

It was a frenetic few months of testing new recipes while still preparing everyday meals. In typical Janet fashion, nothing was wasted and many of the new dishes were tried on visitors. Katherine Symonds was one of them and observed that 'the whole house reeks with recipes and some of them are excellent but I doubt whether the plain cook of England will be able to understand them all. However it is a blessing to us all and perhaps we may be able to make them intelligible'. Fortunately her doubts proved baseless. Janet was able to make the recipes simple and workable and the English cook appreciated her efforts.

After more than three months of activity, the recipes were laid down and the introduction written. Janet dedicated the book to Mary Fraser Tytler, the much younger second wife of George Federick Watts, the artist who had drawn and painted Janet as a young woman. The dedication reads, 'Dear friend, will you accept this little book? It may sometimes bring a thought of Italy into your beautiful Surrey home'. Mary was almost vegetarian so it seemed fitting to dedicate the book to her. Janet was fond of Mary — an artist in her own right — and made a point of visiting her and Watts when she was in England. Sometimes she sent them wines from Poggio Gherardo and recently had dispatched sweet-smelling Parma violets from the garden to arrive fresh for Watts' birthday.

The final collection of recipes that ended up in *Leaves from Our Tuscan Kitchen* was typical of the dishes prepared and eaten in villas and grand houses in Italy. Even allowing for the fact that cooking for an expatriate family gave him more freedom to explore ideas, in general terms, Giuseppe's culinary style was typical of the place and time he worked.

While he used olive oil freely, as was becoming increasingly common with the great expansion in olive production, his training had imbued him with an appreciation of butter and cream too. There are recommendations for artichokes with cream and instructions for asparagus with butter, cream and split almonds, another for beetroot cooked with cream and a dish of delicate sweet leeks baked with cream. There are, however, even more dishes flavoured with olive oil and lemon juice or parmesan cheese and herbs. And none of this is to overlook the fact that Giuseppe would have used the traditional cooking base, pork fat, too when the flavour was required.

To the English audience, *Leaves from Our Tuscan Kitchen* was a breath of fresh air. The approach it took was completely different to the comprehensive household management books that dominated the scene. Books like Mrs Beeton's *Book of Household Management* which had come out in 1861 and the earlier *Modern Cookery for Private Families* by Eliza Acton, dating from 1845, although justly popular were, by comparison, not expansive on the subject of vegetables.

Mrs Acton's approach emphasizes freshness and delicacy and includes interesting recipes for such vegetables as jerusalem artichokes, dressed dandelions and sorrel. Indeed her descriptions of light, well-dressed salads of young leaves and baby vegetables are delightful. Nonetheless, her choice of ingredients and the methods of dealing with them are limited. It is no surprise that she devotes considerable space to different ways to cook the ubiquitous potato.

By way of introducing the topic, she wrote, 'There is no vegetable commonly cultivated in this country, we venture to assert, which is comparable in value to the potato when it is of a good sort, has been grown in suitable soil, and is properly cooked and served'. It appears boiled, mashed, roasted, crisp, scooped, formed into croquettes and served a la crème.

Nearly twenty years later, Isabella Beeton published her famous *Book of Household Management* in twenty-four monthly parts. Like Artusi, her market was the housewife of the burgeoning middle classes. More than a book of recipes — many of which were taken from earlier books including Eliza Acton's and included without attribution — it was, as its name makes clear, a complete set of instructions for the smooth running of the house. It provided a vast quantity of information including detail on rates of pay for servants and numbers of servants appropriate to various levels of household income.

When it came to vegetables she took a semi-scientific approach in her descriptions. Her writing is weighed down with the nutritional and biological detail accompanied by illustrations perhaps better suited to a botanical text. In keeping with the didactic intent of the book she provided information on seasonality, portion sizes and cost per weight.

Among the recipes themselves, there are a few happy surprises including a salad made of endive, mustard and cress, boiled beetroot and hard-boiled egg. But such fresh and enticing combinations are few and far between. Elsewhere, beetroot, cabbage and broccoli are boiled. Globe artichokes are boiled, fried or alternatively served *a l'italienne* which in this case meant boiled and served with mushroom-flavoured gravy! Jerusalem artichokes are similarly boiled, mashed or combined with brussels sprouts and served with white sauce.

Like Mrs Acton, Isabella Beeton devoted most space and the greatest enthusiasm to the potato. Included were suggestions for steaming, mashing, or according to a German method, serving with some butter and a little vinegar. Alternatively, potato could be mixed with parsley and formed into little rissoles coated with breadcrumbs and fried over the fire in hot lard. She also recommended a simple potato salad dressed with tarragon vinegar and minced parsley.

In most cases the vegetables of Victorian England were simply intended to accompany more substantial meat courses. The devotion to meat among families that could afford it is almost unimaginable today. For a mid-summer dinner party, Mrs Beeton recommended several meat courses. She suggested starting the meal with soups and fish dishes. These might be followed by entrées of stewed pigeons, sweetbreads, savoury rissoles and veal cutlets.

The next course included a further four or five meat dishes for guests to enjoy: roasted fowls, bacon and beans, tongue garnished with small vegetable marrows, a haunch of mutton and perhaps a braised ham. The last of the meat courses would be game birds; wild duck, grouse and partridge, accompanied by plates of sweet-flavoured puddings and jellies. In summer, a suitable selection could include a cherry tart, whipped strawberry cream and *vol-au-vent* of plums and meringues.

The final course would be dessert — a light course of fruit, nuts and ices. 'It may be said', writes Isabella Beeton earnestly, 'that if there be any poetry at all in meals, or in the process of feeding, there is poetry in the dessert'.

Coming after this, Janet's little book of 159 pages specializing in vegetables was radical. It did not confine the 'poetry of eating' to sweet courses, but showed what pleasure could be had from simply giving more attention to hitherto neglected ingredients. It had no argument with meat, but rather took

LEAVES
from
OUR·TUSCAN
KITCHEN
or
How to Cook
Vegetables
by
JANET·ROSS

LONDON: J. M. DENT & SONS LTD.
NEW YORK: E. P. DUTTON & CO. INC.

The title page as it appeared in early editions of
Leaves from Our Tuscan Kitchen.

it for granted that the English cook was well served by existing publications. By moving meat to one side, Janet placed the vegetable at the centre of the table.

The Italian approach is to serve meat with few if any vegetables; a simple salad or perhaps some roasted potatoes flavoured with rosemary usually being enough. Vegetables are savoured without distraction, often as a course on their own. Janet's book showed the English how to follow suit — how to transform vegetables into the most delectable dishes. The text was laid out alphabetically according to vegetable and included additional sections on pasta, rice, salads, sauces and soups. Pasta, especially macaroni, had appeared in earlier English cookbooks but Janet's recipes were altogether broader in scope.

The range of possibilities she offers for preparing artichokes demonstrates the horizons she was opening up for the British cook. Janet recommended the popular Italian method of picking and eating the vegetable when it was still young — barely half grown. The section began with artichokes *alla Barigoul*, which were artichokes stuffed with forcemeat made of salt pork, shallots and mushrooms, parsley, salt, pepper and nutmeg. The resulting little packages were tied with string and braised in broth. The broth was reduced a little in the cooking and made a good sauce to pour over the artichokes for serving. An alternative method suggested a stuffing made of minced chicken and ham flavoured with parsley and spices. The artichokes were then baked and served with a cream sauce.

Simpler recipes suggested dressing steamed and quartered artichokes with fragrant olive oil, lemon juice, salt and pepper, or simply grilling artichoke halves on the grate and serving them with an oil and lemon dressing. Another suggested accompaniment for artichokes was a sauce made of capers, tarragon, chervil, gherkins (pickles), and egg yolk, mustard, oil and wine vinegar.

The versatile globe artichoke could be baked with parmesan cheese and butter, or served with a more elegant hollandaise sauce. Lastly, she included recipes perfected with the Tuscan cook's mastery of the frying pan. Wonderful *carciofi fritti*, tiny, tender artichokes, lightly floured and quickly fried, squeezed with lemon juice and served immediately.

Janet urged her readers to use first-rate ingredients — the butter and cream should be sweet, the oil pure, the eggs fresh, and the herbs, basil, marjoram, tarragon, chervil and parsley, just picked.

There are recipes for flans and moulds, summer salads and soups and delicate purées. There are clear directions for the making and filling of tortellini and instructions for lightly fried, crescent-shaped stuffed pasta pockets, as well as gnocchi made with wheat flour and gnocchi made with semolina. Sauces have an important place too, and Janet encouraged the reader to give them due attention and use only the best ingredients. In all their simplicity, the recipes displayed a level of enthusiasm and freshness unknown in English cookbooks of the period.

Another obvious point of difference between Janet's approach and the English tradition was her inclusion of brightly coloured Mediterranean vegetables and pulses, capsicums (peppers), eggplant (aubergine), pumpkin (winter squash) and lentils. The last of these, Mrs Beeton had reminded the reader, 'is not used for human food [in England] although considered the best of all kinds for pigeons'.

Janet had recipes for lentils cooked with rice, puréed, flavoured with chopped anchovy, minced shallots, olive oil and some butter, or warmed with finely diced ham, onion and a little good stock.

Although tomatoes were known and used in England, they were not prominent in English cookbooks. In *Leaves from Our Tuscan Kitchen*, Janet afforded them the attention they received in the Italian kitchen. Similarly, she included recipes for vegetables that had once been popular in England but had subsequently gone out of fashion; one such was the leek.

After tomatoes, in the alphabetical order of the book, came truffles, treated as a vegetable in their own right. Interestingly, Janet is on closer ground to accepted British taste here, for both Eliza Acton and Isabella Beeton included a couple of similar recipes for cooking truffles. As well as varieties imported to England from Italy and France, truffles were found locally on the downs of Hampshire, Wiltshire and Kent among the oak and chestnut forests. Even so, in England the cost of the little morsels made them strictly the domain of the well-off, whereas in Italy they were more accessible.

Janet had suggestions for truffles cooked with cheese and served very hot with croutons; she recommended truffle omelette, stewed truffles and sautéed truffles. Though she was aware that the truffle was an occasional treat rather than an everyday ingredient for her readers, the recipes she recommended were unpretentious. In keeping with her general intention, the focus was on food that could be prepared in the domestic kitchen.

Though Janet aimed to inspire the reader with a wide variety of vegetables, she stopped short where she knew English cultivation to be scarce or non-existent. Subsequently the early editions of the book contained no recipes for such Italian staples as fennel and zucchini (courgettes). Apart from realistically dealing with the lack of availability of some vegetables, Janet did little to 'protect' the reader. She assumed a good amount of enthusiasm for new experiences and treated the English cook as intelligent and competent. The fact that the reader may never have had the pleasure of eating a plate of spaghetti with fresh anchovies or freshly fried hot crumbed eggplant before was no reason to hold back.

The sections on rice and pasta were a delight to the adventurous English cook or even to the reader seeking to recreate something of their travels abroad. Recipes for macaroni cooked in veal stock, layered with grated gruyere cheese, topped with breadcrumbs and baked in the oven, or *Macaroni alla Siciliana* reminiscent of some great southern feast, are evocative and enticing. In the pasta section there was also a recipe for spaghetti with a sauce of mushrooms, truffles, tongue and tomatoes, and another for tortellini filled with a delicate fresh curd, served steaming hot with parmesan cheese.

Two of the most interesting recipes in this section were Giuseppe's specialities. *Agnellotti alla Poggio Gherardo* are little pasta pockets stuffed with a mixture of finely chopped boiled chicken, hare or pheasant mixed with truffle and bread soaked in veal stock. *Risotto alla Poggio Gherardo* is Marsala flavoured risotto with the addition of some minced chicken or duck livers and mushrooms.

Leaves from Our Tuscan Kitchen came out in 1899 and sold well from the start. Mary Tytler wrote immediately back, 'I am delighting in your recipes — we all are — the cook tries her hand at one every day, and they are delicious. How I envy your Giuseppe and your lovely old kitchen'. This was exactly the response Janet had hoped for.

But the book's success extended way beyond the small numbers of English vegetarians. Dent's instincts had served him well and the book proved very popular, being reprinted eleven times up until 1936. In 1908, Janet made some additions in 'obedience to requests from friends', for some additional simple recipes and a few light soups. (A revised edition was also produced in the 1970s by Janet's great-great-nephew, Michael Waterfield, with a new edition in 2006.)

The success of the book not only brought in welcome revenue but also extended Janet's reputation to a wider circle of readers. As the years passed, many who had not read her articles or books became devotees of the recipes. Elizabeth David, writing fifty years later echoed Janet's enthusiasm for the Italian attitude to vegetables. As a collector of cookery books, David was familiar with *Leaves from Our Tuscan Kitchen* and referred to it in her own 1954 book on the subject, *Italian Food*.

The writing of *Leaves from Our Tuscan Kitchen* put Janet years ahead of her time. In advocating the pleasures of vegetables she was leading the English cook towards new and exciting possibilities; the impact of her little book resonating for years afterwards. It was to become a classic and even today earns its position in the cook's library. Reading it is to be delighted all over again by the possibilities of the vegetable and be transported back in time to the kitchen at Poggio.

Family and Neighbours

Miss Bartlett had not heard of Alessio Baldovinetti, but
she knew that Mr Eager was no commonplace chaplain.
He was a member of the residential colony who had made
Florence their home. He knew people who never walked about
with Baedekers, who had learned to take a siesta after lunch,
who took drives the pension tourists had never heard of, and saw
by private influence galleries which were closed to them.
Living in delicate seclusion, some in furnished flats, others in
Renaissance villas on Fiesole's slope, they read, wrote, studied
and exchanged ideas, thus attaining to that intimate knowledge,
or rather perception, of Florence which is denied to all who carry
in their pockets the coupons of Cook.

E.M. FOSTER
A ROOM WITH A VIEW (1908)

AS the new century dawned, Janet was working on a book on Florentine villas, a limited edition, published in 1901. It was a beautifully produced book with line drawings and reproductions in photogravure. In the meantime, the popularity of *Leaves from Our Tuscan Kitchen* only enhanced Janet's reputation as an Anglo-Florentine icon. The year the book came out she was fifty-seven years old. Henry was seventy-nine and as astute and kindly as ever. He continued to take pleasure in his vast orchid collection, in reading and in conversation with his wife and others who came to the house. Lina, now twenty-five, had grown to be a very attractive, independently minded young woman. She owed much to Janet and Henry — they had furnished her a broad education and a wonderful house filled with interesting people. Much of who she was could be traced to their influence, and yet she was now just as strongly drawn to her own generation and the times she lived in. Increasingly, she saw the world from a different point of view to that of her aunt and uncle.

She would often go down to I Tatti on her own account. She was only ten years younger than the Berensons and was very much drawn to their general intellectual interests and the company they kept. There she would meet more people her own age. The Berensons' circle, while it overlapped with the Rosses', was younger and had what might be described as a more modern outlook or sensibility. Bernard and Mary were regular visitors at Poggio, but increasingly when they did venture up the hill they found Janet's gatherings rather a lottery; sometimes fun, and other times somewhat oppressive. One Sunday Bernard returned home after a short time, only to report, somewhat snidely, that he had been confronted with 'a large miscellaneous company of second-rate celebrities boring each other to death'.

Despite this, the firm friendship between the two households had grown stronger rather than weaker over time. Janet and Mary were especially close and reliant on each other. Janet's willingness to smooth Mary's path in getting the household established at I Tatti was much appreciated. Mary's task was made all the more difficult by Bernard's high expectations and she sometimes found herself overwhelmed by his demands. So if she could not solve a domestic problem herself, Mary was still likely to pay a visit to Janet. She had neither the patience nor disposition to imitate Janet exactly, but she appreciated any help and advice that was offered.

From Poggio, Mary bought her olive oil, wine, vinegar and tomato sauce and she took Janet's advice to find the best suppliers of other staples. In addition to the purely practical, Janet made some gestures that were especially thoughtful. On one occasion earlier in Bernard's career, Janet had smoothed his way with his rich American patron, Isabella Stewart Gardner, with a wonderful gift. Janet undertook to send the grand Bostonian lady a collection of fifty different wild tulip bulbs. This entirely original present was beyond the realm of monetary value and could not fail to impress a wealthy woman. Mary was deeply touched, calling Janet 'the source of all material blessings'.

In return, the Berensons included Janet, Henry and Lina on their art pilgrimages. Small groups of family and friends would be led by their expert guides in the direction of a possible Fra Angelico in a remote convent, or to confirm a Piero della Francesca in a village church. There was always the thrill of finding something extraordinarily beautiful.

Lina's eager and open mind, especially loved these outings. She found Bernard and Mary's conversation and ideas stimulating. By contrast, Janet's interests and inclinations were well formed by the time she encountered the Berensons, and although she appreciated their extraordinary knowledge of Italian art, she was less interested in their intellectual ruminations. Janet's intelligence was of a practical nature; she was a keen observer and an acknowledged agriculturist. She was not reflective by nature, nor was she an abstract thinker.

Poggio Gherardo and I Tatti were separated by about ten minutes on foot, so it was natural that the two households had become close. Such was the relationship that Mary, in a curious annual inventory she kept, had included the Rosses and Lina listed among the friends she and 'B.B' had in common. Mary also placed Janet and Henry in a second category of friends called 'those who matter in everyday life here'. Lina was added under a third heading called 'my real world', the only non-family member to be included.

The Rosses and Berensons often dined together, visited old and new friends together and called in on one another when ill or in need of company. Bernard appreciated Janet's looks and character, her books, success on the farms and her artistic ability. Bernard was also very taken with Henry's tales of the East; pig-sticking on the mounds of Ninevah, tales of the tribal Kurds and the splendid lives of the Pashas. Henry's magical powers of storytelling had not diminished with time. The atmosphere he conjured up mesmerized delighted visitors, just as it had thrilled the eighteen-year-old Janet at the Gordon Arms. One night Henry held his audience spellbound with another tale from his early days in Egypt, at the conclusion of which Berenson turned to Lina and with a sigh of satisfaction said, 'that is epic — it is Homeric!'.

At moments like these, Henry dominated and everyone, including his wife, was enthralled. But over the coming years he suffered a gradual deterioration in health culminating in a series of strokes. Each of these required extended convalescence and rehabilitation. Janet of course, was fastidious in her care of him. She made him comfortable and kept him company by sitting with him and reading aloud from his favourite books.

As part of his rehabilitation, she accompanied him on expeditions to spa towns for curative rests and treatments. Once they went to the popular baths at Chianciano near Siena and another time, on the recommendation of a friend, they set out for an extended stay at Valdieri, 4,600 metres (15,000 feet) above sea level in the Piedmont Alps. Each day Henry was immersed in hot sulphuric waters in the hope of restoring some movement to his now crippled hands. The air was so fine in the mountains that they decided to ask their old friend Carlo Orsi to join them. He had been suffering from some respiratory problems and Janet thought the mountains would do him good.

Henry loved the mountains and they decided to make a return visit the following year, 1896, to stay for a couple of months. This time though, Carlo Orsi was too sick to join them. Janet had been to see him just before she left and thought he looked very weak. Soon after their arrival in the mountain town, news came that Carlo had died.

Henry's treatment did at last have some positive effect and when they got back to Poggio, Janet took advantage of his renewed energy to begin transcribing her husband's letters covering the first twenty years he lived in the East. Reading his letters was a reminder of his wonderful use of language, his perception and insight. His time there was undoubtedly the most remarkable period of his life and nothing since had matched it for sheer adventure. Though he demurred and claimed no one was interested in his old stories, Janet pushed on. She was determined that his intimate knowledge of Eastern manners and customs should not die with him.

Janet worked until late into the night copying and arranging the letters. By day she would check names and places with Henry, making sure she had both the classical and modern place names correctly aligned. Fortuitously publisher Joseph Dent (her own publisher for *Leaves from Our Tuscan Kitchen*) paid another timely visit and Janet gave him a couple of the letters to read. Quick as ever, he proposed publishing them under Henry's name, edited by her. The resulting book, *Letters from the East 1837–1857* was a public confirmation of her esteem for Henry, a gesture that carried echoes of Sarah Austin's determination to edit and publish John Austin's best work for posterity. Henry continued to understate the letters, saying they were not worth printing, but he was quietly pleased.

During the period of Henry's declining health, Lina fell in love with a young artist called Aubrey Waterfield. She met him in Oxford during a visit to England. She was on a trip to catch up with friends and relatives, although she makes no mention of her cousin Alick. In Oxford she was the guest of cousins Sir William Markby and his wife Lucy — the same cousins who had missed out on dinner with Samuel Clemens at Poggio. The Markbys knew Aubrey's aunt and, through her, asked the young man to join them for a dinner in Lina's honour.

Lina was immediately taken with his looks. He was tall with fair hair and blue eyes. And then she liked the way he talked amusingly about his Oxford experiences. In the following days she was introduced to his circle of young friends. It was the first time she had spent a whole week with people her own age. Lina also met and liked Aubrey's family. They were easy, hospitable people. His father was a classical scholar and highly regarded headmaster before he became a banker in later life, and his mother was devoted to good causes and country life. With Janet's permission, Lina asked Aubrey to Italy the following summer. Janet agreed because Aubrey's uncle had been helpful to her at the time of the bank crisis.

It was soon clear to anyone looking — and Mary Berenson was — that while Aubrey and Lina were falling in love, Janet was positioning herself against any idea of marriage. Her growing irritation was palpable throughout the summer. Any attempt at charm by Aubrey fell flat until he no longer persevered. Although he was perfectly respectable, he had no money or prospects to speak of. Moreover, any marriage would clearly be based on romantic attachment, which in Janet's view provided the flimsiest foundation for a lasting union.

A later picture of Henry at the front steps of
Poggio Gherardo.

Janet was not just caught unawares, she was angry. Although she had never explicitly laid out any aspirations for Lina, she had clearly not imagined the option of marriage to a struggling artist. Janet felt that Lina and Aubrey were directly challenging all that she stood for and all that she had provided for her niece. She had rescued Lina from her hapless father and paid her more attention than she gave to her own son. Now her niece seemed intent on making a miserable future for herself despite all Janet's best efforts. To make matters worse for Lina, her gentle uncle agreed with Janet.

Maurice had died in 1896 at the age of forty-six from pneumonia and the horrible condition known as general paralysis of the insane. The insanity was the consequence of the syphilis he had contracted as a young man. Janet and Lina both had cause to be disappointed in Maurice. He had squandered every opportunity given him and all but deserted his daughter. Perhaps because of Maurice and the opportunities he had wasted over a lifetime, Janet had an abhorrence of unreliablity, real or imagined, in men. She gave the impression that she considered Alick to be tarred with the same brush as Maurice and now Lina seemed to be foregoing all sensible opportunity in preference for another ne'er-do-well.

On a subsequent visit to England, Lina announced by letter her plans to marry. But she was not far enough away to avoid the wrath from Poggio. She was inundated with missives from Janet referring to her 'miserable engagement' and describing the 600 pounds that the two proposed to live on as a 'miserable pittance'. Janet went so far as to warn Lina of the detrimental effect news of the engagement was having on Henry. The tone of the letters reached an almost hysterical pitch. Dejected and cut adrift, Lina sought some level of reconciliation, finally getting a concession that she could visit Poggio on the understanding that the subject of marriage not be discussed. 'We shall go on as before, you my dear child and I your old aunt.'

When she returned to Florence, she found Henry in better shape than she imagined from Janet's letters. It was a great relief to be home and — temporarily at least — restored to her aunt's affection. But since her return there was a change in the way she viewed Janet and Henry. Details that she previously overlooked now struck her. Her letters to Aubrey are frank, especially concerning the Ross marriage. It did not occur to her that Janet's behaviour might be related to a fear of losing both husband and niece. On the contrary she interpreted it as simple callousness, 'It is very sad, for what will she do with "freedom" when she has got it, I know not. She hardly realises now what Uncle Henry has been in her life'. She went on:

> *Aunt Janet is always looked upon by the world as the strong character and the brilliant one, but ask B.B. or the Lawsons who have eyes and they will say differently. I know that Uncle Henry has suffered for he has told me, and I know what his mental endowments are. He has more literary feeling and gift of expression than any of us on the hillside. His letters we are reading now, though in a different way, are as brilliant as Grannie Lucie's. It is odd to see her surprise, now*

Aubrey Waterfield self-portrait. Later included by Lina in her autobiography.

Lina before she married.

on reading his letters and journals to find what a really great person Uncle Henry is. It comes late but all the same it is good to find him appreciated — in his eighty-second year after being with him forty years! It didn't take other people as many weeks to discover Uncle Henry.

Despite the more friendly terms arrived at between Lina and Janet, there was to be no wedding at Poggio. Janet would not have it. Before long, her hostility to the marriage took on a rigidity from which it was impossible to retreat. But Lina would not back down either, so she returned to England and prepared for her wedding there.

Then came news that Henry was deteriorating. Aubrey telegraphed Janet to say that if Mr Ross were so ill, he and Lina would get married immediately and come over, but the suggestion was politely declined. They tried a second time, but were told there was no room in the house because Alick was coming. The petty nastiness continued and there was little Lina could do about it. Janet's position was impregnable. She refused to have anything to do with the wedding, which eventually went ahead in London on July 1, 1902.

Henry died three weeks later, on July 19. Janet was sixty, Alick was forty and Lina twenty-eight. Henry left his money and property to Janet. At the time of his father's death Alick Ross was probably based overseas. At some point he had left the world of stockbroking to look for employment elsewhere. He moved to Russia and worked there for a number of years at the Russian Court. With his excellent language skills — French, German and Italian — he found work as a companion to three teenage children of the Grand Duke Vladimir and his wife, members of the extended royal family. While he was there he learnt Russian. He was certainly not present at Lina's wedding.

Whether he actually did return to Poggio in his father's lasts weeks and days is not certain. To Lina, Janet had claimed he was coming, but that was the only mention of him. Likewise because of the tension between Janet and Lina, the exact nature of Henry's final illness remained unclear. He had been left unwell by debilitating strokes, but six months before he died, Janet was describing him as gravely ill while at the same time Lina found him, 'such a wiry, healthy and equal-tempered man that I have every hope that he may be spared us many years yet'. Each had reason to view the situation as they did. Janet perhaps wanted to make Lina feel responsible for her uncle's decline. Lina refused to accept such a posssibility.

Later the same year Lina and Aubrey travelled to Florence and prudently took up an invitation from Mary Berenson to stay at I Tatti. This was a safer option than risking insult by staying with Janet. Mary was drawn to the drama of the situation and had been naturally sympathetic to the young couple from the start — a point of grievous irritation to Janet. Mary thought Lina was well and happy and clearly the dominant partner in the new marriage. Observing the young couple, the Berensons detected traces of Janet's relationship with Carlo Orsi. The significant difference being Janet would not have formalized any attraction to an artist by marriage.

One day Lina went without Aubrey to see Janet. She was dreading their first encounter since her marriage. Years later, in her autobiography she wrote:

> As I left the Berensons and walked up the hill to Poggio I felt very moved and a great deal troubled at the thought of seeing Aunt Janet without Uncle Henry to smooth the way for me. I shall never forget our meeting. I might have been a stranger who had come with a letter of introduction and after a little talk we parted. I wondered afterwards if I were to blame as, perhaps, I could have broken down the barrier between us but my senses seemed numb and I let the opportunity pass. She may have felt as sad as I did.

Janet had time to prepare herself for Henry's death, but when it finally happened the emotional loss was overwhelming. Their marriage had not been based on a great romantic or physical passion, but their bond had been a solid one. She had greatly admired him and remained devoted to him. He was a foil to her enterprise and she had relied on him and at times, taken him for granted. If she had not reflected on this reality before, she certainly did now. Lina, still in England before she returned to Florence with Aubrey, knew how keenly Janet would feel the loss. 'I was so sorry for my aunt and felt selfish that I could do no more than write her a letter, trying to tell her how much I realised her loneliness.'

Without Lina and Henry, Janet felt isolated in the big house. She tried to keep up a routine, but the joy and pleasure of conversation and company were gone. She was lonely, physically exhausted and without the comfort of family. When her physician, Dr Giglioli visited, he was alarmed enough to order complete rest. In an attempt to recover, she took herself to the thermal baths at Lucca where she remained more or less in bed for seven weeks.

When she finally came home, she received the news that her newly published revised edition of Lucie's *Letters from Egypt,* with a moving introduction written by George Meredith, was selling well. He was now an acclaimed man of letters, president of the Society of Authors and considered 'a living treasure'. He was sought out by the rich and famous and within a few years would be honoured with an Order of Merit.

But this good news about the book did little to lift her mood. For months she remained isolated and depressed. Mary Berenson tried to offer comfort although Janet was still irritated by Mary's encouragement of Lina and Aubrey. Stubborn and proud, Janet made things hard for herself. In early November Mary found Janet, 'ill and lonely and old and full of herself, in the hands of her servants, bitter against Lina — a sad spectacle — yet [with] something of the old lioness about her still'.

Aubrey and Lina dressed as Romeo and Juliet after their engagement. The costumes were suggested by Mary Berenson as a theatrical act of defiance against Janet. The picture was included in Lina's biography.

A CASTLE IN TUSCANY

Mary persevered though, and over the coming years became a mainstay in Janet's life. She and other old friends could forgive some of Janet's gruff ways because they loved her.

For Mary, the friendship with Janet was an unlikely one. She felt they disagreed on almost every point of thought or conduct that one could disagree on. But she found her friend and neighbour so complete, so characteristic of the age and milieu of the England in which she had grown up, overlaid sometimes very strangely with adventures in Egypt, that whatever their disagreements, there was no denying Janet was a wonderful if sometimes maddening original.

With time, Janet did rally. Slowly her former energy and enthusiasm returned. She responded warmly to Mary and others who came and wished her well and even found herself helping the Berensons sort out a few problems at I Tatti. Fixing the practical problems of friends, as she had done with Symonds, Clemens and so many others, was a clear sign that her mood was lifting. Janet's efforts were mostly appreciated although she did sometimes misjudge the situation. On one such occasion Mary mentioned that Bernard was looking for an assistant — he probably had a bright young graduate in mind for the job. Mary returned home with the 'appalling' news that Janet had offered herself to his service. The friendship was strong enough though, that no offence was taken when the offer was not taken up, and over the next twenty-five years, Janet and the Berensons remained close and would become at times intimately dependent on each other.

After Henry

For indeed it is true —— why should we deny it any
longer? Florence is no more: there remains beside the Arno,
between the hills where once Florence stood, the most beautiful
museum in the world, the one city in Italy that seems to have lost all
character, to be at various seasons almost English or German or American,
and save in the dog-days perhaps, never really Tuscan at
all ... And yet —— for beauty is immortal —— in spite of all these changes,
though the electric trams rush around the Duomo and have quite spoiled a
great part of the Lung' Arno, though nearly all the statues are fig-leafed
and in prison, and the pictures are invisible because of the crowds which
follow some jackanapes quoting Browning, Florence remains one of the
loveliest of the dead things of Italy —— yes a beautiful Museum full of
priceless masterpieces.

EDWARD HUTTON
COUNTRY WALKS ABOUT FLORENCE (1908)

OTHER neighbours offered support too. One of these was Fritz von Hochberg who lived close by and had come to know the Rosses not long before Henry's death. He and Henry found much in common and enjoyed each other's company. Observing Janet's isolation he devised a radical plan.

One November afternoon sixteen months after Henry's death Janet was in her study, pondering, in a rare moment of reflection, her future. Suddenly the door was flung open and there before her stood Fritz. Without apologizing for the interruption, he announced that he had sold his house and booked a passage for himself and Janet to Egypt leaving the following Tuesday. He instructed her to meet him at the main railway station in Florence at midday on that day. That is all she need do, everything else was arranged. But, she stammered, she had no proper clothes for such a journey. 'Oh', said Fritz, 'there's no but in the matter. You must come.' He then made hasty goodbyes and turned on his heel muttering something about being very busy. He was a very impulsive character, but Janet was fond of his ways. As the door closed she was left to contemplate how she might get herself ready in time.

Fritz was the son of Prince Pless of Selisia, one of the wealthiest of the German princes. Just before the 1895 earthquake, a friend of Janet and Henry's had brought him over to look at Poggio. At one point he wandered out onto the terrace and casting his eye across the vista, he spotted a nearby house known as Villa Hall. Janet told him it had once belonged to Cenni di Giotto, a relation of the great painter, and was later lived in by the patrician Florentine family of Valori. More recently, another local family had enlarged the villa and laid out the garden. There and then, in a moment of excitement, the newcomer decided he wanted to buy the place, but Janet told him he would have no chance as the current owner, Mrs Hall was a recluse and would not sell.

Then came the earthquake and Villa Hall was all but destroyed — the one good thing to come out of the earthquake, in Janet's view, who had a low opinion of the house and its owner. To avoid the expense of rebuilding, the allusive and luckless Mrs Hall put the place on the market and Fritz was able to buy it. This is how he became a neighbour to the Rosses.

Fritz renamed the house Villa Montalto — a simple translation of his own name into Italian. He was his own architect and landscape gardener, and with his considerable talent he managed to transform the place. The villa he built was a fusion of the German and Italian architectural styles of the period, not uninteresting though somewhat out of context with the landscape. The garden, however, was a marvellous testament to his expert botanical knowledge. His love of plants and gardens saw him quickly establish a firm friendship with Henry. Seeing his obvious talent, Henry more than once lamented what a pity it was that his new friend was not required to work for a living, in which case he may well have fully exploited his gift.

After Henry's death, Fritz continued to be a regular visitor to Poggio. On one of his visits he and Janet had talked loosely of travelling together to Egypt, but she thought nothing more of it. On Janet's first Christmas Eve without Henry, Fritz invited her to dinner to see his magnificent German Christmas tree. This was in the days when the Christmas tree was still a very Teutonic tradition that had only recently been exported to England by Queen Victoria's German husband, Prince Albert. The glitter and sparkle of the decorated tree was a complete novelty to the locals. Janet joined Fritz in distributing to the servants the Christmas presents piled up underneath.

Now he planned to distract her with an elaborate trip back to Egypt, a place she had not seen in thirty-five years. Rather than allow her time to ponder and possibly decline the offer, he had gone ahead and made all the arrangements. She would have to get herself ready in the four short days she had available before they were to depart.

The prospect of travelling east in such agreeable company was too good to refuse. Henry, when he was alive, had no desire to return to Egypt, but now Janet was free to do as she pleased. Janet, of course, arrived punctually at the station platform. Fritz was there to meet her and together they found their compartment and settled in. On a late autumn day in November 1903 the train slowly pulled out and set off on the track towards the port city of Genoa. From there Fritz had organized cabins on board a fabulously comfortable German steamer. The luxury was a revelation compared to the hulk she had boarded nearly forty years earlier in 1867 when she first made the trip. Fritz was an ideal companion — an experienced traveller with an inquiring mind, who admired and understood Janet.

As the kindly Fritz had intended, leaving Poggio behind gave his friend a new lease of life. On the boat there was time for for treasured memories of Egypt to come flooding back, time for the anticipation to build. But the suddenness of the departure also meant Janet had precious few moments to reflect on how much things might have changed in the many years since she had left.

Sure enough as the steamer sailed into Port Said past the statue of her old friend, the father of the Suez Canal, de Lesseps, she felt a wave of disappointment come over her. When they disembarked she 'found an evil-smelling, large, dirty town, instead of the pretty little place I remembered so well'. By the time they arrived in Cairo, the feeling was all consuming. The city was so changed that she felt displaced and completely unsettled.

In Cairo, nothing was quite as she had recalled. A few landmarks were familiar but they appeared strangely dwarfed by the new and unfamiliar. The city had sprouted masses of big hotels and the new trams rattled their way along the roads so pedestrians had to jump clear. Amid all the rattle and noise there were no donkeys for hire anywhere. There were no owners calling out 'come 'long, Ma'am, Gladstone, very good donkey' or 'here, lady, this Bismark, good donkey' which she remembered so vividly.

The smells too were quite different to anything she remembered. Relaxed street life had been transformed by mechanization to make the place fast and unforgiving. Janet and Fritz stayed at the huge Continental Hotel where Janet got the impression they were regarded as numbers rather than human beings. In the whole city, she could find little that remained unchanged except the carpet and the tent bazaars. She felt like a relic from another age that no one knew or cared about. On the positive side, she could see that the prosperity was striking and the better physical health of the people was an undeniably great achievement. But with few exceptions Janet felt alienated and invisible as she had never felt before.

The place reminded her of her spirited youth, a young woman with her life ahead of her. Now she was older and could not help but feel nostalgia for those times. Much of these feelings she kept to herself, not wanting to spoil Fritz's trip.

If she went to see Lucie's grave in the City of the Dead, outside Cairo, she made no record of it, but she insisted on taking Fritz on an overnight train up to Luxor to show him where Lucie had once lived. The train — another change for the better — was a far cry from the terribly slow boat trip she had made with Henry all that time ago. Arriving at the ancient capital, there was more disappointment. It was obvious that even here, far from the hubbub of the big city, little remained intact. It seemed to Janet that even the topography had shifted, that the Nile had changed its course and was further away from the village. There were no visible traces of her mother's life, or of the people who had known her. Janet retreated to her memories of the indescribable beauty she had been fortunate to witness when she and Henry had made their last trip to see Lucie before leaving Egypt.

The one small pleasure she found was the lovely Hotel Savoy in Luxor. It was cool and well run and had a pleasant garden that offered relief from the overwhelming heat and dust outside.

Further up the river at Philae, the ancient temple complex so loved by Lucie, the shock was even greater. The beautiful sights were not simply changed; they were gone, mostly submerged beneath the waters of the Aswan dam. Trees were dead and dying, and tangles of collecting flotsam were all about. The sky was still and quiet. The water birds, pelicans, wild geese, ducks, plovers and masses of small birds had all but disappeared. The bewildered visitors were told that Italians who had come to work on the construction of the great dam had shot all the birds. Janet was left feeling utterly dismayed and consumed by a hatred of utilitarian science that had destroyed such loveliness.

They were to have travelled on to Khartoum, but Fritz developed appendicitis and remained very sick for some time. Far away from modern medicine, this was definitely not a good place to be so ill. This unfortunate turn of events meant they had no choice but to stay at nearby Aswan for the weeks until he finally recovered. By then it was time for Janet to return to Italy because she was expecting the Markbys at Poggio. Fritz had no urgent need to move and stayed on until he was fully recovered. On the way back down the river Janet made another short stop in Luxor.

Fortunately these last couple of days turned out to be the most satisfying of the whole expedition. Entering the lobby of the Savoy again she was approached by an old German gentleman, who in an extraordinary feat of recognition, asked whether she was the daughter of Lucie Duff Gordon. He was Dr George Scheinfurth, a well-known traveller and Egyptologist whose name was certainly familiar to Janet. He knew some people who remembered Lucie and took Janet to meet them.

One was the German Consul, a local by the name of Todoros. Janet remembered him as a skinny young boy who had been taught English and German by Lucie. It was his father who had given Janet the alabaster kohl jar in 1867, which she had treasured all these years. Janet asked him if he remembered Lucie, which of course he did. He told her he remembered her daughter too, the young Mrs Ross, who rode better than any Bedouin. Janet interrupted to explain that she was Mrs Ross. He looked at her incredulously, 'What so old!' Janet's response was to remind him that he was no longer the young boy either.

George Meredith, the acclaimed writer of later years.
Portrait by G.F Watts.

Then on the train south to Port Said to catch the boat home, Janet had a second happy encounter. She had written to an old friend, Sheik Saoud, who she fondly remembered as a brilliant young huntsman and rider at Tel-el-Kebir in the 1860s. She suggested meeting him at the station, as her train was due to pass by Tel-el-Kebir on its run south. He wrote back, delighted at the prospect.

As the train ambled into the station and she peered through the window searching for someone she recognized, she felt a sudden sense of disappointment when it appeared that no one was there to meet her. Then at last a solid, well-dressed Bedouin came up and called her name. Saoud could not immediately recognize the young woman he remembered, but after studying Janet he recognized the woman from his youth in her eyes. She discovered that the young boy she had known had become, since his father's death, Sheik of his tribe in the Suez desert. He invited Janet to come and spend a few days with him, promising her a good horse. Janet knew that she had to keep travelling to arrive back in Tuscany for her guests and could not accept the invitation, but it was offered with such generosity and warmth that it compensated for the all the other disappointments of the trip.

> He and I were almost the only ones left of those joyous days in the desert … Saoud was a middle-aged man, I was a white-haired old woman. Tears came thick into my eye as the train moved out of the station and I waved a last farewell.

When she finally arrived home there was a great relief. Back with all that was familiar and with old friends for company, she discovered an energy that had been missing since Henry's death. The feelings of despair and loneliness no longer plagued her. She was eager to see people and check progress on the farms. She even accepted an invitation from James Lacaita, her old friend from Puglia, for her and her cousins to travel south and stay with him at his estate Leucaspide. Perhaps the trip with Fritz for all its difficulties and disappointment had made a difference. His extraordinary generosity and kindness consolidated a firm friendship between the two and it certainly restored her enthusiasm for life at Poggio.

In the summer of 1904 Janet went to England. While she was there, her old friend Frederick Watts, the painter, died. This was the end of another enduring friendship stretching back over most of her life. One of the few remaining intimates from those days, was George Meredith and she was eager to see him. She wrote asking if she could visit and received a heartfelt response, 'It will be a revival of old pleasures to see you, with some clouds of memory overhead, but no longer obscuring. The death of Watts will have grieved you as it has me. My friends are dropping to right and left, and I ask why do I remain'. Quite what he meant by 'clouds of memory overhead' is not clear. Was it a specific reference to his sense of loss all those years ago when Janet married Henry or was it a more general reference to the slow but sure disappearance of the world they had known and loved. Meredith was now an acclaimed living monument, having achieved all the recognition that eluded his youth.

He had gone on to marry a second time in 1864, a practical domestic woman, Marie Vulliamy. She was very unlike his first wife but the marriage was happy and produced two children, William in 1865 and Mariette in 1874. The family lived in a cottage on Box Hill near Dorking in Surrey. In 1886 Marie died of cancer and in 1895, Arthur — Meredith's child from his first marriage, whom Janet had cared for when he was a small boy — died too.

With the passing of years Meredith, now seventy-six, had become quite deaf — still Janet found all 'the old fire and brilliancy'. They talked for over two hours about old times and old friends, most of them dead. As she rose to leave, he commented that she had something of his fictitious heroine, Rose Jocelyn, in her still. He was flattering her as he had often done so many years before and she enjoyed it. Janet described the encounter as a 'revival of old pleasures'. This was the last time she saw him before he died five years later, but she always preferred to remember him as the 'lithe, active companion who so often strode along by the side of my cob over the Copsham common, brandishing his stick and talking so brilliantly'.

Like the trip to Egypt, Janet's time spent in England that summer provided a fillip. Despite her good humour, however, there was no evidence that she saw Lina while she was there. After their extended honeymoon in Italy, Lina and Aubrey had returned to England and settled in the town of Sandwich in Kent. Their first child, Gordon, was born in 1903 and Aubrey was painting with some success. While Lina was wondering what she might do next Joseph Dent paid her a visit and asked her to write a history of Rome to be illustrated by Aubrey. The young couple jumped at the proposal. They decided to leave the baby and his nurse with Aubrey's family while they travelled to Italy to research.

When Janet returned to Poggio after England, she felt an urge to take up the pen once more, the first time since Henry had died. The void left by Henry's death and her alienation from her immediate family was gradually filled by a resurgence of writing. Without obligations to an unwell husband and the farms in good condition and returning some income on the sale of wine, oil, vegetables and fruit as well as the vermouth — Janet was free to devote herself to the work of research and writing.

The new edition of *Letters from Egypt* with Meredith's introduction had continued to sell well and was reprinted in 1903. The following year Dent published a collection of some of Janet's best articles under the title *Old Florence and Modern Tuscany* which included some pieces she had written for journals years before. At the same time, Janet began a book on *Florentine Palaces and Their Stories* that came out in 1905. And soon thereafter she started work on another book, this one on *The Story of Pisa* published in 1909, also for Dent — another in his series on Italian cities. The same series that Lina and Madge had contributed to with *The Story of Perugia* published in 1898. For this one she had to visit Pisa and work in the archives. By 1906, Janet, now aged sixty-four, had written or edited twelve books. She enjoyed writing and was showing no signs of slowing down. She was moved to write on subjects that she knew well and that she thought would be of interest to her audience, and in most cases she hit the mark.

163

AFTER HENRY

Thomas Lindsay as Janet knew him.

About this time she began a friendship with a man who would encourage her to go further with her writing. The man was Dr Thomas Lindsay, a sturdy, handsome Scotsman about the same age as Janet. He had a full, clipped beard and a penetrating gaze. His obvious intelligence and warmth made him a likeable and popular character. She found herself immediately attracted to him. Janet met him when he was a guest at the house of a Scottish neighbour of hers. His wife had died three years before he met Janet, leaving him with five grown up children, two daughters and three sons.

In his youth he had been a brilliant student of philosophy but eschewed a career as a university teacher to take up ministry in the Free Church of Scotland. By the time Janet met him, his career had come full circle and he was principal of the Free Church of Scotland's theological college in Glasgow. (Though Janet had no idea of this when she met him because he did not wear clerical clothes outside Scotland.) Experience had taught him that the wearing of a dog collar abroad was 'a sort of placard. "Enquire here for everything," especially to ladies, who demand string, paper, ink, pens, the names of hotels and proper tips to give, etc etc'. He was simply introduced to her as Dr Lindsay and there was nothing about him to suggest he was a cleric. She liked his conversation and felt they had much in common. The same day she invited him to stay at Poggio as soon as it suited him.

The encounter came at a critical time for Janet, as she noted some years later. 'To gain a real friend is an event in one's life more especially when youth is long past and only the memory of old friendships is left. So 1906 was a red-letter year.'

Thomas Lindsay seemed enchanted by Janet's life and interests and over the following years made it his business to visit her regularly, either alone or with one of his children. During their time together, Janet, Lindsay and anyone else staying in the house would often head off to some nearby festival or in search of a particular painting or fresco recommended to them by Bernard Berenson. One year they went to Lucca to see the Festa of the Volto Santo that takes place on September 14. The festival is a celebration of a crucifix brought to Lucca in 742 and placed in the church of San Martino. 'Lucca, generally so tranquil, was in a ferment of excitement when we arrived in the afternoon. In the cathedral, all hung with crimson damask, vespers were being celebrated … The illumination of the facade of San Martino, the great lines of the architecture picked out with hundreds of small oil lamps, was wonderfully beautiful.' Another summer they went to the city of Ravenna on the Adriatic coast north of Tuscany. Their objective was to see the superb early mosaics in the Byzantine churches, about which Thomas was particularly knowledgeable.

Although his academic preoccupations were philosophy and later the Reformation, his interests were broadly based. He seemed to welcome distractions that might take him into the realms of ancient history, literature, language or a dozen other subjects. He was extremely generous with his time and knowledge and enjoyed searching things out for Janet. She once described him as being like a rotary bookcase that could be turned around to provide any required reference. Their enquiring minds seemed to fire off each other.

He tried to come south each year and Janet travelled to Scotland as often. Between visits, they kept up a frequent correspondence. Every few days they exchanged letters brimming with news and ideas.

Janet working at Lucie's writing desk.

She turned to him when she encountered obstacles in her research and he invariably added some useful perspective. When Janet was working on *The Story of Pisa*, she wrote to him inquiring about medieval statistics she had come across in the archives. His response was typically knowledgeable. He began an explanation of the numbers of people involved in medieval crusades, adding 'As to your troubles about statistics I think no one can accept medieval or even classical statistics — only no one can correct them'.

In addition to the parcels of books travelling between Florence and Glasgow, Janet made sure the Lindsay house was stocked with vermouth and other good things from Poggio. There developed between them an intimate fondness that, typical of Janet's relationships, existed outside the physical. She thought him the kindest and most indulgent of men and rejoiced in her good fortune to have met him. He was always ready to assist her in her research or show some kindness. When he travelled to London he always offered to find material for her at the British Museum, other times he happily went over pages of her work she sent him for comment. It gave him considerable satisfaction to be of help. But best of all, he liked her company and found her energy and intelligence stimulating.

Despite their obvious compatibility and the pleasure they brought each other, there was no question of marriage. Their lives were deeply rooted in the places they lived and neither would have wanted to move on a permanent basis away from everything familiar and important to them. Moreover they were both emotionally and materially independent people who would have little to gain from the formal arrangement of marriage.

In regards to Janet's writing, Lindsay was generous with his time and knowledge and like others before him, such as Symonds, he actively encouraged her. To this end he was rigorous in his criticism and she accepted much of what he said. His feedback acted as a stimulus to this particularly prolific period of writing. Moreover, it was a time in which she undertook some of her most complex and demanding work.

She began the difficult task of translating unpublished letters of three generations of the famous Florentine family, the Medicis — Cosimo, Piero, Lorenzo and their wives and friends. This was a significant endeavour. Deciphering historical manuscripts is made particularly difficult by archaic handwriting and idiosyncratic spelling contractions. Although Janet was assisted in this code-breaking exercise by library staff, it was a considerable task. The finished book, *The Lives of the Early Medici as told in Their Correspondence* was published by Chatto and Windus in 1910. It was an accomplished scholarly work that showed off her great ability as a translator and storyteller, and was favourably received.

Its success was due to her determination and ability to concentrate. She was probably more intellectually focused now than ever before. These translations were new ground and she was making it her own. The book received due recognition and even today is regarded as a significant work. Janet now in her late sixties had rediscovered the purpose and fulfilment she needed to reach her intellectual peak. She had much to be thankful for.

In the intervening years Lina and Aubrey were spending more and more time in Italy. A couple of years after the publication of their book *Rome and its Story* in 1904, they moved to an old manor house, Northbourne Court, near Canterbury in Kent. Aubrey was painting and Lina doing some work for *The Times Literary Supplement*. Although they had to be careful with money, they managed well enough to travel to Italy every few months. This established a pattern that lasted for years to come. In Italy, they set up house in an ancient fortress attached to the little town of Aulla about 25 kilometres (15½ miles) inland from the town of La Spezia on the Ligurian coast.

Aubrey had come across Aulla while still at Oxford and first took Lina there after they finished work on the Rome book. Initially they rented it very cheaply from its English owner and furnished it with a couple of camp beds and some rugs. Eventually they bought furniture, made repairs, planted a beautiful roof garden and had Gordon and his nanny join them. Janet thought they were mad to live in such a place. Although La Spezia was less than 150 kilometres (93 miles) from Florence, the life they led was a world away from Poggio Gherardo.

They and their friends in Italy and England led an altogether more bohemian life than Janet. Their domestic arrangements especially, were more relaxed than those of the older generation. Lina made an effort to visit Poggio from time to time because she retained a genuine affection and appreciation for her aunt, but she found these visits easier without Aubrey. To a young couple in the prime of their lives, Janet appeared increasingly out of step. All the more so because Janet and Lina had not really reconciled their differences, they simply avoided the fraught issues.

When she came to visit her aunt, Lina joined Janet's Sunday afternoon gatherings — a tradition which continued — and mingled with old friends and new visitors. One who saw her across the crowded room one Sunday was Virginia Woolf, now a close friend of Madge Addington-Symonds. Virginia, apparently knowing little of Janet's background or that she was a writer, described the scene in a letter to Madge:

> We had a tremendous tea party one day with Mrs Ross. She was inclined to be fierce, until we explained that we knew you, when she at once knew all about us – our grandparents and aunts and uncles on both sides. She certainly looks remarkable, and had type written manuscripts all scattered about the room. I suppose she writes books. There, numbers of weak young men, and old ladies kept arriving in four wheelers; she sent them out to look at her garden. Is she a great friend of yours? I imagine that she has had a past – but old ladies, when they are distinguished, become so imperious. Lina Waterfield also came in for a moment, but I hardly spoke to her. She has beautiful eyes. The garden; though it rained, was wonderful; I could fancy you wandering about it, and eating un-ripe oranges. Florence was lovely, more lovely than seems possible.

Not all younger people found Janet so fierce. There were some whose appreciation of her came more easily. One was Frank Crisp. He had turned up in the summer of 1908 with a letter of introduction from Ambrose Poynter, the Englishman who had travelled with Janet to Pulgia all those years ago when

Janet was researching her book *The Land of Manfred*. Crisp was an easy-going twenty-five-year-old, a tall figure with a pale complexion. He had been awarded a Royal Academy travelling scholarship enabling him to travel and paint on the Continent. He had spent a month in Rome and had now turned up in Florence. He planned to spend time in the galleries and pursue his art. Janet took an immediate liking to him and after this initial visit he returned often to stay. He painted several portraits of Janet and after some persuasion, Mary Berenson sat for him too. The picture of Janet liked most is a rear side view of her at her writing desk which she later chose as the frontispiece for her autobiography.

Another young man who developed a close friendship with Janet was the English-born travel writer Edward Hutton who had moved in nearby with his wife. He was completely won over by her, so much so that he dedicated his *Country Walks about Florence* to her in 1908. At the time he was immersed in an exhausting study of Boccaccio and according to Janet had overworked himself. She decided to step in and with 'the authority derived from age and white hair', decreed a day's rest. In order to take him away from his desk she suggested he 'should explore the country around Florence and write a much needed book about the beautiful walks, the wayside tabernacles, and the old world villages'. In the introduction to the book, he attributes his discovery of the delights of the Florentine countryside to her influence:

> And then came one who drew me out of the whirlwind, and in her beautiful palace, where the ladies of the Decameron told the deplorable, delicious tales which have always delighted the world, she lured me back with songs to the appearance we call reality … Now, when she had cured me I began to go into the lanes, into the woods, into the little villages among the children, back into the world, — a new world.

Some time later, Janet and Hutton collaborated in editing a collection of the poetry by Lorenzo d' Medici published in 1912 as *Lorenzo d'Medici, Poesia Volgari*.

That same year Janet wrote *The Story of Lucca* — a follow up to the earlier *The Story of Pisa* — and her autobiography, *The Fourth Generation*. This was an extended sequel to her *Three Generations of Englishwomen*, so well received twenty-four years earlier in 1888. It was an account of Janet's life as she wished it to be drawn. Just as she had in telling the stories of her forebears, if Janet had nothing positive to say on a subject she preferred to ignore it altogether. Despite the book's popularity, to those who knew her, the omissions were obvious.

From the time of her marriage to Aubrey, Lina is not mentioned again, and Maurice's financial and marital difficulties are avoided, as are his illness and death. Likewise, Ouida is left out. Most obvious of all however is the complete absence of Alick. Although his birth is mentioned in passing in *Early Days Recalled* (Janet's earlier autobiography), here he simply does not exist. This seems all the more curious when it appears that privately Janet still considered Alick as her son and heir. Lina recalled that during the First World War, some years after *The Fourth Generation* was published, Janet had specifically outlined her intention to leave Poggio to Alick for his use during his lifetime. Yet only a few years earlier she had excluded him from her life in the most public way. Whether this was the result of some passing irritation with her now middle-aged son or whether it was the culmination of a lifetime's mismatched relationship is not clear, but by any standard, it was extraordinary. Janet ended the book by describing her life as 'a happy one on the whole, save that I am rather solitary and feel the void left by the death of old friends. [Although] I have, it is true made others'.

Years before, Kinglake had suggested that such a book would appeal to the reading public and his instinct was right. She had known some of the most interesting people in Victorian England and Italy and the story she tells is intriguing for that alone.

Janet was seventy and although she continued to write, *The Fourth Generation* marked the end of this period of intense literary activity. Two years later Lindsay died and Janet was without an intellectual confidant. She was unlikely to enjoy such companionship again and felt a great sense of loss. Her personal despondency seemed to be reflected in the broader political front where the talk was increasingly about war.

Later Years

Regrets, regrets, how many there are in life for most of
us. My great regret is, and still comes back to me, to
have been tongue-tied at crucial moments when a few
words might have cleared away much unhappiness. Aunt
Janet was also loath to show her real feelings and I
realised too late how much she loved me. She too, never
knew my feelings of love and admiration for her. A wall
seemed to separate us at times and there was even a
streak of Scottish dourness in both of us.

LINA WATERFIELD
A CASTLE IN ITALY (1961)

IN August 1914, with Germany and England on the verge of war, Janet had the somewhat
perverse idea of visiting England. Refusing to be cowed by incessant speculation, as she saw
it, and growing fear, she set off northwards, travelling across Europe as it prepared for conflict. Fritz
von Hochberg had invited her to stay with him at a house he had recently bought near Southampton.

The preparations for war caused her to delay in Paris, so by the time she arrived in England she
was tired and needing a rest. She had barely arrived at Fritz's new house when he received a message

from the German ambassador in London, requesting that, as a German citizen — and a noble one at that — he return to Germany immediately. As he threw his things together, Fritz asked if Janet could look after his house and horses while he was away. By nature Janet was one to take things in her stride, especially some of Fritz's hastily announced plans, but this time she was genuinely open-mouthed. Even if she wanted to argue the point, there were more pressing practical issues to deal with so she kept quiet. Fritz was short of money and under the circumstances could not draw any funds from an English bank. Janet gave him what cash she had and took herself off to pawn a necklace to raise some more. That was all the time they had. She gave him the money, wished him well and he was gone.

The next morning an English officer turned up insisting on searching the house for bombs that were rumoured to be there. He wanted to talk first with the person left in charge and was surprised to be introduced to an imperious old English woman sitting up in bed. Apparently, when Fritz's belongings were being moved into the house, the driver of the truck warned removalists to be careful handling the transport crates as they may explode. In the current near hysterical environment, an overheard joke developed into an imminent German plot and the house was to be searched. The officer did his job and was satisfied there were no bombs. Unfortunately for him, Janet insisted he do the job thoroughly. After all, she was a friend of the German gentleman's. The officer must search her drawers and trunk too, just to be sure. Her point was made and the embarrassed officer left.

Janet had taken a small stand against the jingoistic bluster of war, but in reality it made no difference. The old connections between England and Germany, friendships, cultural esteem and family connections that she had always taken for granted counted for little in the face of the populist frenzy.

Once Janet had finalized some longer term arrangements for Fritz's house and horses, she set off. She went to visit various friends and extended family members ending with a visit to see Lina at Northbourne Court in Kent. There were now three Waterfield children. In addition to Gordon, there was Johnny, born in 1909 and Corinthia, known as Kinta, born in 1911. With war about to be declared, Lina and Aubrey had returned to England with the children, not knowing when they would see Aulla again. Fortunately, Janet's timing coincided with Aubrey's absence in Canterbury where he was helping run a tea and recreation centre for soldiers.

To Lina's great relief, Janet managed to be completely charming to everyone. Now taking the war more seriously, Janet was concerned about the proximity of the place to the coast. She spent a considerable amount of time looking around for suitable refuge points in the event of an air attack, finally settling on the entrance to an old tunnel she discovered in the garden. The threat of danger caused Janet to reflect on the rift between Lina and herself — it was time to let go of the years of anger and resentment she had harboured, if not to openly express remorse. She was perfectly capable of putting aside her grievances in the wartime environment and the warmth she showed was reciprocated. The thaw continued even after Janet's return to Poggio and she wrote to Lina suggesting that she and the children come to stay while Aubrey was absent on war duties.

Janet in her later years continued to be involved in
the vintage.

Janet was alone in a big house and wanted to help Lina if she could. Moreover, shortly after she returned to Poggio at the beginning of 1915, she was shaken by the terrible news that Frank Crisp who had joined the army as Second Lieutenant in the Grenadier Guards stationed in Flanders, had been killed in action. Janet was stunned. She had been concerned for her young painter friend from the time he joined up. Like Carlo Orsi before him, she had loved Frank dearly. Mary Berenson claimed that Janet had once confided that if he died, she wanted to die too. Even if Mary was exaggerating, it was clear that Janet dreaded losing her young friend to the fighting. So it was an awful job that fell to Mary when she received the news from Edward Hutton along with a request that she break it to Janet. The death of the fine young artist confirmed in Janet's mind that now was a time for families to be together.

After mulling over the pros and cons of her aunt's offer to bring the children to Poggio, Lina finally decided to leave Gordon at prep school and to bring the two younger children, five-year-old Johnny and three-year-old Kinta, to Florence. If Lina had doubts about the invitation, especially about breaking the family up and leaving Gordon and Aubrey behind, she was persuaded that the warmer climate and good food at Poggio was better than she could provide in England. At this stage, Italy had not entered the war and there was no rationing, so milk, wheat, oil, wine, fruit and vegetables were readily available.

Their arrival was met with a very warm welcome from Janet and all the domestic staff, including Davide who ran the household and Agostino, who had been cooking at Poggio now for the last seven years. Janet had made an apartment on the east side of the house ready for Lina and the children. Meals were eaten together with Janet in the dinning room, and Lina and Janet spent many long hours talking in the drawing room. At other times it was a blessing for Lina and the children to retire to their own rooms where Johnny and Kinta could be messy and Lina had a place to set up her typewriter and work on correspondence. They had a big living room that opened onto a terrace overlooking olive groves and vineyards.

The abundance of food was very welcome. Kinta, writing years later, remembered delicious fried vegetables served as hors d'oeuvres; tiny zucchini (courgette) and slices of young fennel dipped in the lightest batter and quickly fried in olive oil, served with pesto or lemon. There was a tasty frittata of cardoons (an edible thistle, like the globe artichoke), and tender, sweet asparagus served in different ways.

Just like his predecessor, Agostino excelled in variety. Asparagus might be *alla Parmigiana*, grilled with cheese, *all'Italiana*, with coddled eggs and cream or *ai gamberi*, with prawns and lemon mayonnaise. Out from the kitchen came delicious morsels of *crostini di fegatini*, minced chicken livers with herbs served on small pieces of fried bread. Then there might be a steaming mushroom risotto or, in the spring, a *soufflé ai piselli* made with the freshest peas from the garden.

For a meat course there were *involtini di vitello*, little rolls of veal wrapped up with ham or mortadella and a sage leaf, or perhaps trout basted with oil and herbs and grilled over the wood fire. Similarly, he might cook a freshly plucked chicken or rabbit on the rotisserie.

In one notable way Agostino did distinguish himself from Giuseppe. He had, Kinta recalled, a genius for *dolci* or desserts. She thought it a pity he never produced a book of his creations as a complement to *Leaves from Our Tuscan Kitchen*. Among her favourites were wafer biscuits filled with cream, delicate mousses and a special pudding of *nocciola* — pounded hazelnuts with egg and cream. For special occasions he made a magnificent 'Mont Blanc', a pile of chestnut purée flavoured with dark chocolate, brandy or rum and covered with peaks of fresh whipped cream to resemble its namesake.

This was the first time in the twelve years since her marriage that Lina had slept in the house and all the old magic of it came back to her. Even so, when they arrived, she could little have imagined that Poggio would become her home for the next four years. In the meantime, mindful that Janet was unused to having young children running underfoot, Lina reminded Johnny and Kinta to keep to their side of the house. 'Our trenches', they jokingly called it.

For the first time in many years, Janet, distracted by the prospect of war, was not working on a book. She believed that now was not the moment to withdraw to research and write — except for the mandatory nightly letter-writing — it was a time for action. Although Italy had still not committed to entering the war, it was thought to be only a matter of time. War was the new reality and the prevailing point of conversation in every household. There were divisions of opinion about whether Italy ought to get involved at all, and if so, on which side. All the talk meant that anxiety and tension crept into everyday life, and anyone fortunate enough to have the choice thought about leaving. Some English friends decided to depart and, of course, Germans were moving out too. For the time being, the prevailing mood put a temporary halt to the longstanding ritual of Sunday afternoon gatherings. For the time being, the Berensons stayed on.

War was not the only menace. Growing social and political unrest had broken out into low level street fighting in and around some of the major cities. Social inequalities and a failure by the central Government to make life better for most people was fertile ground for discontent. Nearly fifty years before, when Janet had first arrived in Italy, there was tremendous optimism for the new nation. It was hoped that a united country under a stable constitutional monarchy would improve the lot of the many Italians living in poverty and hardship. But in the time since unification little had been done to address the disparity between the heavy taxes levied on the poor and the huge sums of money that the rich continued to spend on themselves. There were significant taxes on salt and grain, for example, but no tax on accumulated wealth. As hopes for a better life for the average Italian faded, socialism became the new motivation for increasing numbers of people.

Victor Emanuel III was king and the conservative Antonio Salandra was prime minister when Italy finally entered the war in May, 1915 on the side of the Allies, against Germany. If it couldn't remain neutral, the fact it sided with the Allies must certainly have been a relief to Janet and Lina who otherwise would have found themselves in very difficult circumstances. (As the experience with Fritz had shown all too well, the situation for enemy alien expatriates was a precarious one.) After months of foreboding, the immediate impact was less than Janet had anticipated and something of an anticlimax. Even after all the young men from the farms were conscripted, for a while life seemed to go on much as usual.

Meanwhile, Lina was pleased to be back among old friends. She spent time at the Berensons who at one point lent their *villino* or cottage to a group of four wild but delightful Australian soldiers on leave. To Lina's astonishment they managed to drink a bottle of whisky a day, each, without getting drunk. As Mary was away, Bernard asked Lina to show the young men around the city. They were eager to see and hear about everything, insisting their guide leave nothing out. They said they did not want to get back to the Dardanelles to find that their mates had seen more than they had.

The impact of the fighting, although slow to be felt at first, did come. Gradually and quietly, life became more difficult and the mood more subdued. With less manual support, the running of the house came to feel like a struggle. The priority of those left behind was to keep the farms working. They had to pick up all the agricultural work left by the young men now at the front. For all of these dependent families to survive, it was imperative that the land be kept productive.

Eventually rations were imposed, further increasing the strain on the women, children and the elderly. Even wood for heating water in the house was scarce. Not only did this mean cold water — not a problem in summer though awful in the winter months — but also that Janet would have to let Henry's orchids die. They relied on a warm humid environment. It was sad but unavoidable under the present circumstances.

Although Janet spent more and more hours just keeping the house and farms functioning, she never thought of leaving. Apart from the fact that this was her home and she had nowhere better to go, she felt it her duty to provide enough for Lina and the children and the farming families who were working harder than ever just to survive. The young *contadini* (farm workers), now soldiers, were depending on them too. Food parcels of home-grown produce were sent off regularly to the twelve men from the farms serving at the front. Such commitment to the men and their families was not necessarily the norm among the expatriates living in large villas dotted around the Florentine hills.

Janet and Lina helped in the field when they could. They joined the old men and the women in the evening to cut fodder for the cows. When Lina was distracted by the sunset, Janet would call out 'My dear child, what are you doing?'. Janet had no time for sunsets and kept her mind on the job. The vintage and olive picking both had to be done with the limited labour available. There were crops to plant, animals to tend and gardens to maintain, all hands were needed.

With the adults so busy, Johnny and Kinta were largely left to their own devices. Kinta in her memoir recalls a happy time where she and her brother made friends with Agostino's son and daughter. The girls made dolls and played nurses, taking it in turns to dress up in a little Red Cross uniform that someone had given Kinta. The boys played hide and seek in the vast, empty oil jars in the cellars, and all four children had competitions to catch lizards and crickets. Their secret kingdom was the *bosco* or wood inside the north gate, where they liked to swing from tree to tree without touching the ground.

There were occasional outings to Florence in the carriage with Janet, for some shopping and, maybe, treats at Doney's. Other times there were visits to neighbours. Looking back from adulthood, Kinta remembered Janet as fair with her and her brother though disapproving of Lina's complacency towards their upbringing. She also remembers Janet's special affection for Johnny. Their great-aunt really warmed to him, paying him extra attention. In the summer, Lina took the children to the beach for a holiday, although Janet felt compelled to stay behind to carry on the necessary work on the farms.

This is how it continued for the next few years. Life for the children was an idyllic one, but the drain on the adults increased as the war dragged on. The effort required to produce the minimum of food seemed to be greater with each passing season. In the winter of 1917, Lina wrote to Gordon, still at school. She told him of the bitter cold in Florence, where snow had lain on the ground for several days, and how it had also rained incessantly for three months. The average person had no fuel, petrol, sugar or butter and everyone was left freezing cold in their houses. At Poggio things were better because Janet had managed to stockpile wood and fuel in the summer, but for most Italians life was miserable.

These were difficult times for Lina and Aubrey too. He had joined up as a private in January 1915 believing he was going to fight a war to end all wars. His decision came as an unwelcome surprise to some of their friends bitterly opposed to the war. Lina was concerned for Gordon, separated from his family. And to add to Lina'a anxiety, the *fortezza* at Aulla was requisitioned by the Italian Government as a garrison.

Janet did her best to soothe things for Lina and the children. She did the same for the Berensons when they decided to leave Florence for Paris part-way through the war. Bernard had work to do and plenty of friends in Paris and Mary, at a difficult point in her marriage, decided to join him there. In their absence, Janet kept a close watch on their house and farms. Mary and Janet kept up a flow of correspondence that was a great comfort to them both. Years later Mary remembered:

> [with] gratitude the fact that when I was away from Italy with my husband in Paris, after America came into the Great War, and was very ill for many months, Aunt J wrote to me every single day, telling me all the news of the smaller world surrounding her castle: the weather almost from hour to hour, the state of the crops in our poderi and her own, so that I did not feel separated from the background of our ordinary Florentine life ...

The illness Mary referred to was a general physical breakdown of her health, the symptoms of which were to plague her for the rest of her life. These health problems were exacerbated by frustrations at I Tatti — Bernard was making great sums of money while she had little and could not assist her daughters in the way she wanted to. At the same time, she was becoming uncomfortable with the luxury at I Tatti while all around workers were struggling. But just as Janet was determined to carry on during the war, so she urged Mary put her, 'whole heart and mind to getting well ... there is nothing like being determined to do a thing — one always succeeds'.

To keep Mary's spirits up she sent a constant stream of local vignettes and gossip. Her letters painted a picture of the difficulties brought on by the war as well as Janet's cheery determination to make the best of it. She may have given up writing books, but nothing, it seems, could stop her writing letters. If she was up past midnight doing them, it made no difference. 'There are no more cats about', she wrote one day, 'they have been eaten; one of the restaurants in town has got into hot water, as they had fourteen in the cellar being fed up, and as the beasts made a great noise the neighbours literally, 'let the cat out of the bag'. The following day she continued:

> *... we get no more rice or pasta and only 600 grammes a head of flour instead of 400 of bread — but out of that we have to make our own pasta ... The miller may only grind a certain amount of wheat a month per head. I've signed the death warrant of my pretty gold pheasants, and I am going to eat them ... I can't wear my rings any more, they flip off my fingers! Post! Goodbye darling your loving Janet.*

Apart from occasional treats like a pat of butter or a delicious rice pudding given to her as thanks for a good turn she had done someone in the village, food was scarce and very low in animal fat. But Poggio's great salvation during the war was Agostino, who did a wonderful job with what he had at hand. Nonetheless, Janet shed pounds from her nicely shaped figure. She had never been prone to fluctuations in weight, but she managed to see the positive side of becoming skinny, declaring it better to be thin than fat. In a derisory aside to Mary she described one local Englishwoman (somehow unaffected by food rationing) as looking like a 'mass of shaking jelly that it was a wonder she did not leave spoonfuls of herself about the room'.

Towards the end of the war, Janet proposed to Mary that she and Bernard lease one of their farms to her. The one she had her eye on was actually farmed by a family called Grassi and according to the *mezzadria* system, if the Berensons agreed to the idea, the family would work for Janet and Davide. In her proposal to Bernard and Mary, she was critical of the current state of the farm in question and promised to get the land back in order quickly and to pay a good return. They accepted Janet's offer. At seventy-six Janet maintained considerable capacity for manual work. It was still her great distraction.

In addition to the farms, in 1918 before the end of the war, Janet opened a *doppo scuola* or after-school program for local children. The idea was to provide a decent meal for the children of Ponte a Mensola after they finished school. The meal had an extra benefit in that it encouraged mothers to stop stinting on themselves in an attempt to feed their children. About seventy local children now enjoyed one decent meal each day and going home with a full stomach. It was hugely satisfying to see the increased energy of the children and the improved well-being of their mothers.

It was such a success that Janet talked to Lina about possibly finding a house to set up another one in Florence. Lina approved of the idea but at the time was fully occupied with a project of her own, establishing the British Institute in Florence. The Institute sought to promote a better understanding

16. Sept. 1918. Poggio Gherardo
                        Settignano. Florence

Dearest Mary

I hope yr. weather is as beautiful
as ours, I'm so glad Lina has fine days up
at Vallombrosa. Mr. V. is there too, but
goes back to Rome from there. Ferrando
came to lunch yesterday, looking much better,
he spoke with tears in his eyes about you
& yr. kindness with regard to the Villino. I suspect
his mother is rather a trial to him. Sunday
is the only day I can give lunch to anyone,
as we get meat on Sunday mornings. I've
begun to eat my pretty gold pheasants,
I'm glad I've no cat, or we might be tempted
to eat that, & a decoction of rats & mice
does not attract me!

Kinta & the maid never arrived yesterday, so the
motor either broke down or wd not take them.
I must send in again to meet them; what
a bore people are!

The people all about are perfectly
furious with the X Rossa, & no wonder.
Hardly any of the 'pacchi' sent through
the X Rossa to the starving prisoners
ever reach them, while those sent by
the post from the families get to

A letter from Janet to Mary shortly before the end of the war. The 'X Rossa'
is the Red Cross.

them all right. I wonder where the fault is. Partly, no doubt, that the Austrians steal as many as they can, witness the wrapping found on an Austrian prisoner, which he was using as a pockethandkerchief!

Almrotte has sent me reprints from the Lancet of articles of his, one — "Acidosis of Shock etc" is very, very interesting. Only I always am so vexed that I don't understand more & am so ignorant. My 70 children hearing I was not well have sent me up a nosegay of common flowers — entirely out of their own heads the nun writes. It shows how civilised they are getting;. They enjoyed the 300 figs I sent, (out of Mrs Lacaita's money), I sd. not dare out of Govt. money as figs cost 15 cents: each!!! I'm afraid I write ill, because I'm still rather a rag, & my pen is not behaving well — Ever my very dear Mary — Yr most affte

Love please to B.B.   Janet.

of England and English culture to an increasingly cynical Italian populace. Lina was alarmed by the anti-British feeling she encountered in Florence and — along with some others, including Janet's friend the writer, Edward Hutton — felt passionately that something needed to be done to counter the untruths and misinformation. The Institute would house a library of English books and host talks on relevant themes.

Janet admired Lina's efforts with the Institute and understood she could not take on more work. Undeterred, Janet redoubled her efforts to get extra food into the farmer's houses. She bought sacks of potatoes and sold them to households at half price, and distributed cigars to the men. Although these were enormously expensive, Janet believed tobacco acted as disinfectant and helped fight off colds and influenza. Needless to say, this was all well received.

Janet's concern and care for ordinary Italians in dreadful circumstances was based on a deep sense of obligation. It was part and parcel of her background and her worldview, a sense of *noblesse oblige*, now increasingly under threat. Political agitation continued throughout the war years, exacerbated by stories coming back from the front of appalling conditions. It was impossible to ignore the mounting unease all around. If Janet, however benignly, thought her loyalty to the people of Ponte a Mensola was enough to protect her from the ugly side of this agitation, she was mistaken.

An Armistice was signed between the Allies and Germany on November 11, 1918. With the war finally over, Lina and the children left Poggio to be reunited with Aubrey. For Janet it was sad to see them go. After four years she had become used to having them around. She had gained great comfort in the laughter of the children and the good company of Lina. Between these two there remained differences, but the war years had renewed the bond. Now she would be alone again. On a more positive note, she could look forward to returning to the life she had known before the war. It would take time, but she was certain the proper order of things would reassert itself.

Italians felt humiliated by what they had been through. Six hundred thousand had been killed and many more wounded, a good proportion crippled for life. To add to the humiliation, Italy was all but ignored at the Treaty of Versailles. There were refugees across the country and desperate shortages of food. In the first days of July 1919, Janet accounted for seven hundred and fifty refugees in the local area needing help. Disease was rife and the Spanish influenza that had ripped around the world in the previous twelve months had left a wake of devastation in Tuscany too. Despite the gloomy situation, Janet remained confident the old way of life would be restored. But returned solders and Italian workers were in no mood to return to the former status quo. The pressure for change simply grew.

All over Italy there was a mounting sense of unease. Law and order was breaking down and apparently little could be done to stop the growing incidence of violence and disruption. A particularly nasty incident in the summer of 1919 brought the unrest literally to Janet's doorstep. On July 4 a mob of men from Monte a Mensola came up the hill and removed all the stores of wine, oil and maize from the cellars at Poggio Gherardo. I Tatti — with the Berensons still away — was also targeted. Janet was furious at having her stores stolen, but it stung all the more that the villains were local people. It was quite incomprehensible to her. She was deeply hurt and responded by turning her back on the people of the village. The day after it happened, Janet wrote to Lina, now back in England, that gunshots had been fired in Florence and she only hoped some of the anarchists had been shot.

Other, seemingly insignificant, incidents revealed much about the way things were changing. Twelve months after the raid on the cellar, the gardener at Poggio threatened to go on strike. He belonged to the local Association of Gardeners which, like most trade organizations, was originally set up to provide a forum for the interests of members. But these associations were becoming increasingly politicized. In this instance the local trades hall officials called together the gardeners and began to talk of a strike. Janet was indignant.

All these years she had worked in good faith under the *mezzadria* system of land tenure and that too was now under challenge. Agrarian strikes were made possible by the labour shortages brought on by war casualties and epidemics. Poggio Gherardo's survival was based on a common understanding between the landowner and those who worked the land. This bond and the daily round of domestic and agricultural activity was what Janet understood and valued. She was seventy-seven and temperamentally ill-equipped to adapt to emerging realities.

She was always firm in her views, but now Janet's opinions about people and the world became unyielding. She simply could not see the need to rethink certain fundamental approaches to the way society worked. One example was her opposition to female suffrage. She would not accept that giving the vote to women was in anyone's interests, an extraordinary argument to be made by a forthright, politically engaged woman. To many of her acquaintances, her views on the subject were extraordinary. Mary was particularly sensitive about Janet's position, but fortunately managed to see some humour in it too. Mary remained loyal, but Janet's intransigence in the face of a changing world was highlighting the differences in their age and outlook.

Janet's frustration inclined her increasingly towards the fascists. Perhaps not entirely surprisingly, their can-do rhetoric provided some comfort in a world that seemed to be falling apart at the seams. Janet was by inclination a liberal, but like many liberals she sensed danger in the growing civil disobedience. Despite the tactics of the fascists, many liberals took them at their word and accepted their growing influence and rough tactics as the best hope of maintaining legality.

In 1921 Janet described for Mary, who was away from I Tatti again, what she called a decent attempt at a revolution in Florence. There were seventy killed and more than four hundred wounded. 'Luckily the Fascisti came to the rescue and the cursed socialists and communists were thoroughly frightened.' The following year she told Mary how impressed she had been at the Fascist Festa at

Settingnano. 'There were flags all over the place and trams running every ten minutes. Everything passed off perfectly, as the socialists kept themselves shut up in their houses.'

Janet was by no means a wholehearted supporter of the fascist policy (for a start, ironically, the fascists supported universal suffrage). More than anything she supported the maintenance of the world she knew and loved, and the Black Shirts seemed the best hope of keeping it. But like Lina and other Anglo-Florentines she was increasingly alarmed at the rising anti-British feeling that had spread as a result of the war and the Treaty of Versailles. Indeed she took to writing her letters on paper emblazoned with pro-English slogans written in Italian. These were reminders of British support for Italian unification and the suffering of the English soldier alongside his Italian brother at the front. Although the letterhead was wartime stock, Janet kept using it periodically up to 1921.

She was not alone in her hopes for the fascists, especially in these early years of their ascendancy. But from the beginning, Lina and Mary and others were wary. Mary recalled in her diary a dinner after she and Bernard had returned to I Tatti that included Janet and Lina in November 1923:

> I really love Aunt Janet, but there again one must not expect real conversation. She has hardened into fixed opinions and narrowed her interests to local events. Lina [now working as Italian correspondent for *The Observer* newspaper] on the contrary, grows and grows, witty and humorous and such a splendid creature.

None of this hampered Janet's reputation as a sort of living legend; among foreign visitors she had become something of an institution. Her Sunday gatherings resumed and were attended by everybody of note visiting the city. She enjoyed the attention, of course, but liked to grumble to Mary about the amount of time she had to spend on flocks of people turning up with letters of introduction. Too many asked her about the past and wanted to hear stories about the people she had known. She was just as likely to recommend they read her books as to waste time answering their questions. If they were interested in the farms and issues of the day she was more obliging.

Many of her visitors were young people starting careers, and to some of them she appeared like a vision from another age. One of these was the young art scholar Kenneth Clark. In September 1925 he travelled to Italy with an English friend who had arranged that they stay with Janet. Many years later Clark recorded his first impressions of Poggio in his autobiographical account *Another Part of the Wood*, published in 1974. In Janet, Clark saw a living document and talented writer, but his impressions of the house are singularly dour. He remembered a long, dark drive, crumbling walls and a large abandoned area in front of the door, guarded by a huge misshapen dog called Lupo. Already chilled by the experience he rang the bell and heard it echoing through the empty corridors. After what seemed like an eternity, it was opened by a small, unfriendly man, and then he saw that the corridors were even longer and emptier than they had sounded. He wrote the memoir many years after the fact but, correct or not, it gives the impression that Poggio had become a bit of a ghost house in the years since the war.

(Despite such ominous beginnings, his time in Florence marked an important beginning for the rising star. Clark was invited to lunch down the hill at I Tatti and it was at this first meeting that Bernard invited him to work on the revision of his collection of Florentine drawings. Clark assisted Bernard for two years and in the process learnt an enormous amount.)

At the beginning of 1927 Janet was writing again, this time, a translation of the travel adventures of a sixteenth-century Florentine merchant, Francesco Carletti. At the same time she started work on a guidebook for the Palazzo Vecchio after hearing that a new one was needed by spring.

In between, she kept an eye on the farms and the accounts. Her present concern was a recent sharp drop in sales of Poggio endives to Germany. Germany was buying cheaper produce from Spain and as a result, Janet had to dump her endives at the local market and take whatever price she could. She had heard there was a similar glut in oranges as Germany had turned to Spain for cheaper supplies.

But even with the ongoing difficulties facing her, Janet's energy was largely undiminished. The years seemed to be taking little toll. Mary compared her to Vernon Lee who was suffering the common ailments of old age even though she was fourteen years younger. Lee was still living in Florence, a feminist and staunch pacifist. During the war years she had continued to write and by now had a large number of publications to her name. In contrast to Lee, Mary could not recall Janet, now eighty-five, ever alluding to getting old. Mary once asked her how old she felt and back came the reply, 'unless I'm ill, I don't feel any age at all, just the age I have always been'. Lina, though, thought Janet felt the effects of the passing years more than she was prepared to let on.

Janet's health was giving out and she must have known something was wrong because in May, 1927, she called Dr Giglioli. This highly respected practitioner in whom she had absolute faith — who over the years had treated patients at Poggio including farmers and their families at Janet's expense — came straight away. He examined the patient and found a cancerous growth behind the vagina. His prognosis was that she would not suffer much pain but was likely to grow steadily weaker. The condition, possibly uterine cancer, was fatal; there was no treatment. In his opinion, the best hope was that her heart might give out first. She might live some months, perhaps longer. If he told Janet the reality of her situation, she did not mention it. He did, however, tell Mary and it was she who contacted Lina.

The heart attack did not come and Janet grew steadily weaker as Dr Giglioli had foreseen. Lina — living at Aulla with her family, but at that moment, in Naples for *The Observer* when she received the news from Mary — arrived shortly afterwards. Though a nurse was employed, Lina planned to stay until

Janet in later years in a beautifully embroidered dress.

the end. She found her aunt by turn restless and fretful or weak and quiet. When Janet was tired, Lina sat by the bed and held her hand. She was inclined to change quite suddenly, one minute resting and the next sitting bolt upright on the pillows reading *The Morning Post* and killing flies with her ivory handled swat. Lina had to give a sworn promise not to come into her room in the night as she was determined to keep her independence to the last gasp.

As her spirit quietened, Janet sometimes still ate with gusto, especially little dishes of eggs or tapioca prepared by Agostino. To drink, she had bowls of mild coffee, as well as brandy and champagne. There was some disapproval in the house about the champagne, but Lina insisted Janet was to have whatever she wanted. In any case after a short period of hilarity it sent her firmly to sleep.

As the summer heat intensified, Lina thought Janet would be more comfortable if a bed was set up in the library, which was cooler. To Lina's relief and surprise, Janet happily agreed to leave the big four-poster bed and Carlo Orsi's naked rear view of her as a young woman. By now even Janet recognized that she was dying.

As the hot weather set in almost everyone, including Dr Giglioli, left Florence. Most of them went to the mountains or the beach. One hot summer's day in late August, Lina was summoned back to the house from the vineyards where she had been walking, by the sound of the big bell in the tower. Janet had died.

Lina had prayed for the end and it came more peacefully than she had dared hope. She set about arranging the library to be filled with plants from the garden. Next to the bed she placed a couple of saintly figures that had long stood on Janet's desk. Nearby she put a lit candelabrum. The farm workers and everyone in the house came in to see her, some kneeling in prayer. Janet had specifically instructed that there be no religious ceremony of any kind, but Lina felt that the private offering of prayer and affection would not contradict her wishes.

The longest serving house staff carried the coffin to the hearse. And a little procession led by Lina and Aubrey — who travelled from Aulla without the children — made its way around the north of the city to Via Bolognese and up to the city cemetery. The urn containing her ashes — into which Lina had placed Janet's wedding ring — was closed and placed next to Henry's. Alick was not present.

At the time she died much of what she knew and valued in the world was in decline. The glory days of the Anglo-Florentines was coming to an end.

Epilogue

During the war, when Lina and the children were living at Poggio, Janet had specifically said that she intended leaving the house and farms to Alick for his lifetime. After his death everything would revert to Janet's favoured nephew, Johnny Waterfield. It was therefore a huge surprise to Lina and Aubrey to discover that in fact she had left the place to Lina for her lifetime, to revert to Johnny once Lina died. Needless to say, when Alick received the news, it would have been a surprise for him, too.

Janet in fact left two wills. One written in English in 1910 dealt with assets she had in England. These were largely investments inherited from Henry, the bulk of which were left to Lina. In the event that Lina died before Janet, the assets would revert to Alick.

In 1924 Janet wrote another will, this time in Italian. With this she intended to assign Poggio and its contents. It was in this will that she decided that Lina, rather than Alick, should inherit the use of the castle until it passed to Johnny. In writing two wills, one in English and another in Italian, Janet was attempting to cover all legal bases, the idea being that the two would complement each other.

The English will, drawing on money in English investments, allowed for those employed at Poggio at the time of Janet's death to receive two months' wages. Some were named specifically for special consideration and considerable legacies, including Davide. All jewellery, lace and clothes were left to Lina.

Surprised as she was, Lina felt no concern for Alick, who, she argued, would be legally entitled to inherit his mother's marriage settlement. At the time of Janet's death this amounted to 30,000 pounds — a little over one million pounds in today's money. Alick did not attend his mother's funeral and there is no reference to correspondence with his cousin about the will.

To Lina the inheritance came as a poisoned chalice. She and Aubrey were happy and settled in their fortress in Aulla, which they had only recently managed to buy after years of leasing. It was a very big wrench to move from the carefree life at Aulla to the responsibility of Poggio, a castle beset with problems. All the difficulties Janet had quietly turned a blind eye to in her last years had to be addressed. To saddle herself and Aubrey with such a weight seemed foolhardy.

Yet Lina was determined to take it on. She remained firmly of the view that Alick was irresponsible and unworthy. Kinta Beevor in her memoir described Alick as having wasted his talents, 'an unfortunate remittance man by then well into his middle age, who must have been embittered from an early age by his mother's regret at ever having borne a child'. In Lina's mind, it was her duty to take on the legacy of Poggio. Kinta thought that the castle's location close to Florence would also have been appealing for Lina, as more suitable for her newspaper work.

The fundamental problem with moving to Poggia was a lack of money. The property had insufficient capital to run effectively. Increasing mechanization of agriculture required significant investment to buy equipment. Lina and Aubrey, despite what Lina had been left by Janet, simply did not have the money needed to sustain it. The new economics of farming not only threatened to sweep aside the time-honoured methods of agriculture, but for relatively small holdings like the farms at Poggio, it placed unsustainable pressure on the mutual obligation of the *mezzadria* system. Poggio would battle to remain viable in the new environment.

Not long after their move into the house, Lina and Aubrey received the rude news that the Italian Government required them to pay an inheritance tax equivalent to forty per cent of the value of the property. This was imposed because, under Italian law, Johnny Waterfield was considered to be outside the immediate family and his inheritance therefore attracted a penalty. Lina managed to arrange to have the tax paid in instalments over a number of years, but it still had to be paid. Janet had not been well advised in making her will.

Their problems only got worse when a year after Janet's death, a letter arrived from Alick's lawyers challenging the will under English law. On behalf of their client, lawyers were demanding a greater share of the estate. Alick had inherited a reasonable sum of money but certainly less than half the value of the estate. Lina was unmoved, indeed she was affronted. Regardless of the financial burden she now carried, she resolved to retain Poggio. She knew that if Alick won the claim, Poggio would have to be sold, which was precisely what Janet had tried to avoid. The reality was, neither Lina nor Alick had the resources to run Poggio as Janet had. Times had changed and the costs of production and labour had risen.

Rather than enter into any conciliation with her cousin, Lina determined to deal with his claim in the courts. She remained steadfastly unsympathetic, preferring to cast her cousin as a case of 'bad blood'. The situation was muddied further because years before at Poggio, when Alick was thirty-six and Lina twenty-four, she believed he tried to seduce her and had never forgiven him. It seems that nothing was made of the incident at the time. It appears as a passing reference in an unpublished biography of Janet written many years later by Lina's eldest son, Gordon.

Alick would have been aware that a successful claim on his part would result in breaking up Poggio. He must have had less emotional attachment to the place than Lina. After all it had never really been his home, but rather, his parents' house that he visited from time to time. In the end, Alick Ross lost the case, although if he had brought the claim in an Italian court, the decision would most likely have gone in his favour. Lina was greatly relieved, but as it turned out, her victory was more of a temporary stay than the promise of a secure future. In reality, the load of running the house and farms, and the turn of history, would ultimately defeat her.

In the meantime, she put all her effort into making a go of it. First, she and Aubrey set about cutting costs. They met some resistance from Davide who had long grown accustomed to running affairs. The kitchen was an obvious place to start, and one of Lina's first economies was to reverse Janet's habit of never allowing cold or twice-cooked food to be served. Though it soon became obvious that cost cutting by itself was not enough. To keep the place going they would have to bring in extra money.

During the next decade Lina continued to work as the Italian correspondent for *The Observer* newspaper — much of her work reporting on alarming political developments in Italy. At the same time she and Aubrey established a small school for girls at Poggio. Aubrey — who had continued to paint and established a reputation as a fine water colourist — had long held the view that conventional education 'trained student's minds, their feet and hands, but never their eyes'. Here was a chance for him to put his ideas into practice. The school was most definitely not to be a finishing school but rather a 'beginning school' as Lina described it, 'not lessons every minute of the day, but the great lesson of learning how to employ their time'.

The school promoted learning by the exploration of ideas among books and paintings. A teacher was engaged to give lessons in Italian language and literature. His name was Professor Scarafia, and his wife, Clementina, became the school accountant and Lina's secretary. The fourteen or so girls who attended were particularly fortunate in being allowed to use the library at I Tatti, including the thousands of photographs of paintings that had been collected by Bernard over his lifetime. They made regular excursions to Florence and were given instruction in painting by Aubrey. It was a sort of modern incarnation of the liberal education enjoyed by Janet and her maternal forebears. The school put Poggio to good use and exploited Lina and Aubrey's talents. At last some of the extra money was coming in.

While the school flourished, the political situation in Italy grew steadily more ominous. Lina who had worked for the *The Observer* for fourteen years found her anti-fascist position increasingly at odds with the views of her editor in London, James Garvin. It was only a matter of time before they agreed to part ways. In the last few years of the thirties, no longer working for the newspaper, she was free to concentrate on Poggio without worrying about outside work. The gardens were in good shape and she managed to keep the house running smoothly. Her own three children were now grown up and leading independent lives. Gordon was married and working as a journalist, Johnny was also recently married and had been teaching in Canada, and Kinta had married Jack Beevor a clever young lawyer. Despite the growing political unease, the last years before the war were productive and optimistic for the school.

In the end though, events got the upper hand. As committed critics of a regime heading to war, there was ultimately little choice for Aubrey and Lina but to leave Italy. It was a dreadful decision to make and they procrastinated until the eleventh hour. They closed the school in late 1939 and finally in June 1940, the day before Mussolini declared war on England, they decided to go. After arranging to give a power of attorney to Clementina Scarafia, and making hasty arrangements to pack their belongings, they said goodbye to friends and staff and set off, back to England. Clementina had agreed to live in the house in order to best protect it. They had no idea when they would be back or what might be in store for those they left behind or for the house itself.

Before long, it was decreed that all English property in and around Florence was to be handed over to the Florentine branch of the Sienese bank, Monte dei Paschi. The bank in turn nominated a custodian. At this point, towards the end of May 1941, Clementina received an immediate order to

A CASTLE IN TUSCANY

leave. She was offered a monthly pension on condition she took no further interest in the estate, an offer she flatly refused. Her principled stand would cost her dearly. She was quickly accused of taking a hostile attitude to the state and warned she would regret her decision.

One week later her husband Professor Scarafia was ordered to leave the couple's own house — where he had remained while his wife stayed at Poggio. He was given no explanation or justification, simply ordered out. For the next three years, the aged professor and his wife were in exile from Florence with practically no means of support. For the last three months of this period the Professor was imprisoned, first in a jail with common criminals and then in a concentration camp. After the intervention of an old friend he was finally released, a broken man of seventy.

The estate was let out for a peppercorn rent to a fascist senator. Acting against the agreed rules of his use of the house, he unlocked doors that had been sealed prior to his arrival and opened trunks full of Lina's possessions. Towards the end of the war when the Italian army collapsed and the Germans invaded Italy, Poggio was occupied at different times by troops. After the German troops came the Allied soldiers. Poggio had seen nothing like it since the days of Sir John Hawkwood and the White Company in the fourteenth century.

In mid-1944 Aubrey died, aged seventy, in London and Johnny, heir to Poggio, was killed by a bomb while on service in Malta.

At the end of the war, Kinta's husband, now Colonel Beevor, visited Florence and was able to write the grieving Lina a thorough account of what he found. In the fighting near the city, there had been a battle around Settignano that went on for two or three days. A machine gun had been set in position on the terrace above the green houses at Poggio. The house was still standing, although most of the windows were gone. It had been targeted by three shells, one through Lina's old bedroom, one on the top floor by the tower and one already patched up in a top floor wall. All the glass and much of the framework in the greenhouses were broken.

In all the confusion of the last weeks of war during the late summer of 1944, British troops had come through the villa and destroyed Aubrey's sketches and given furniture away. They found remnants of fascist material belonging to the senator and had assumed that the British owners of the house were fascist sympathizers. Most of the furniture, including Janet's writing desk had gone. Only some tables and chairs and bedsteads remained. The books in the library had not been taken but many letters and personal effects were missing. Worst of all was the damage to the farms. In the closing months of the war, they had been used as a carpark for heavy armoured vehicles and had been all but destroyed. While the farming families did what little they could, their vines were smashed and many trees knocked over.

In the midst of such vandalism the good news was that no one from Poggio had been lost, although just before the liberation of Florence Mary Berenson had died at I Tatti. Bernard, being Jewish, had gone into hiding, but Mary had been too unwell to leave with him. He later emerged unscathed to discover that in his absence, his house with the ailing wife inside, had been occupied by German troops.

EPILOGUE

When it was all over, Lina returned to Poggio to see for herself what she could retrieve, and received a warm welcome from the house staff and the farm workers. Before leaving England, she had accepted an offer from Kemsley Newspapers — publishers of *The Sunday Times* among other titles — to send them news from Italy. Back at Poggio and with the help of Clementina Scarafia, she was able to restore some order. Janet's writing desk miraculously turned up in Bologna and a small table once belonging to Kinglake was found. Old friends and neighbours like Bernard Berenson kindly lent or gave whatever was needed to make the place habitable. But it was an uphill battle.

The war and its aftermath placed unsustainable pressures on the *mezzadria* share-farming system that underpinned the farms at Poggio. The system had been under pressure for some time, the war just exacerbated this decline. Increasingly, young men from the country were drawn to the cities in search of better work prospects and a higher standard of living. Now labour had to be paid for with wages.

For a time Lina, now in her seventies, took some English visitors at Poggio as paying guests. After the war years, there were many in England happy to pay to come and stay. Usually they were friends, or friends of friends, and provided Lina with company in the evenings, leaving her free during the day to write. Clementina looked after the money side, and it barely occurred to Lina she was running a hotel. But it was tough going, all the more so given that Lina had been required to pay another round of death duties as a result of Johnny's death. Janet's dream of keeping Poggio intact was failing.

Ultimately, the impossible demands of upkeep at Poggio reached the point that Lina decided to sell. In 1950 she put the place on the market and sold it to an Italian industrialist. She was encouraged by what she understood was the buyer's guarantee to keep the farms and castle intact. The guarantee, however, proved worthless. Within no time, most of the land in front of the terrace was subdivided. The olive groves and vines that ran down the hill to the south gate were converted into small lots on which modern family villas sprang up.

Poggio Gherardo and the remaining garden was sold to a congregation of Antonian priests who established a shelter for needy children within the old rusticated walls. Many of the girls and boys who live in the castle today, are children of struggling migrants from the east and south who have come to Italy looking for a better life.

Alick Ross appears to have had no children of his own and the passage of his adult life is hazy. After the years spent in Russia he turned up in Austria. From 1920 he was a Captain in the British Delegation of the Inter-Allied Military Commission of Control, stationed first in Vienna, then moving to Budapest the following year. In Vienna, he shared a room for over a year with Pietro Gerbore, a native of Florence who went on to become an Italian diplomat. It is from Gerbore's account we can draw the faint picture we have of Alick's latter life.

The gates to Poggio Gherardo as they appear today.

Gerbore remembered Alick as a man approaching fifty, (although he would in fact have been closer to sixty years old), as an 'exquisite gentleman of the late Victorian type — humorous, suave and cultivated'. 'He was poor, but always well dressed, well shaved, humorous and gentle.' He liked pretty women and good wine and, according to Gerbore, he was a thrifty man. Alick talked openly of his Tuscan childhood and, with affection and devotion, of his mother. He talked about her life and the lives of Lucie and Sarah Austin. But he also spoke plainly about the dislike that his mother had taken to him as a child and the lack of family life he had experienced. Despite talking about his family he gave the impression he had been estranged from them for some time.

During his early years in Budapest, Alick was in correspondence with Joseph Dent on publishing-related matters. His letters sought assistance with such things as finding an English magazine to publish an article written by a young Slovenian woman or suggesting publication of an English translation of a book on Austria by a French historian. In one letter written in 1923, he sought Dent's help in his effort to become Hungarian correspondent for *The Times* newspaper. In a follow-up letter, Alick implies that in the meantime he has already been recommended for the job by *The Times* special correspondent in Vienna, and is optimistic. Whether the job ever transpired, we do not know. Throughout the correspondence, Dent is courteous and prompt, helping where he could. Although Dent was writing to Janet at the same time, there is no mention of her in letters between the two men. Nor did Dent refer to Alick in correspondence with Janet during this period.

Gerbore did not see Alick again until 1936. In the meantime Alick continued to serve in Eastern Europe. In July 1927 — as Janet was close to death — a letter written by Alick appeared in *The Daily Mail*. The letter argued against the harsh effects on Hungary of the 1920 Peace Treaty of Trianon. Its author, Alexander Gordon Ross, was described as the former General Secretary of the Delimitation Commission of the Czecho-Slovak-Hungarian Frontier.

The next time Gerbore saw Alick, he had long lost his claim to a share of Poggio. On discovering that he had effectively been cut out of the property, he borrowed money from friends to return to England to contest the will. What happened to the inheritance of 30,000 pounds that Lina claimed he received from Janet's marriage settlement is unclear. Gerbore remembers him returning to Budapest poor and defeated. By now he was living with a Hungarian family and engaged in a business arrangement with an Englishman, probably selling insurance.

Gerbore returned to Budapest again in 1942 but he could find no trace of his old friend. Alick had vanished, nobody knew where. Gerbore's best guess was that he had been interned as an enemy alien or had simply died.

Years later Pietro Gerbore, since retired from foreign service, was asked to write a review of Lina's autobiography, *A Castle in Italy*, published in 1961, and in the process wrote to her asking why she referred to her 'unworthy' cousin. In her reply she evaded the question. 'As far as I know', wrote

Gerbore, 'he had only two weaknesses; both in Vienna and in Budapest he never failed to find a lady friend very suitable to him. And every night he liked to empty a bottle of red wine'.

Alick and Janet, he concluded, 'were people from another world, a sort which you do not meet any more and which made Europe worthy [of] being lived in'. In Gerbore's mind mother and son were linked together by a common culture, although one which failed to emotionally bind them in their own lifetimes.

Janet's fractured relationship with Alick was the great unresolved tangle of her life. All the more so for a woman who set much store by family and loyalty. Janet's legacy remained with the many who had known her great capacity for friendship and her success on the farms. Later generations enjoyed her intelligence and ability as a writer and her little book of Italian vegetable cookery has stood the test of time. Through changing fades and fashions, it continues to bring a 'thought of Italy' into the modern kitchen.

Today, Poggio Gherardo is barely recognizable. If you take the number 10 bus from Florence to Settignano and get out at Ponte a Mensola, you can look up the hill and still see the imposing square form of the castle. But the shape is all that is left of the castle that Janet so loved. The walls have been rendered and washed a yellow colour and all the windows have been replaced with shiny metal frames. Off the main road, the smaller Via Poggio Gherardo leads up the hill past the north gate. On the left of the gate is a little tablet fixed into the pillar inscribed, Villa Ross. This is all that remains of Janet's civilized and ordered world.

Giuseppe in the kitchen at Poggio Gherardo. This was
the frontspiece for the early editions of
Leaves from Our Tuscan Kitchen.

Food from the Kitchen at Poggio Gherardo

Giuseppe Volpi and his successor, Agostino, prepared wonderful food in the kitchen at Poggio Gherardo over many years. Between them, they spent more than sixty years carefully applying their methods to create dishes for Janet's family and friends.

They used the best seasonal produce, always fresh and, wherever possible, grown or raised at Poggio in the garden or on the farms. Their techniques were often age-old, yet both men possessed a versatility and lightness that set them apart. Many of their dishes can be easily reproduced today using the same simple approach and techniques.

There are no smart fandangle gadgets or obscure ingredients. The flavourings appear and reappear like familiar notes; parsley, parmesan cheese, nutmeg, good fresh stock, olive oil and lemon juice, although the balance may vary from dish to dish according to the requirements of the main ingredient.

I have included here some recipes from the first edition of *Leaves from Our Tuscan Kitchen* as well as including a small number of other dishes that made an appearance in Janet's dinning room. As much as any others, these few recipes give a sense of Janet's taste and ideas about food. The meals at Poggio were carefully prepared and unpretentious.

In most cases I have adapted the recipes adding standard metric and simplified the instructions. This makes them useful while retaining the intention of the original. The few recipes I have included appeal to me because of their uncomplicated attention to flavour and their use of ingredients that are sometimes undervalued. Their simplicity makes them suitable for every kitchen and you will find yourself using them over and over again.

The vegetable recipes are arranged alphabetically, followed by a few of Giuseppe's pasta and rice dishes. Lastly, I have included some recipes for dishes eaten at Poggio but not included in Janet's cookbook.

ARTICHOKES

The globe artichoke is an under-utilized vegetable, yet it is quite delicious, versatile and easy to deal with. A dish of perfectly fried tender baby artichokes served with wedges of lemon is a great Tuscan favourite, for nobody fries with the lightness of touch of the Tuscan cook. Similarly, whole artichokes, stuffed and braised make a wonderful first course. Alternatively, they can make a lovely light meal, served alone accompanied simply by fresh bread and a green leaf salad. Giuseppe had any number of ways of making a wonderful dish of artichokes.

There are several varieties of this lovely winter vegetable. Some are large and quite dense, best suited to braising and stuffing, others are small and cone-shaped and ideal for pickling, frying and grilling. They range in colour from a dusty darkish green to deep purple. At Poggio Gherardo, artichokes were grown in the usual Italian way in the spaces between olive trees and vines. In the hills around Fiesole and Settignano, they are still grown this way today. Whichever artichoke you choose, make sure it is firm.

To clean them, take off the tough outside leaves, leaving the heart and surrounding tender leaves. Cut the stalk down to about 1 cm (½ in) and take off the top third of the globe. You should be left with a cup-shaped artichoke. As you finish each one, put it in a bowl of water to which you have added the juice of a lemon or a dash of vinegar. This is simply to stop them discolouring while you clean the rest. This is the method of preparing artichokes for any dish.

Artichokes 'Fritti'

The best results come with using small artichokes that are well-trimmed. There may appear to be a lot of wastage with this vegetable because so many tough outer leaves must be discarded. However, what is left has a fine nutty taste. The artichokes can be dipped in batter and fried or rolled in breadcrumbs and fried. Both are excellent, although I think the domestic cook achieves the most consistent results using breadcrumbs. Whatever you decide, they must be eaten immediately they are cooked, piping hot, dusted with a little salt and served with lemon. They can also be served with other fried vegetables such as fennel.

Agostino served both accompanied by a fragrant pesto. This sauce has been vastly over-exploited in recent years and commercial versions never live up to the beauty of the original sauce. Reduced to its basic ingredients, the crushed, fresh picked basil produces a wonderful flavour and smell to the dish.

6 tender small/smallish globe artichokes, 1 egg – beaten in a bowl, 100 g (3½ oz) fine dry breadcrumbs, olive oil – for frying, salt, lemon – to serve.

Quarter the artichokes if they are small. If they are larger they can be sliced. Now blanch them by dropping them in a pot of boiling, lightly-salted water. As soon as the water returns to the boil, tip them out into a colander and allow to cool. Dip the quarters or slices in the beaten egg and then roll in the breadcrumbs. The artichokes can be prepared to this point, a few hours ahead. Just before you are ready to eat, heat plenty of oil in a frying pan until it is just about to smoke, add the artichokes and cook on all sides until golden and crunchy. Drain quickly on absorbent paper and serve immediately scattered with salt and lemon wedges.

Artichokes 'alla Barigoul'
Braised artichokes stuffed with mushrooms and herbs

This is one of Giuseppe's recipes for artichokes served at Poggio as an entrée or a light main course. Cooked this way they are ideal served with a fresh green salad and some good bread.

6 large globe artichokes, 1 medium sized onion – finely diced, 2 tablespoons butter, 200 g (7 oz) mushrooms – very finely diced, 2 tablespoons finely chopped parsley, 1 tablespoon finely chopped fresh chervil, salt and fresh pepper, 6 small whole mushrooms (optional), another onion – sliced, 1 carrot – sliced, 250 ml (9 fl oz) white wine, 500 ml (17 fl oz) chicken stock, 2 tablespoons breadcrumbs.

After cutting the stems off the artichokes and removing any scrappy outer leaves, place them in a heavy pot or ironware casserole. Ideally they should be a snug fit in the pot otherwise they will float around. Pour on enough water to barely cover them, bring to the boil and cook for three minutes.

Remove them from the water and drain well. With a sharp knife, cut off the tips down to about two-thirds of the artichoke and pare the bottoms so they are free of any outer rough fibrous leaves too. Now gently open the mouth of each artichoke wide enough to allow you to remove the choke from the base of the interior. Giving the choke a slight twist can do this.

In a frying pan over moderate heat, cook the diced onion with the butter until soft but not brown. Then add the mushrooms, parsley, chervil, breadcrumbs and salt and pepper to taste and cook for a further five–ten minutes.

Spoon the mushroom and onion into the cavity of each artichoke and, if you wish, place a whole mushroom on the top of each one. Take a heavy-bottomed dish, again, just large enough to allow the artichokes to hold each other upright during cooking. Into the dish put the sliced onion and carrot and then the filled artichokes. Next put the wine and stock into the dish with the stuffed artichokes, cover and place in a 190°C (375°F/Gas 5) oven for one hour.

Serve warm with some of the juice spooned over and some finely chopped parsley.

Artichokes 'alla Graticola'

Artichokes on the gridiron

This is a very simple but delicious way to cook artichokes. This recipe relies on the quality and tenderness of the young artichokes as well as good quality salt and freshly ground pepper. The kitchen at Poggio had an open fire and grid and these were easily prepared. These artichokes are especially good with grilled meat which might be cooked alongside them. Because they are so simple they make a wonderful vegetable to cook at any picnic with an open fire.

12 small tender artichokes, olive oil, lemon juice, salt and pepper.

Wash the artichokes and remove the stalks, the hard outside leaves and the points of the leaves. Next cut them in half and place them cut-side down on a hot, lightly oiled gridiron. Cook for about three minutes, then turn and cook for another three minutes until tender. Make sure that any flame is low so that the little artichokes do not burn.

Remove from heat and drizzle with good olive oil, lemon juice and salt and pepper. Serve immediately.

BEETROOT
The magnificent colour of the beetroot is reason enough to enjoy cooking with it. Moreover, when it is young, it is sweet and tender and very good eating. Giuseppe used the whole plant in a number of ways. He cooked the bulbs *alla Parmigiana* — baked with parmesan cheese or cooked slowly with fresh cream. Here is a recipe he cooked to make use of the tasty little stalks or mid-ribs of the beetroot leaf. Italians are also fond of cooking the leaves with a little oil and garlic.

Beet 'Gnocchi'

These lovely light gnocchi use ricotta cheese rather than potato as the central binding agent. The resulting little sausage-shaped mounds are delicate and require a light touch, but they are worth every effort. When you next buy or harvest a bunch of beetroot, don't waste the stalks.

1 tablespoon butter, 200 g (7 oz/1 cup) young beetroot stalks, 120 g (4¼ oz) freshly grated parmesan cheese, 150 g (5½ oz) ricotta cheese, 3 or 4 eggs, pinch grated nutmeg, salt and pepper, some plain flour for spreading on the work bench, extra grated parmesan cheese, extra butter.

Warm the oven to 70°C (150°F/Gas ¼). Put a knob of butter in an ovenproof dish and put in the oven to keep warm.

Wash the stalks and blanch them in boiling water. Drain and refresh with cold water. Then dice them very finely with a sharp knife.

Next mix the diced stalks with the parmesan and ricotta cheeses, three of the eggs, nutmeg, salt and pepper. It is safer to use fewer eggs at this stage. Depending on the size of the eggs the mixture can get too soft and the gnocchi will not hold together. Combine everything thoroughly until it makes a fairly dense paste. If it is too dry, add the extra egg and combine again.

Put the mixture on a well-floured table or bench and shape into a long sausage roll about the width of your thumb. Then cut into lengths about 2 cm (¾ in) long.

Have ready a pot of just boiling salted water on the stove and very gently put in a few of the gnocchi at a time, only as many as will allow for a single layer to cook and rise to the surface. Once they come to the top, just as carefully take then out with a little flat sieve scoop or a slotted spoon. Put the gnocchi in the pre-warmed serving dish and return it to the oven while you repeat the exercise with the remaining uncooked gnocchi. When they are all cooked, sprinkle with a generous amount of grated parmesan and small knobs of butter. Serve immediately.

FRENCH BEANS Small tender beans have a wonderful flavour and make

a welcome addition to any meal. Beans are easy to deal with, and with a minimum of effort and some regard to freshness, wonderful results are achieved. At Poggio Gherardo, delicate beans were grown in the *orto* or kitchen garden and picked when young and tender. Sometimes they were simply served with butter and maybe a little lemon juice, salt and pepper. Other times they were dressed in a slightly more complex sauce. Either way the flavour of the beans predominates.

It is important not to overcook beans. Blanching the beans for a few seconds in boiling water, then placing them under cold running water to stop the cooking is a useful way to avoid overcooking. They can then be combined with other ingredients and will require very little additional cooking.

French beans 'alla Crema'

400 g (14 oz) beans – trimmed, 1 tablespoon butter, 200 ml (7 fl oz) cream, 50 g (1¾ oz) grated parmesan cheese, 1 egg yolk, pinch allspice, juice of ½ a lemon, salt and pepper.

Blanch the beans in boiling salted water until just tender. Put them in a frying pan with the butter and cook until just shiny, a couple of minutes on moderate heat. Remove the beans to a warm serving dish. Next, make a sauce by combining the cream, parmesan cheese, egg yolk and allspice into a little sauce and just bring to the boil. Remove from the heat and add the lemon juice, salt and pepper and pour over the beans. Serve hot.

BROAD BEANS Broad (fava) beans are a wonderful late-winter vegetable and are very good braised or sautéed with a little olive oil, herbs, garlic and lemon juice. Before the use of olive oil became so widespread in Italian cooking in the later-nineteenth and early-twentieth century, a simple dish of broad beans flavoured with garlic would have been made using pork fat rather than olive oil as it is today.

It is preferable to use small sweet beans if possible. Older, larger beans tend to be dry and have tough skins that should be removed. In Tuscany, it is common to serve new season young beans in their skins with a small bowl of sea salt for dipping. Such young beans are also excellent in another Tuscan favourite, *pinzimonio*, a dish of the most tender, raw, young vegetables arranged around a bowl of new season olive oil. Broad beans, slices of tender fennel bulb, sweet stalks of celery and other early-spring vegetables are dressed only with the fragrant new oil and some salt and pepper.

Broad beans 'al Burro'
Broad beans cooked with ham and butter

1 thick slice double smoked ham, 1 stick celery, 3 garlic cloves, 4 peppercorns, 1 small bunch parsley, 1 bay leaf, salt and pepper, 500 g (1 lb 2 oz) young broad beans shelled, 2½ tablespoons butter.

Put all the ingredients except the beans and butter in a heavy-based saucepan and add about 750 ml (26 fl oz/3 cups) of water. Bring the water and ingredients to the boil and allow it to continue boiling for 10 minutes. Now add the beans and cook until just tender — this will be a mater of a few minutes. Drain the beans and discard all seasonings except the ham. Cut the ham into small dice and return to the saucepan with the beans and the butter. Let the butter melt and combine with the beans and serve.

Broad Beans 'alla Romana'

500 g (1 lb 2 oz) young broad beans – shelled, 2 tablespoons olive oil, 3 garlic cloves – finely sliced, 4 sage leaves, 400 g (14 oz) tomato passata (puréed tomatoes) or diced tomato, salt and pepper.

Have ready a large saucepan of boiling water. Put in the beans and as soon as the water returns to the boil, drain the beans and refresh them under cold running water. Put the oil, garlic and sage leaves together in a saucepan and cook gently until the garlic is just soft, then add the drained broad beans and coat them in the flavoured oil. Finally add the tomato, salt and pepper. Bring back to the boil and serve.

Capsicums 'al Forno'
Baked capsicums

For four people you will need: 2 large capsicums (peppers) of any colour, although the red and yellow ones are sweeter, 150 g (5½ oz) fresh breadcrumbs, 150 g (5½ oz) combined minced (ground) veal and pork, 1 garlic clove – finely chopped, 1 small handful parsley – chopped, salt and pepper, olive oil, juice of 1 lemon, 150 ml (5 fl oz) good stock (optional).

Cut the capsicums in half lengthways and remove any seeds and filaments and parboil in salted boiling water for 3 minutes. Combine the breadcrumbs, minced meat, garlic, parsley, salt and pepper together and add enough olive oil and lemon juice to moisten and make the mixture shine. It should not be too wet. Put the capsicums in an ovenproof dish and loosely fill each half with the mixture. Add the stock or the equivalent amount of water to the dish and bake in a moderate oven at 190°C (375°F/Gas 5) for 30 minutes. Just before serving drizzle a little more olive oil over the capsicums.

FENNEL This delicately flavoured bulb is extremely versatile. It is lovely in a salad, shaved finely and dressed with olive oil, a little wine vinegar and salt and pepper. Eaten this way it is refreshingly crunchy. As it is a winter vegetable it is well suited to being braised or roasted, puréed or fried.

Fried fennel

A dish of fried fennel makes a good accompaniment to fried artichokes. The delicate flavour of these vegetables seems to be captured and enhanced inside the crunchy crust. The two vegetables can be mixed together in the same dish too. They are both available at the same time of year, which makes them perfect partners. Although it was eaten at Poggio, Janet did not include a recipe for fennel in the first edition of *Leaves from Our Tuscan Kitchen* because she thought the vegetable was not readily available to the English cook.

FOOD FROM THE KITCHEN AT POGGIO GHERARDO

If you are to serve this as a dish by itself the following quantities are appropriate. Use half amounts if you intend making a dish of mixed fried fennel and artichokes. 3 medium fennel bulbs, 2 eggs beaten in a bowl, 150 g (5½ oz) fine, dry breadcrumbs, olive oil – for frying, salt, juice of 1 lemon.

Trim the fennel bulbs by cutting off any tops and removing any discoloured or damaged outer layers. Slice the bulbs into 5 mm (¼ in) thick slices from the top of the bulb towards the base or core.

Bring a saucepan of salted water to the boil and drop the slices in, first the ones with the most core, as these are a little tougher than the others. When the water has returned to the boil, cook for a further 1–2 minutes. The fennel should be tender but certainly not mushy. Allow to cool. Dip the slices into the beaten egg and then into the breadcrumbs. Heat plenty of olive oil in a frying pan and when it is just about to smoke, add the slices of fennel and cook on both sides until golden. Place on absorbent paper briefly and then serve immediately with salt and lemon juice.

LENTILS
Lentils are not only delicious but also very nutritious. While Mrs Beeton viewed them as little more than birdseed, Italians appreciated their flavour and texture. Lentils can make a welcome alternative to the potato as an accompaniment to other dishes. To my mind, the best variety is the Puy lentil from France and now grown in other countries too and readily available in good grocers, however, the larger varieties will also give good results. A common cooking method is to simply boil lentils, which is a great pity because this method fails to take advantage of the way this wonderful pulse absorbs flavour. Giuseppe had a number of flavoursome ways for preparing the earthy lentil.

Lentils 'in Istufato'
Braised lentils

The anchovies in this recipe may suggest too robust a flavour for those who do not like the salty fish, but in fact the result is really delicate and makes an excellent accompaniment to a young roast chicken or spatchcock. With the addition of a simple salad there would be no need for other vegetables. The finely chopped onion, celery, carrot, garlic and rosemary make the classic *battutto*, used in so much Italian cooking as the basis for flavouring.

Olive oil, 1 medium onion – finely chopped, 1 carrot – finely chopped, 1 tablespoon finely chopped celery, 1 garlic clove – finely chopped, 2 anchovies – finely chopped, 500 g (1 lb 2 oz) Puy lentils – washed (if not available you can use the common greeen or brown lentil), 1 small sprig fresh rosemary – finely chopped, salt and pepper, 500 ml (17 fl oz/2 cups) good veal stock.

Warm the oil in a frying pan and add the onion, carrot, celery and garlic and cook gently for about 7 minutes, or until they become fragrant and soft. Add the anchovies and cook until they disintegrate. Next add the lentils, rosemary, salt and pepper and the stock. Cover the pan and cook on medium heat for 20–30 minutes. Check from time to time that the lentils are not cooking too fast or becoming dry. If so, add a little more stock — the lentils should be soft but firm. They should not loose their shape and become mushy. Serve hot. This dish can be prepared a little ahead of time and gently warmed through at the last minute.

Peas 'all Antica'
Old-fashioned peas

1kg (2 lb 4 oz) fresh, shelled peas, 1 trimmed lettuce, 2½ tablespoons butter, salt, 1 tablespoon sugar, 3 tablespoons cream mixed with 1 egg yolk, pepper.

Put the peas, lettuce, butter and a pinch of salt into a saucepan with enough water to half cover the peas. Cover and simmer for 15 minutes. Remove the lettuce and add the sugar and stir, then add the cream and egg yolk. Cook for a further 5 minutes, season with pepper and serve. This is enough for four.

SOUPS
Many of the recipes for soups devised by Giuseppe were puréed or put through a sieve, making them smooth and subtle. This is in contrast to some of the hearty rustic soups that are popular in Tuscany. I have included three, each one quite delicious.

Chestnut Soup

The chestnut is not, strictly speaking, a vegetable, but it is remarkably versatile, finding a place in both savoury and sweet dishes. It has long been associated with peasant food and before the introduction of the potato, was widely used as a farinaceous staple. In Tuscany chestnut cake or *castagnaccio* — a humble flat cake made of chestnut flour and flavoured with rosemary and pine nuts — is widely available in late autumn and early winter when chestnuts come into season.

1kg (2 lb 4 oz) chestnuts – to yield 500 g (1 lb 2 oz) peeled chestnuts, 2½ tablespoons butter, 125 ml (4 fl oz) white wine, 1 litre (35 fl oz/4 cups) good chicken or game stock, 1 garlic clove – finely chopped, 100 ml (3½ fl oz) cream, salt and pepper.

Score the chestnuts across the rounded side of the shell. This will help the shell and inside skin to come off more easily when they are cooked. Then either boil them in water for 15–20 minutes or roast them in a 120°C (235°F/Gas ½) oven for 15–20 minutes. Allow them to cool just a little — in their water, if boiled — and begin to peel them, getting off both layers. This is quite straightforward but requires a little patience. It does not matter if some chestnuts crumble a bit as they are soon to be puréed.

In a saucepan, moisten the chestnuts with the butter, wine and a little stock. When they have absorbed most of the liquid, add the garlic and cook gently for 5 minutes more. Now add the remaining stock and simmer for 30 minutes. Allow to cool a little, then purée or pass through a coarse sieve, pressing any leftover chestnuts through with pressure from the back of a spoon. Put back in the saucepan, add the cream and salt and pepper and simmer for a further 15–20 minutes. If the soup is a little too thin, continue to cook to allow more evaporation. Giuseppe liked to serve this and many other soups with croutons or sippets — small pieces of fried bread. Although these are somewhat out of fashion nowadays, when freshly fired in good oil, they are delicious.

Palestine Soup

Jerusalem artichokes are knobbly little tubers that often require a few minutes to peel. The skin is not thick and comes off easily with a potato peeler. Alternatively, the skin can be scrubbed off with a clean scourer. Once this is done, everything else is straightforward.

500 g (1 lb 4 oz) Jerusalem artichokes – skinned and roughly chopped, 1 onion – chopped, 1 garlic clove, 1 stick celery, 100 g (3½ oz) butter, 60 g (2¼ oz) ham – chopped, 1 litre (35 fl oz/4 cups) chicken stock, 250 ml (9 fl oz) milk.

Put the Jerusalem artichokes, onion, garlic and celery in a saucepan with half of the butter. Cover and stew over a low heat for 10 minutes or until the vegetables are well sweated. Next add the ham and then the stock and simmer uncovered for about 30 minutes, or until all the vegetables are soft. Allow to cool a little then purée or pass through a coarse sieve, making sure that the soft vegetables are pushed through using the back of a spoon. Return to the stove and add the milk and season. As with many of his soups, Giuseppe suggested serving this with croutons or sippets. This soup is equally well served with a sprinkling of finely chopped chives.

Sorrel Soup

This is another lovely soup with a distinct green colour and a lemon flavour.

2 bunches sorrel – washed and dried, 3 tablespoons butter, 1 tablespoon flour, 300 ml (10½ fl oz) chicken stock, 200 ml (7 fl oz) cream mixed with 2 whisked egg yolks, salt and pepper.

Chop the sorrel finely and cook it with the butter until it becomes a pulp. Sprinkle the flour over and stir in thoroughly. Now add the stock and bring to the boil. Lower the heat and add the cream and egg yolks. Season and serve. Once again, Giuseppe would serve this with croutons or sippets, though a sprinkling of chives does very well too.

SPINACH
Spinach is now widely available all year round and is justifiably popular for its lovely fresh taste and versatility. In Italy it is often simply wilted and dressed with good fresh oil and a little seasoning. Otherwise, it might be cooked with a little oil and some finely chopped garlic or alternatively sweetened with the addition of sultanas and pine nuts. It is also extremely good mixed with puréed haricot beans or mashed potato to make little fried croquettes, or in the Italian equivalent of the soufflé, the *sformato*. Of course, it also makes a delicious filling for ravioli when mixed with very fresh ricotta cheese.

Spinach Soup 'alla Modenese'

This is a warming soup that is light and refreshing. It is similar to the well-known *stracciatell*, soup made with beaten eggs and cheese poured onto boiling broth. For the best results, a well-flavoured chicken or veal stock will make all the difference.

1 bunch spinach – washed, 2 eggs, handful grated parmesan cheese, 100 g (3½ oz) butter, pinch grated nutmeg, salt and pepper, 1.5 litres (52 fl oz/6 cups) well-flavoured stock.

Boil the spinach for a few minutes until soft and when cool, chop it as finely as possible. Next, beat the eggs and mix into the spinach along with the cheese, butter, nutmeg, salt and pepper. Just before serving, bring the broth to the boil, reduce the heat to a simmer and pour in the spinach mixture. The egg will cook very quickly and you need to stir a little so that the mixture breaks up evenly in the broth. Serve at once. Giuseppe recommended it be served with croutons but it is very good with a little more cheese on top too.

TRUFFLES
Truffles remain a rare treat, but it is worth including this simple dish for eggs with shaved black truffles, for its simplicity and wonderful perfumed flavour. Giuseppe and Janet suggested a number of ways to enjoy truffles, some of which remain curiosities of their time. One such

is a recipe for truffles cooked in Champagne and stock to be served in a folded napkin. Another calls for twenty-four truffles to be cooked with cream, a wonderful delicacy to share with friends, but with the current cost of truffles, way beyond the scope of most households today. More accessible is the lovely truffle omelette that makes a wonderful light meal.

Omelette with black truffles

This is enough for two omelettes: 4 big fresh eggs, small pinch nutmeg, salt and pepper, 1 tablespoon butter, dash olive oil – for frying, 50 g (1¾ oz) fresh black truffle – shaved.

Beat the eggs well and season with nutmeg, salt and pepper. Put an omelette pan on the stove and when it is hot, add the butter and a tiny drizzle of olive oil. When the bottom of the pan is well-coated with melted butter, add half the egg. Let it settle for a moment then pull in the edges and allow some of the runny centre to flow to the outside of the pan. Now strew half the shaved truffle over the top of the omelette and fold the top over and tip onto a warm plate. Repeat for the second omelette. Alternatively, you can make one 4-egg omelette and cut it in half before serving immediately. This is a wonderful breakfast or a light lunch followed with a fresh salad and good bread.

Maccheroni 'al Forno'
Baked macaroni

Leaves from Our Tuscan Kitchen includes a number of macaroni and other pasta dishes. Macaroni *alla Siciliana* was an elaborate mould made of alternate layers of forcemeat – ham, veal, hard-boiled eggs, herbs, cooked macaroni and parmesan cheese. This would have made a grand start to any meal.

I have included this more straightforward recipe for baked macaroni, because it is quite unusually cooked in veal stock. It is a simple but rewarding dish to serve on a cold day. This will serve six people. At Poggio this would be served as a first course.

500 g (1 lb 2 oz) macaroni, 2 tablespoons butter, Gruyere cheese – grated, salt and pepper, 1 litre (35 fl oz/4 cups) good veal stock, 400 g (14 oz) some dry breadcrumbs to scatter on top.

Cook the macaroni in the stock until *al dente*. Take an ovenproof earthenware dish and grease with a little of the butter. Put a layer of the drained macaroni in the dish and sprinkle with a layer of cheese and salt and pepper. Repeat the process until the dish is full, finishing with a good layer of cheese.

Add a little of the cooking stock to the macaroni, just enough to keep it moist. Lastly sprinkle the top with breadcrumbs and dot with the remaining butter.

Bake in a 200°C (400°F/Gas 6) oven for 20 minutes. The top should be brown and the juices from the broth absorbed by the macaroni.

Maccheroni 'alla Quaresima'
Macaroni for Lent

This is extremely easy and always good.

500 g (1 lb 2 oz) macaroni, 6 anchovies – finely chopped, 3 garlic cloves – finely chopped, good handful parsley – finely chopped, 2 tablespoons olive oil, 250 ml (9 fl oz) white wine, 250 ml (9 fl oz) fish stock (optional), black pepper, parmesan cheese – grated.

Cook the macaroni in boiling salted water until *al dente*. While it is cooking, in a frying pan, gently cook the anchovies, garlic and parsley in some olive oil. The anchovies should almost disintegrate. When the macaroni is cooked, drain and add the anchovies, parsley and garlic, together with the wine and fish stock and pepper. If not using fish stock you may substitute a little water or add a little extra wine. Heat thoroughly on the stove and serve immediately with parmesan cheese.

Onions ' Farcite'
Stuffed onions

4 large onions, 1 slice bread without crusts, a little milk for soaking the bread, 150 g (5½ oz) finely diced ham, 2 tablespoons chopped parsley, 2 tablespoons grated parmesan cheese, salt and pepper, 2 tablespoons breadcrumbs, butter to grease the dish with.

Skin the onions and parboil them in a saucepan of salted boiling water for a few minutes. Remove from heat and carefully take the onions out of the water and allow to cool a little. In the meantime, soak the bread in the milk. When it is saturated squeeze it out.

Carefully cut the onions in half across the middle, and with each half, scoop out the centre and chop finely. Add the chopped onion to the ham, parsley, bread, and parmesan cheese, salt and pepper. Combine thoroughly and fill each onion half with the mixture. Sprinkle with breadcrumbs and put in an ovenproof dish greased with plenty of butter. Pour a little water into the dish; just enough to give some moisture and to prevent the onions from burning. Cook in the oven at 180°C (350°F/Gas 4) for about 30 minutes.

Tomato Jelly Salad

This is in fact a wonderful little jelly with an intense tomato flavour. As an entrée on a hot summer day or evening, it is perfect. I have eaten a version of this at the celebrated Cibreo restaurant in Florence. There it was unadorned except for a drizzle of verdant olive oil and a sprinkle of little basil leaves. It can be accompanied by prawns or tuna mayonnaise or celery and mayonnaise as Giuseppe suggested. My preference is to leave the jelly unencumbered.

Giuseppe set the jelly with calves' feet, but powdered gelatin can simply be used today. More importantly, the success of the jelly is dependent entirely on the flavour of the tomatoes used. It can be made in a single jelly mould or ring, or in individual moulds.

A little nut oil or olive oil to smear the inside of the moulds, 3 teaspoons gelatine powder, 500 g (1 lb 2 oz) flavoursome, ripe tomatoes – peeled, seeded and diced, 1 onion – finely chopped, 1 tablespoon red wine vinegar, ½ teaspoon fresh thyme, 1 bay leaf, 2 cloves, 1 teaspoon sugar, salt and pepper, olive oil for drizzling on top, a small handful basil leaves for scattering.

Depending on the size of your mould this amount will be enough for 4–6 people. Slightly smear oil on the inside of the mould/s and put to one side. Dissolve the gelatine powder in three tablespoons of boiling water.

In a saucepan, bring to the boil the tomatoes, onion, vinegar, thyme, bay leaf, cloves and sugar. Continue cooking until the tomatoes are soft. Remove from the heat and discard the bay leaf then pass through a coarse sieve. Extract all the juice by pushing the tomato through the sieve with the back of a spoon. Adjust the seasoning with salt and pepper. Now add to the tomato juice, the dissolved gelatine powder. Stir well until the gelatine is thoroughly dissolved.

Pour the tomato juice into the mould/s and chill until set. Just before serving, turn the jelly out. Drizzle with a little olive oil — a fresh intense green olive oil looks very good with the red colour of the jelly. Scatter with some small basil leaves and serve.

Risotto 'alla Poggio Gherardo'
Risotto with mushrooms and duck livers

This beautifully flavoured risotto was perfected by Giuseppe in the kitchen at Poggio using Marsala, rather than the usual dry white wine, in the early stages of cooking.

Duck livers are especially good for this because they are less prone to overcooking than chicken livers, but either is fine. Italian arborio rice is an important element in the dish because it has a great capacity to absorb flavour, which is what risotto is all about. It is readily available in speciality shops and supermarkets.

200 g (7 oz) mushrooms – finely diced (any type of mushroom is suitable although fresh porcini if you are lucky enough to have them or the flavoursome Portobello are particularly good. The mushrooms should be clean but not washed), 1 tablespoon olive oil, 2 medium onions – finely chopped, 2 tablespoons butter, 300 g (10½ oz) arborio rice, 100 ml (3½ fl oz) Marsala, 1 litre (35 fl oz/4 cups) well-flavoured warmed chicken stock, 200 g (7 oz) ducks livers – cleaned and finely chopped, 1 tablespoon freshly grated parmesan cheese and more to serve, salt and pepper, 1 teaspoon fresh thyme.

In a frying pan, cook the mushrooms with a little olive oil for 7–10 minutes, until they are quite reduced, then put to the side.

In a heavy-based saucepan over a gentle heat, sauté the onions in a little butter and olive oil until soft and translucent. Be careful not to burn them. Next add the rice and mix thoroughly. After a couple of minutes the rice should be well coated and shiny.

Turn up the heat and add the Marsala, allowing the liquid to reduce quickly. The rice will start to accumulate flavour. Next, add a ladle of stock and add the stock slowly, one ladle at a time, stirring all the while as the liquid is absorbed before adding the next ladle. Continue this process adding the stock ladle by ladle until there is only one ladleful left. The risotto should have swelled in volume and be almost creamy in consistency but with the individual grains still discernable.

Before adding the last ladle of stock add the chopped duck livers and stir for a couple of minutes, then add the cooked mushrooms. Continue to stir and add the final ladle of stock. The final stir should be for about 5–7 minutes. This will allow the chopped livers to just cook through.

Remove from the stove and add the remaining butter and the grated parmesan. Check for seasoning and stir again for a minute or two. The whole process should take about 30 minutes. At the last minute sprinkle a few fresh leaves of thyme on top.

Serve immediately with extra cheese. This will serve six people as a first course.

Monte Bianco
Pureed chestnut 'mountain'

This refined dessert is one that Kinta Beevor remembers fondly from her time at Poggio in *A Tuscan Childhood*. It was made by Giuseppe's successor, Agostino, who produced wonderful puddings and sweet dishes. It is certainly worth making the effort to peel the chestnuts for this. The flavour and texture of fresh chestnuts are far superior to any pre-prepared purée.

There are a number of recipes for this dish but the general intention is to create a mountain of light chestnut purée topped with cold whipped cream — the snow.

Some recipes call for dark chocolate and a little rum to be added to the chestnut purée, others keep the purée plain. Both methods are good.

450 g (1 lb) fresh chestnuts, milk – enough to cover the chestnuts in a saucepan, 175 g (6 oz) dark cooking chocolate – optional, 4 tablespoons rum – optional, 450 ml (16 fl oz) pouring (whipping) cream, 2 teaspoons castor sugar.

Score the chestnuts across the rounded side. This will make it easier for the shell and inside skin to come off when they are cooked. Then either cover with water and boil them for 15–20 minutes or roast them in a slow oven for 15–20 minutes. (I have read a recipe that adds a pinch of fennel seeds to the chestnuts as they boil in the water.) Allow the chestnuts to cool just a little — in their water if boiled — then begin to peel them, removing both layers of outer shell and inside skin. It does not matter if some crumble a little as they are soon to be puréed.

Now put the peeled chestnuts in a saucepan with enough milk to cover them and boil slowly for 25–40 minutes depending on how fresh the chestnuts are, until they are tender and all the milk has been absorbed. If you are going to add chocolate, melt it in a small bowl in a low oven while the chestnuts are cooking. The chestnuts are cooked when they are tender but have not disintegrated. Let them cool.

Next, put the chestnuts through a potato ricer, letting the mixture fall into a mixing bowl. Now add the melted chocolate and rum if you are using them, and put the mixture through the ricer again. This time let the chestnut mixture fall directly onto the serving dish. Continue this until you have used all the purée and have in front of you a 'mountain' shape. The shape does not have to be perfect and under no circumstances should you try to interfere with it using your hand or a fork. The whole idea is that the purée remains light and airy. Next, whip the cream and sugar together and then dollop 'the snow' on top of the 'mountain'. Serve with extra whipped cream for those who would like more. I have also read of crystallized violets scattered on the cream for decoration, which would certainly look very pretty.

Asparagus with coddled eggs and cream

Kinta Beevor also recalls Agostino serving various asparagus dishes including one with coddled eggs and cream. The eggs and delicate spears form a simple but rewarding combination. This dish is at its best when the eggs are really fresh, the asparagus recently cut and the herbs straight from the garden. This recipe requires glass or ceramic egg coddlers, which are available at good cookware shops.

3 tablespoons butter, 4 large eggs, salt and pepper, 1 tablespoon each of finely chopped parsley, chervil and tarragon, 16 spears asparagus, 2 tablespoons pouring (whipping) cream.

A CASTLE IN TUSCANY

First, brush the inside of coddlers with melted butter, and then into each one crack an egg. Add a little salt and pepper and screw on the lids. Place the coddlers in a wide-open saucepan filled with simmering water two-thirds up the sides of the coddlers. Let the water boil for 5 minutes, then remove from the heat and take the coddlers out of the water. In the meantime, get four serving plates ready and on each one place a little dish of the finely chopped herbs, mixed together. Now cook the asparagus in boiling water until just tender, drain, roll them in a little butter and divide equally between the four plates. Next unscrew the lids from the coddlers and add a little cream to the top of each soft-cooked egg. Place the coddlers on the serving plates alongside the asparagus and herbs and serve. The asparagus spears are dipped into the egg, then the herbs and eaten directly.

Roast Beef with Salsa Verde
Roast Beef with Green Sauce

When Janet and a party of friends and visitors went out to pick the vintage they were rewarded with lunch cooked by Giuseppe and brought out to the vineyard. On one occasion Janet described a steaming mushroom risotto, followed by a roast sirloin of beef cooked in the kitchen and delivered hot to the hungry grape pickers.

A beef fillet would do as well and would certainly be easier to prepare and eat for a picnic. Served at ambient temperature with a bowl of green sauce, some fresh bread and wine, this makes a grand lunch.

Every Tuscan house has a version of roast beef or *rosbiffe* — roast steer — as it is commonly called, often cooked on the stove with oil and garlic and other flavourings rather than in the oven. Both approaches give a good result.

For six people: 1.25 kg (2 lb 12 oz) beef fillet, salt and pepper, 1 good-sized sprig fresh rosemary, olive oil, 1 small handful fresh sage, 125 ml (4 fl oz) red wine.

Turn the oven to 200°C (400° F/Gas 6).

With a knife, make four little incisions in the fillet and in each one place a little salt and a sage leaf. Make the fillet into a nice looking even shape by folding the thin ends under and tying the length and breadth of the whole thing with string. This will give a good final shape.

Put an ovenproof dish on the stove and add a little oil and brown the fillet all over. Season and sit the fillet on the sprig of rosemary. Finally, add the wine. Put in the oven for 30–40 minutes depending on how well-cooked you would like it. Ovens vary considerably, but you can test the meat by placing a metal skewer deep into the middle, waiting 1 minute before pulling it out. Put the skewer on your lip. If it is warm your meat will be medium-rare. If it is hot, the meat will be well done. The colour of the juice that comes out of the meat is another good indicator. Red juice is rare, pink is medium and clear is well done. This fillet should be rare or medium-rare.

Take the meat out of the oven and let it rest somewhere warm. If it is to be eaten hot, let it rest for at least 15 minutes. If it is to be taken on a picnic it should be served at room temperature. For a picnic, it can be made the day before.

Green Sauce

There are many variations on this admirably versatile sauce. Some are quite piquant, others more subtle. In one form or another it is a very good accompaniment for roast beef as well as boiled meat and poached fish. This version relies on the addition of a little potato and hard-boiled egg yolk to give it a smooth delicacy.

These quantities will yield a bowl of sauce sufficient to serve 4–6 people.

1 small potato, 2 hard-boiled eggs, 1 good bunch parsley, 1 gherkin (pickle), 3 anchovies (if using salted anchovies, they should be rinsed, cleaned and their heads removed), 1 garlic clove – peeled, 200 ml (7 fl oz) olive oil, 2 tablespoons white wine vinegar, salt and pepper.

Boil the potato until it is tender, remove from the water, let it cool a little and peel. Put it in a bowl and mash together with the two egg yolks. Next, chop the parsley, gherkin, anchovies and garlic together on a good-sized chopping board. The mixture needs to be fine but retain some texture. A sharp knife or *mezzaluna* (a half-moon-shaped Italian chopping knife, held by two hands and moved in a rocking motion) will achieve the best result and only takes a few minutes.

Add the chopped parsley mixture to the potato and egg yolk. Now gradually add the oil until a thick-sauce consistency is achieved. Lastly, add the vinegar, salt and pepper. This will keep in the refrigerator for several days quite happily.

Nearby the farm workers were served a big dish of steaming white beans with *polpette*, little sausages of minced meat and rice.

White beans with meatballs

This dish of beans and meatballs prepared for the farm workers to eat at the harvest picnic is typical Tuscan workers fare. White beans — *fagioli all'uccelletto* — meaning 'beans like birds' accompanied by sausages or meatballs or even simply dressed and eaten alone are perennially popular, especially in the cooler months. Any workers' *trattoria* will have some version on the menu. Freshly cooked and well-flavoured, white beans evoke the rustic origins of Tuscan cooking. Giuseppe had a number of ways of cooking beans. At Poggio these beans would simply be left to simmer gently on the back of the stove, with Giuseppe passing an eye over them every now and then. This is a good thing to make on a cold winter day.

Either fresh shelled or dried beans can be used for this, though dried beans take longer to cook. Haricot beans are good but others can be used too. To make enough for 4 people you will need: 300 g (10½ oz) beans – soaked overnight and drained, sprig sage leaves, 1 tablespoon olive oil, 2 garlic cloves, olive oil for dressing, salt and pepper.

Simply put the beans in a pot big enough to take them and cover with water to about 2 cm (1 in) above the top of the beans. Add the sage, olive oil and garlic and turn up the heat. Once the water reaches boiling point, turn down to a gentle simmer and leave for about 2 hours for dried beans and about 40 minutes for fresh beans. Watch that the water does not evaporate too quickly. If this occurs, just add a little extra water. When the beans are cooked, the water and oil should be mostly absorbed. Remove the sage and garlic. Prepared this way they need only be dressed with some good fresh olive oil and a little salt and pepper. Served with meatballs they make a delicious and hearty meal.

Meatballs

There are many variations of meatballs in the Italian kitchen, but typically they would include some bread soaked in milk as a binding agent, in other words, they are not overly meaty.

For enough little meatballs for 4 people you will need: 400 g (14 oz) minced (ground) meat (veal or a mix of veal and pork), 2 thick slices bread soaked in milk, drained and squeezed, 1 egg yolk, handful chopped parsley, 2 tablespoons grated parmesan cheese, good pinch grated nutmeg, salt and pepper, some dry breadcrumbs for coating, oil for frying.

Mix all the ingredients together except for the dried breadcrumbs and olive oil. Once everything is well integrated, make into little balls. Roll in dried breadcrumbs and fry in the oil over a fairly high heat until golden all over. Watch the breadcrumbs do not catch and burn. If this starts to happen reduce the heat. These can be eaten hot or at room temperature sitting on top a of pile of beans.

End Notes

Introduction

'converted into another dress shop' Subsequently, after considerable public pressure, the proprietor of the dress shop decided to re-open a version of Cafe Giacosa right next door. The new Giacosa, though smaller in scale and somewhat flashier than its predecessor, is a welcome return to the street. The coffee is excellent and the pastries are very good.

Chapter One: Florence

'The eighteenth-century writer' Hester Piozzi published her recollections in 1789 as *Observations and Reflections made in the Course of a Journey Through France, Italy and Germany*.

'*Pictures from Italy*' The novel by Charles Dickens was first published in 1846.

Chapter Two: England

'precisely what Sarah Austin wished to avoid' The letters notwithstanding, today Herman von Pückler-Muskau is remembered less as a writer than as the creator of a beautiful garden at Muskau. The park is laid out on both sides of the River Neisse, which forms the modern Polish, German border, with two-thirds of it on the Polish side. In 2004 it was given a UNESCO world cultural heritage listing.

'*Shagpat* was deemed a great success' Tales of the Orient enthralled the Victorians, and the Duff Gordons were no exception. Lucie and Janet had read and loved *The Arabian Nights*. Lucie also became interested in first-hand accounts of life in the East.

Chapter Three: A Life of Her Own

'a heroine who deserved to be a heroine' Janet revelled in the role of literary muse, although she later realized she was probably more hindrance than help. 'With the magnificent impertinence of a sixteen year old I would interrupt Meredith, exclaiming; "No. I should never have said it like that" or 'I should have done so and so".'

'another possible cause was that an abortion had made her so sick' Katherine Frank in her biography of Lucie, *A Passage to Egypt, The Life of Lucie Duff Gordon*, makes this suggestion. It is entirely feasible.

Chapter Four: A Place to Live

'this amounted to about 600 pounds' The receipt for the purchase of *The School of Pan* refers to Italian lire 27,000 despite the offer being made in gold Napoleons. For significant purchases, Henry and Janet like other expatriates and wealthy Italians were able to use both pounds sterling and gold French Napoleons. The pound sterling had a good reputation. It was pegged to the gold standard and was widely accepted and the Rosses had ready access to money in pounds sterling.

French Napoleons were also widely accepted. Moreover, in 1865 — in what is considered by many as a forerunner to the Euro — France, Italy, Switzerland and Belgium established the Latin Monetary Union, making their currencies interchangeable. Greece joined in 1868 and other countries subsequently joined. The First World War saw differing rates of inflation in these countries and the union was dissolved.

'They also agreed to pay Tricca 10 per cent' Signor Tricca was keen to make a profit for himself; after all it was pretty clear that the Cardinal was more concerned to be rid of the offending painting than selling it for its real value. Tricca knew the painting had the potential to be resold for a much larger sum and he was ensuring he would receive his share for spotting the painting in the first place and bringing it to the Rosses' attention.

Chapter Five: Sketching the Landscape

'Sir James Lacaita' Born Giacomo, Sir James was the epitome of the Anglo-Italian. He was a moderate liberal in politics, imprisoned in 1851 in Naples for having supplied the English Government information on misrule under the Bourbon Monarchy in the Kingdom of Naples — an area including much of the lower part of the peninsula and Sicily. After intervention from the English and the Russians, Lacaita was released and went to live first in Edinburgh where he married Maria Carmichael. He later moved to London where he made friends in literary and political circles. In 1855 he became a naturalized British subject and for a few years was professor of Italian at Queen's College. Later he was private secretary to Lord Lansdowne for a period. When he returned to Italy in 1860 he was actively interested in a number of British companies operating in Italy. One of these was the Anglo-Italian Bank, an affiliate of the Florence Land and Public Works Company, the entity responsible for the remodelling of Florence when it was the capital.

'Marianne North' The daughter of a Liberal Member of Parliament, Marianne North was born in England. Her first passion was singing, but when she lost her voice she spent more time sketching, especially plants. Much of her adult life was spent travelling far and wide in search of exotic plants to paint. From 1871–85 she visited America, Canada, Jamaica, Brazil, Tenerife, Japan, Singapore, Sarawak, Java, Sri Lanka, India, Australia, New Zealand, South Africa, the Seychelles and Chile. Her energy and achievement always impressed Janet. Some of the plants she painted were new to science and one genus and four species were named after her.

Chapter Six: A Castle in the Country

'Fyvie Castle in Aberdeenshire' The oldest parts of the castle date back to the thirteenth century. The castle is reputed to have a curse, causing the death of the laird and blindness of his wife should he try and enter a secret chamber deep within. Janet came to visit once and, together with Lina, she discovered the door to the secret chamber and persuaded her brother to enter it. Janet was so attracted to the castle's myths and legends that she produced a small book on Fyvie.

Chapter Seven: Friends and Visitors

'Professor Daniel Willard Fiske' A neighbour of Janet's, Fiske lived at Villa Landor on the edge of Fiesole. The villa was previously known as Villa Gherardesca and was home to the English poet Walter Savage Landor, who lived in Florence for many years. Fiske was a highly educated man of letters who excelled in many fields. He was the first librarian of Cornell University, a bibliophile, great chess player and Egyptologist. Many American writers and scholars visiting Florence stayed with him and his wife.

'her cousins who were visiting from England' Sir William Markby served as a judge on the High Court of Calcutta from 1866–78. He went on to become the first Reader in Indian Law at Oxford in 1879. Janet was always fond of Sir William and his wife and they continued to visit Poggio until the end of their lives.

'Charles Dudley Warner' An essayist, travel writer and editor; many of Warner's pieces were carried in *The Atlantic Monthly* and *Harpers*. In 1873 he and Mark Twain collaborated on the novel that coined the phrase, 'The Gilded Age' — *The Gilded Age: A Tale of Today*. The novel is set at a time when many great family fortunes were being made in America's rush towards industrialization and is is critical of the lavish spending and often-questionable politics of the day.

'Charles Loeser' One of the first Americans to buy the paintings of Cezanne, several of which he left to American collections, Loeser left a significant collection of fourteenth to sixteenth century paintings and sculpture to the city of Florence in 1928. Today it is housed in the Palazzo Vecchio.

'Isabella Stewart Gardner' Amassing the bulk of her collection in a remarkably short period of time, Stewart Gardner became a serious collector of Dutch and Italian paintings in the 1890s. Beginning in 1894, Bernard Berenson, then a young art historian, started to recommend Italian paintings for acquisition. He was just as new at this as Mrs Gardner was, but within two years he had guided her towards a collection that included Botticelli's *Lucretia*, Titian's *Europa*, Vermeer's *The Concert* and a self-portrait by Rembrandt.

I Tatti The villa today is home to Harvard University's Centre for Renaissance Studies. The house, together with Berenson's magnificent library and unmatched photographic archive of Renaissance art, was left to the university after his death.

Chapter Eight: Leaves From Our Tuscan Kitchen

'Artusi's collection' The Italian title of this excellent book is *La Scienza in Cucina e l'Arte di Mangiar Bene*. Random House published an English translation by Kyle Phillips in 1996. Another English translation came out in 1997. Pellegrino was the original star of Italian food writing. As Kyle Phillips III says, before Marcella Hazan and Giuliano Bugialli, there was Pellegrino Artusi. His book is still selling in most bookshops in Italy and has had 111 printings. More recently Artusi has been criticized for undermining regional diversity because he deliberately chose to express a national view. Such criticism unfairly overlooks the fact that he was writing at a time of newfound national optimism.

'well-established traditions' Although written in Italian, *La Cucina Fiorentina par Louis Monod*, edited by Giuseppe La Russo and Mauro Pratesi has an illuminating introduction outlining the experience of the professional cook in Florence during this period. Giuseppe La Russo is a journalist and food writer based in Florence. He is an authority of the history of Tuscan food.

'zucchini (courgettes)' Extraordinary as it may now seem, the zucchini did not become commonly available in England until after the Second World War. Doyenne of English food writing Jane Grigson says that two recipes for zucchini appeared in the 1931 publication *What Shall We Have Today?* written by Marcel Bouleston. These are among the first in an English cookbook. But it was only after 1960 that Elizabeth David was able to say that 'enterprising growers are supplying us little courgettes as an alternative to gigantic vegetable marrows'.

Chapter Ten: After Henry

'Seeing his obvious talent' Today, a remnant of landscape design work by Fritz von Hochberg can be seen in the old Polish city of Wroclaw. Fritz and a Japanese gardener, Mankichi Arai, collaborated to create a Japanese garden for the World Exhibition of 1913. Today the garden has been restored and is open to visitors. In another quite separate tribute to his talent, a lovely, pink, fragrant tea rose hybrid was named in his honour.

'*We had a tremendous tea party*' Virginia Woolf wrote her description of Sunday afternoon at Poggio to Madge Vaughan (now married to Will Vaughan who later became Headmaster at Rugby School) on May 8, 1908. Virginia was thought to have had a crush on Madge, who was thirteen years her senior. There has also been speculation that Madge was the model for Sally Seton in *Mrs Dalloway*.

'Edward Hutton' Best known for his writing on Italian subjects, Hutton is the author of travel books covering nearly the whole of the peninsula and Sicily. He also wrote about Greece and Spain. Among his best-known travel books are: *The Cities of Umbria, Florence and Northern Tuscany, Siena and Southern Tuscany, Venice and Venetia, Rome, Naples and Southern Italy*. He also wrote a highly regarded biography of Boccaccio. In 1917 Edward Hutton was one of the founders, with Lina Waterfield, of the British Institute in Florence.

Chapter Eleven: Later Years

'The British Institute of Florence' This was founded in an attempt to improve the image of England and the English in Italy. During the war there had been stories circulating of aristocratic Italians planning welcome parties for the Germans when they won the war, as they surely would. Socialists took advantage of general ignorance and blamed the poor treatment of Italian solders at the front on the British. In some remote places it seemed there was even confusion as to which side Italy was fighting for.

'**ill-equipped to adapt to emerging realities**' To make matters worse, the government promised soldiers land on their return to civilian life, but no plan was ever prepared or perhaps even intended to realize the promise. In 1919–20 country workers in some parts of the country illegally occupied land out of frustration with the unfulfilled promises and the government seemed unable to contain a situation it had in part promoted. Some retrospective sanction of land occupation was given by the government, which only made landowners indignant.

'**growing influence and rough tactics**' Fascism initially had the look of a democratic movement. The fascist manifesto actually called for greater democratic rights and a limited number of socialist ideas. These were slowly abandoned over the following years, as it took on its recognizable, anti-democratic and anti-socialist shape.

'**Many years later Clark recorded his impressions**' What Kenneth Clark does not reveal in his memoir is that Janet Ross was the great-aunt of his friend Gordon Waterfield — Lina's eldest child — and that prior to his visit to Italy he had fallen in love with, and would ultimately marry, Gordon's fiancée, Jane Martin. Neither Janet nor Lina, nor indeed the Berensons would have known about this at the time of Kenneth's visit.

'**Francesco Carletti**' He initially set out from Seville in 1594 on a short slave-trading expedition that turned into an eight-year round-the-world tour. He detailed his experience in *Ragionamenti del mio Viaggio Intorno al Mondo*. He was one of the first Europeans to travel as a passenger all round the globe. He visited not only Mexico and Peru, but also exotic eastern regions on which few Europeans had set eyes—Japan, Macao, Malacca, and Goa.

Epilogue

'**Janet in fact left two wills**' Her English will was amended by two codicils added in 1921 and 1924 respectively. These did not affect the intent of the will. They were minor changes to the amounts of money left to individuals.

'**Lina returned to Poggio to see for herself what she could retrieve**' Kinta Beevor in *A Tuscan Childhood* gives a moving account of her mother's return to Poggio after the Second World War. The touching welcome of the farm workers and the support of the friends add poignancy to the distressing scene of war wreckage and vandalism.

'**It is from Gerbore's account**' In the 1970s Lina eldest son, Gordon Waterfield, a distinguished journalist and writer, worked on a manuscript of Janet's biography. In his research, he entered into correspondence with Pietro Gerbore, by then, a retired diplomat living in Florence. From this exchange of letters comes the last account of Alick Ross's life, fifty-seven years after he was last heard of.

4   '**The letter argued against the harsh effects**' Reference to Alick's letter appeared in a pamphlet written in 1939 by the British press baron Lord Rothermere, owner of *The Daily Mail*, *The Evening News* and until 1931, *The Daily Mirror*. Rothermere had developed a passionate interest in European politics, noticed the letter in one of his newspapers and agreed with its argument. The Treaty of Trianon was signed at Versailles a year after the Treaty of Versailles itself was agreed.

Further Reading

There are innumerable books on Florentine themes. Memoirs penned by enthusiastic travellers are as prolific as modern cookbooks on the subject of Tuscan food. Among so many, there are some books of Florentine history, the Anglo-Florentine experience and Italian cookery that deserve mention here. I have included titles relevant to Janet Ross's life and the Anglo-Florentine community. I have also added a few books useful to the interested visitor. Not all the books are in print but with modern search engines it is quite possible to track down and order out of print editions.

Harold Acton, *Memoirs of an Aesthete*, Methuen, London, 1948, and *More Memoirs of an Aesthete*, Methuen, London, 1970. Harold Acton was born in 1904 and therefore of a different generation to Janet and even Lina. He was born at Villa la Pietra, just north of Florence on the Via Bolognese. Acton was educated in England where he was a 'bright young thing' in the 1920s and was the inspiration for Anthony Blanche, the homosexual undergraduate character in Evelyn Waugh's novel *Brideshead Revisited*. During his long life he was a poet, novelist, historian, university lecturer, Royal Air Force officer, and philanthropist, but Acton's true vocation was that of an aesthete.

Harold Acton and Edward Chaney, *Florence, A Traveller's Companion*, Constable, London, 1986. This is a compendium of well-chosen extracts through the ages, including Giovanni Boccaccio on the Black Death, Giorgio Vasari — the sixteenth-century writer and painter on Giotto's tower, and the death of Elizabeth Barrett Browning at her house in Florence. There are also twentieth-century accounts by D.H. Lawrence and Dylan Thomas.

Kinta Beevor, *A Tuscan Childhood*, Viking, London, 1993. Kinta Beevor is the daughter of Lina Waterfield and her account complements her mother's earlier autobiography. She tells the story of her early life spent in Italy with her parents, both at the Fortezza at Aulla and with Lina and Janet at Poggio Gherardo during the First World War. She returned to Poggio in the late 1920s after Janet's death. This is a modern, sympathetic and beautifully described view of her Anglo-Italian experience. It continues the story past Lina's death to Kinta's much later return to Italy with her adult son. Kinta includes many well-known characters associated with Florence in the first half of the twentieth-century.

E.M. Foster, *A Room with View*, Edward Arnold, London, 1908, available in Penguin. This is a wonderful social comedy and always a pleasure for the visitor to read in situ. Lucie Honeychurch's Florence is immediately recognizable. This is Florence through the eyes of the English middle class and altogether less grand than Henry James. These are the visitors — clutching their guidebooks — that so irritated the permanent residents of Fiesole and the nearby hills.

Katherine Frank, *A Passage to Egypt*, Houghton, New York, 1994. The story of Janet's mother, Lucie Duff Gordon, her marriage and life in England and then the extraordinary years living in Egypt at Luxor on the upper reaches of the Nile. This is a sympathetic portrait of the achievements and tragic death of Lucie, a woman of integrity and intelligence.

Lotte and Joseph Hamburger, *Contemplating Adultery: The Secret Life of a Victorian Woman*, Macmillan, London, 1991. This study of the marriage of Sarah Austin provides a rare insight into the intimate life of a Victorian woman. The Hamburgers have managed to see beyond the formality and composure of Victorian mores, to reveal one woman's inner emotional workings. That she happens to be Janet Ross's grandmother is interesting enough, but her story is compelling because it brings the Victorian experience to life.

Olive Hamilton, *Paradise of Exiles; Tuscany and the British,* Andre Deutch, London, 1974. A guide to notable English visitors and those that stayed longer. It includes entries for English mercenary Sir John Hawkwood through to D.H. Lawrence and sculptor, Sir Henry Moore.

Christopher Hibbert, *Florence: The Biography of a City,* Viking, London, 1993. Hibbert is the author of many books of history and biography. In this book he has written the most accessible and comprehensive history on the city. As a general introduction, it has not been bettered.

By the same author is the excellent *The Rise and Fall of the House of Medici*, London, 1974 and now available in Penguin. This is essential reading to any visitor wanting to understand the fundamental place of this famous family in the life of the city.

Edward Hutton, *Country Walks about Florence,* 1908. Dedicated to Janet Ross, this guide to walks around Florence is as useful today as it was when it first came out. It is, however, long out of print, but if you happen to come across a copy, it will be a useful addition in planning outings from the city.

Henry James, *Portrait of a Lady*, Macmillan, London, 1881 and reprinted by Penguin, 2003. This classic portrait of American innocence abroad is regarded as the best of Henry James early books. Isabel Archer has many similarities to Isabella Stewart Gardner, the early patron of Bernard Berenson.

Francis King, *Florence, A Literary Companion,* John Murray, London, 1991. The book is divided into two parts, the first on literary visitors and the second on the places they lived. Samuel Rogers, Bryon and Shelley, the Brownings, Henry James, Mark Twain and many more make their appearance.

Ross King, *Brunelleschi's Dome, The Story of the Greta Cathedral in Florence,* Chatto & Windus, London, 2000. If every city has its iconic landmark in Florence it must be the cathedral dome. King reconstructs the intriguing story of its conception and building. He reveals the petty jealousies, bureaucratic meddling and engineering feats that lay behind this architectural masterpiece.

Caroline Moorhead, *Iris Origo Marchese of Val d'Orcia,* John Murray, London, 2003. This is a biography set among the Anglo-Italian community after Janet. Janet and Iris's mother knew one another and shared many friends, and Lina Waterfield was friendly with Iris, the daughter of Sybil and William Cutting. Sybil was English and William, American. Her father died when Iris was still young, leaving her alone with her mother in the very grand Villa Medici in Fiesole.

Mary McCarthy, *The Stones of Florence,* Harcourt Brace, New York, 1959. This book has more recently been published in one volume with McCarthy's other classic, *Venice Observed* by Penguin. Written some forty years ago, it is the twentieth-century classic account of the city and a great asset to the modern traveller. Elegant prose and keen observations make it a delight for anyone who has spent time in the city.

Nicky Mariano, *Forty Years with Berenson,* Knoph, New York, 1966. Nicky Mariano was Berenson's assistant and discreet lover for many years. She lived at I Tatti and managed to get on extremely well with both Mary and Bernard. This is a personal account of the man and his legacy.

Iris Origo, *War in Val d'Orcia,* Johnathan Cape, London, 1947. This is a personal account of Origo's life in Italy during the Second World War. War for an expatriate posses particular difficulties; Origo was married to an Italian and decided to stay and deal with the consequences. The account is beautifully written.

Iris Origo, *Images and Shadows: Part of a Life,* Harcourt Brace, New York, 1970. This is Origo's autobiography, a beautifully written account of her family background and her early life in 'villadom' in Florence.

Ernest Samuels, *Bernard Berenson: The Making of a Legend,* Harvard Press, 1987. This excellent biography gives a well-drawn portrait of a complex man, rising from humble beginnings to achieve the status of a living legend.

Barbara Strachey and Jayne Samuels eds, *Mary Berenson: A Self-Portrait from her Letters and Diaries,* Hamish Hamilton, London, 1983. Edited by Mary's granddaughter and the wife of Bernard's biographer. Mary's story includes many of the thinkers and writers of her day who came to I Tatti to share the life she and Bernard had established.

Some Cookery Books

There are so many Italian cookbooks it seems almost pointless to mark any out for special mention. Nonetheless the few included here are invaluable to anyone interested in the subject.

Pellegrino Artusi, *The Art of Eating Well,* Random House, New York, 1996. There are two translations in English. One by Murtha Baca and Stephen Sartarelli, University of Toronto Press, 1997. The other is a translation by Kyle M. Phillips III. This is a handsome and delightful book.

Boni, Ada, *Il Talismano della Felicita.* First published in 1929. Boni is the heir to Artusi. She presents 1100 recipes and many coloured plates. And where Artusi included recipes from readers beyond Emilia Romagna and Tuscany only in later editions of his tome, Boni is committed from the start to including recipes from across the peninsula. There is a translation in English by Mathilde la Rosa.

David, Elizabeth, *Italian Food,* 1954. As with all Elizabeth David's books, this is beautifully written and well researched. It was a revelation to the English cook when it first came out and remains today an inspiration to anyone interested in Italian food. In her typically thorough way, she added an excellent section on Italian cooking books.

David, Elizabeth, *An Omelette and a Glass of Wine,* 1984. This is a collection of essays previously published in other magazines and journals. There are a number on Italian subjects and a wonderful tribute to Isabella Beeton and her book.

Janet, Ross, *Leaves from Our Tuscan Kitchen,* revised by Michael Waterfield, Grubstreet, London, 2006, previously published by Penguin, Hammondsworthy, 1977. This revised edition has modernized techniques and in some cases updated ingredients. A few of the original recipes have been excluded altogether on account of them being less relevant to the modern cook and modern eating habits. By the same token a few new recipes have been added. This is part of the natural mutation of a cookbook that has been around for over a hundred years and still in everyday use.

Slow Food Guides. A very successful offshoot of the International Slow Food movement that was established in Italy in 1986 and now claims 80,000 members world-wide. *Slow Food* aims to promote the pleasures of the table from the homogenization of modern fast food. The movement promotes gastronomic culture and agricultural diversity. The publishing arm of the movement produces some very worthwhile guides for the visitor. *Osteria d'Italia,* Slow Food, Editore Bra, Italy, is published every two years, most recently in 2005, and recommends inns and trattoria in towns and cities across the peninsula that reflect the Slow Food ethos. Recommendations are made by local members of *Slow Food* which means that entries vary according to individual tastes. Nonetheless, the guide is the most reliable source of information on eating out in Italy. This has become an indispensable guide.

Acknowledgements

This book evolved from an interest in a little cookbook. Along the way it has benefited from contributions from many people. Among those who shared their knowledge and time, I would like especially to thank Janet's descendents whose contribution has been invaluable. From the outset, Janet's great-great-nephews have provided long-distance support and encouragement. Nigel Beevor has given invaluable assistance at every turn. Hugh and Antony Beevor and Michael Waterfield have also given their time answering questions. Much of the material in this book is based on letters and documents in the Waterfield Collection, British Institute of Florence and I am grateful for the access I have had to read and make use of it.

Alyson Price, at the British Institute of Florence, has been invaluable in so many ways. Her knowledge of the subject and her keen eye and intelligence made the process of researching much easier. The time spent at the British Institute, working quietly in the beautiful Harold Acton library overlooking the Arno, gave me nothing but pleasure. Alyson has been a wonderful guide and this book would not have come into its present form without her.

Others who have provided help include Fiorella Superbi, Archivist at Villa I Tatti, The Harvard University Center for Renaissance Studies, Florence, who allowed me access to the diaries and letters of Mary Berenson. Marilena Tammassia, Head of the Photographic Department at the Uffizi Gallery and Marion Kolanoski at the Staatliche Museen zu Berlin. I am also thankful to the General Manuscripts collection, Wilson Library, The University of North Carolina at Chapel Hill for allowing me access to the records of the publisher J.M. Dent and Sons.

Closer to home, I am most grateful to Kay Scarlett for taking the book on and to Vivien Valk and her team for the lovely design and Emma Hutchinson for her sharp questions. Thanks to Jeanne Ryckmans for championing the cause. Hazel Flynn has been a joy to work with. She has been a wonderfully supportive editor, giving helpful, commonsense feedback all the way through. This book is all the better for her contribution.

Lastly, I would like to thank Phillip Keir for his love and support. From the beginning he has provided invaluable feedback and generous encouragement without which this book would not have been written.

First published in 2006 by Pier 9, an imprint of Murdoch Books Pty Limited

Murdoch Books Australia
Pier 8/9
23 Hickson Road
Millers Point NSW 2000
Phone: +61 (0)2 8220 2000
Fax: +61 (0)2 8220 2558
www.murdochbooks.com.au

Chief Executive: Juliet Rogers
Publishing Director: Kay Scarlett

Commissioning Editor: Hazel Flynn
Design Manager: Vivien Valk
Concept and Design: Reuben Crossman
Project Manager and Editor: Emma Hutchinson
Production Manager: Megan Alsop

National Library of Australia Cataloguing-in-Publication Data
Benjamin, Sarah.
A castle in Tuscany: the remarkable life of Janet Ross.

ISBN 9 78174045 8863.

ISBN 1 74045 886 9.

1. Ross, Janet, 1842-1927. 2. Women food writers -
Biography. I. Title.

641.092

Printed by 1010 Printing International Limited in 2006. PRINTED IN CHINA.

Picture credits:
Pages 14, 20, 29, 46, 51, 52, 58, 71, 76, 83, 86, 91, 92, 98, 109, 110, 115, 116, 121, 122, 129, 138, 142, 150, Lina Waterfield
photograph 152, 164, 166–7, 174, 180–1, 186 and 196 courtesy of the Waterfield Collection, British Institute of Florence.
Pages 36, 45, 136, Aubrey Waterfield portrait 152 and 155 courtesy of the Beevor family.
Pages 64–5 courtesy of Staatliche Museen zu Berlin, Gemäldegallery, photo by Jörg Peter Anders.
Page 97 courtesy of Pensione Scoti and the Circolo dell' Unione.
Pages 102–3 courtesy of Gabinetto Fotografico della Soprintenza Speciale per il Polo Museale Fiorentino.
Page 160 courtesy of the National Portrait Gallery, London.
Page 192 courtesy of Sarah Benjamin.

Every effort has been made to contact copyright holders for the images in this book. The publisher would be grateful if notified
of any corrections that should be incorporated in future reprints or editions.